Science

科学箴言录

Maxims

俞乔力［著］

作家出版社

Book

由探索而认知，由逻辑而预言。

Cognition by exploration, prediction by logic.

永远不要被一厢情愿所麻痹，因为驱动事物演绎的逻辑是唯一的，不受人类愿景的任何影响，因此探索真理就成为我们仅有的责任。

Never be paralyzed by wishful thinking, because the logic that drives the things deduction is unique and unaffected by the human vision, so the search for truth becomes our only responsibility.

将灵魂献给：
承受我们生命、
宽容我们无知、
分担我们屈辱、
静候我们启迪的故土，
以及故土中
穿行、欢唱的河流。

Dedicate souls to:
the homeland that bears our lives,
tolerates our ignorance,
shares our humiliations,
waits for our inspiration,
and the river that walks and sings in the homeland.

Any life is something that captures opportunity in the environmental change.

There is no flicker without darkness.

A flower is a prophecy of the fruit.

Exploration must be a long and lonely mission.

God gives us the hand to capture opportunity.

Birds without concern can fly into heaven.

Will is to turn every position of life into a fulcrum of freedom.

The creativity that we retain is nature in being unbound by morality.

Silence is the contemplation of the universe.

Every moment of youth is the time to sow seeds.

Poetry is returning the inevitability of things to nature.

We are choosing interests, and God is choosing us.

All hearts that are throbbing by life are noble.

凡是生命，就是在环境变迁中能够捕捉到机遇的事物。

没有黑暗就没有闪烁。

花朵是对果实的预言。

探索必然是漫长而孤独的使命。

上帝赋予我们的手，用来捕捉机遇。

没有牵挂的鸟儿，才能飞进天堂。

意志，是要把生命的每一个位置都变成自由的支点。

我们保留的创造力，正是不被道义所束缚的本性。

寂静是宇宙的思索。

青春的每一刻都是播种的时机。

诗意，在把事物的必然性回归自然。

我们在选择利益，上帝在选择我们。

所有因生命而悸动的心灵，都是高贵的。

序言 | Preface

第一次读作者的《科学箴言录》，感觉同《道德经》《易经》《黄帝内经》一脉相承，但又没有文言文的晦涩难懂。书中通过一些简洁的、浅显易懂的大白话，表述深刻的科学哲理和自然规律，正所谓“大道至简”。

作者总结 44 年科学实践经验，经过提炼而撰写成 4000 条科学箴言，内容涉及科学仿真、技术发明、经济推广、艺术设计、哲学方法、人性需求、认知过程等多个方面，从科学、哲学、艺术、人性、认知、经济等六个维度进行方法论指导，对于高中生、大学生、硕士研究生、博士研究生、博士后、青年教师、科学研究人员、企业产品开发人员等进行科学探索，深具指导意义和启迪价值。

自古以来，科学技术就以一种不可逆转、不可抗拒的力量推动着人类文明向前发展。从 5G 迈入规模化应用的关键期，到“中国天眼”发现 660 颗新脉冲星，从“神威 · 太湖之光”超级计算机首次实现千万次并行第一性原理计算模拟，到我国首艘弹射型航空母舰“福建号”成功下水；“盖有非常之功，必待非常之人”，人是科技创新最关键的因素，各行各业的科研工作者们如果能够把这本《科学箴言录》放在身边，经常研读，对于科研工作必定事半功倍。

书中“年轻就是憧憬未来的勇气”“青春的每一刻都是播种的时机”“越有知识，越能感受无知的边界”“师天下者无敌”“阳光和彩云总是眷顾山峰”等语句激励年轻人，要勇于探索，不要骄傲自满；书中“成功取决于我们在多大程度迎接挑战”“在持续地跌落中，鸟儿进化出翅膀”“所有的绝壁和断崖迫使我们腾飞”“强者被苦难塑造”，是作者在嘱托我们的科研工作者在遇到困难、碰到挫折时不要灰心、气馁，熬过去了就是黎明和曙光。

作者也从科学术语的角度阐述了可持续发展的真谛：“熵是最具科学和哲学双重意义的概念，对其全面理解和应用有待于科学家和哲学家的共同努力”“负熵是对人类社会发展机会的度量，意味着差别、梯度、动力，意味着有序、活力、生命，意味着逻辑、道德、法律，意味着语言、思想、精神”“可持续的普遍性是伟大的标志”，作者在嘱托我们的科研工作者，科研创新要着眼于熵减，这才是可持续的、符合自然规律的，才能最终实现多赢、实现成功。

希望更多的有识之士能够把这本《科学箴言录》放在手边，作为指导书、参考书，定期研读、思索，在成功道路上，它能助你一臂之力！

刘　东

2022年11月30日

作者简介 | Author Biography

俞乔力，男，满族，1963 年 5 月生于天津；教授级高级工程师，总工程师；中国民主同盟盟员；中国科学技术大学和西安交通大学专业博士实践导师。主要专长为暖通空调、工程热物理、太阳能热利用、热能工程、海水淡化。1985 年 7 月获同济大学供热通风与空气调节工学学士学位；1994 年 7 月获中国科学技术大学工程热物理工学硕士学位；1997 年 7 月获中国科学技术大学工程热物理工学博士学位；1999 年 7 月清华大学反应堆工程与反应堆安全博士后出站。1985 年 7 月—1991 年 9 月，化学工业部第三设计院助理工程师；1999 年 7 月—2000 年 9 月，清华大学助理研究员；2000 年 9 月—2009 年 3 月，大连冷冻机股份有限公司 / 大连冰山集团有限公司教授级高级工程师、首席科学家、上市公司董事；2009 年 3 月—2015 年 9 月，合肥天鹅制冷科技有限公司首席科学家、总工程师、技术中心主任；2015 年 9 月—2022 年 3 月，上海汉钟精机股份有限公司总工程师；2022 年 4 月至今，上海齐耀动力技术有限公司资深工程师。中国制冷学会高级会员；中国制冷空调工业协会高级会员；国家能源局能源装备评估系统专家；中国技术创新管理协会理事会理事；国家火炬计划专家库备选专家。

Chou Qiaoli; male; the Manchus; was born in Tianjin in May 1963; professor-level senior engineer; chief engineer; leaguer of China Democratic League; professional doctoral practice supervisor of USTC and XJTU. The main expertise is HVAC, engineering thermal physics, solar thermal utilization, thermal engineering, desalination. He received his Bachelor of Engineering in Heating and Ventilation and Air Conditioning Engineering from Tongji University in July 1985, his Master of Engineering in Thermophysics from USTC in July 1994, his Ph.D. of Engineering in Thermophysics from USTC in July 1997, and his postdoctoral exit certificate of reactor engineering and reactor safety from Tsinghua University in July 1999. Assistant Engineer of the Third Design Institute of Ministry of Chemical Industry in July 1985—September 1991; Assistant Research Fellow of Tsinghua University in July 1999—September 2000; Professor-level Senior Engineer, Chief Scientist, Director of listed company of Dalian Refrigerator Co., Ltd. / Dalian Iceberg Group Co., Ltd. in September 2000—March 2009; Chief Scientist, Chief Engineer, Director of the Technical Center of Hefei Swan Refrigeration Technology Co., Ltd. in March 2009—September 2015; Chief Engineer of Shanghai Hanbell Precise Machinery Co., Ltd. in September 2015 to March 2022; Senior Engineer of Shanghai QiYao Power Technology Co., Ltd. since April 2022. Senior Member of China Refrigeration Society; Senior Member of China Refrigeration and Air Conditioning Industry Association; Expert of Energy Equipment Evaluation System of the State Energy Administration; Member of the Board of Directors of China Technology Innovation Management Association; National Torch Program Expert Library Alternative Expert.

主持开发的产品："地源热泵采暖空调热水三用机"获国家火炬计划项目证书；"户式采暖空调热水三用机"获国家重点新产品证书；"水源超高温热泵机组"获第 24 届国际制冷、空调、供暖、通风及食品冷冻加工展览会"新品推荐"奖；"户式空调热水机组"获 2006 年大连市技术发明一等奖；"新景煤矿直冷式乏风水汽能热泵供热"获 2018 第十四届中国分布式能源国际论坛"分布式能源优秀项目特等奖"。在核心期刊发表论文 100 余篇，其中 EI 收录 14 篇。获权发明专利 25 项；获权实用新型专利 85 项；实审发明专利 56 项。通过高精度仿真设计，主持开发产品 100 余款；完成节能工程项目 100 余项。

Presided over the development of the product: "ground source heat pump heating and air conditioning and hot water tri-use machine" won the National Torch Plan Project Certificate; "house heating and air conditioning and hot water tri-use machine" won the National Key New Product Certificate; "water source super-high temperature heat pump unit" won "New Product Recommendation" award by the 24th International Refrigeration, Air Conditioning, Heating, Ventilation and Food Refrigeration Processing Exhibition; "house air conditioning and hot water unit" won "2006 Dalian City Technology Invention the First Prize"; "Xinjing Coal Mine straight-cooled exhaust water-steam energy heat pump heating" won the 2018 14th China Distributed Energy International Forum "Distributed Energy Excellent Project Special Award". Published over 100 papers in core journals; of which EI included 14 articles. 25 patents for inventions; 85 patents for utility models; and 56 patents for real-time inventions. Through high-precision simulation design, presided over the development of more than 100 products; completed more than 100 energy-saving projects.

创建新兴产业：1.首创热阻－热容网络传热数值方法及其循环耦合迭代计算方法，并首次用于动态仿真太阳能集热系统，与中试结果平均误差为3%，博士论文的9位外审全部获优。2.发明电子束湿法烟气脱硫工艺以修正美国VAC公司的电子束半干法烟气脱硫工艺，并以专利技术实现清华核研院的中试试验及北京第二热电厂的样板工程。3.发明空气源采暖空调热水机，并负责起草中国行业标准与国家标准，专利技术被日本、美国、欧洲列为产品规范。4.发明低环境温度空气源热泵，并负责起草国家标准。5.发明水源超高温热泵，并负责起草中航工业标准与国家标准，产品广泛应用于盘锦油田、金枫酒厂。6.发明煤矿乏风热泵，全面取代现有煤矿乏风热泵技术，已广泛应用于100多个煤矿。7.发明煤泥干燥烟气热泵，用于驱动煤矿分布式供热系统，并完成煤矿样板工程。8.发明高温热泵驱动巴氏杀菌机，并完成金凤酒厂样板工程，节汽量达1/3。9.发明凝汽源蒸汽热泵驱动多效蒸馏装置，并完成中国纸业的样板工程，节省运行费达2/3。

Creating new industries: 1. Initiated thermal resistance-thermal capacity network heat transfer numerical method and its circular coupling iteration calculation method, and for the first time for dynamic simulation of solar heat collection system, with the average error of the pilot results to 3%, the doctor thesis won all excellence of 9 external review. 2. Invented the electron beam wet flue gas desulfurization process to modify the electron beam semi-dry flue gas desulfurization process of the United States VAC Company, and thus to achieve pilot test of Institute of Nuclear Energy Design and Research of Tsinghua University and the Beijing Second Thermal Power Plant model project with the patented technology. 3. Invented air source heating and air conditioning and hot water machine, and was responsible for drafting its China industry standard and national standard, patented technology was listed by

Japan, the United States, Europe as a product specification. 4. Invented low ambient temperature air source heat pump, and was responsible for drafting its national standard. 5. Invented water source super-high temperature heat pump, and was responsible for drafting its China Aviation Industry Standard and national standard, products were widely used in Panjin Oil Field, Jinfeng Winery. 6. Invented coal mine exhaust heat pump, a comprehensive replacement of the existing coal mine exhaust heat pump technology, has been widely used in more than 100 coal mines. 7. Invented coal mud drying flue gas heat pump, was used to drive the coal mine distributed heating system, and completed the coal mine model project. 8. Invented high-temperature heat pump to drive pasteurization machine, and completed the model project of Jinfeng Winery, the amount of saving steam up to 1/3. 9. Invented the condensate steam source steam heat pump to drive the multi-effect distillation device, and completed the model project of China Paper, saving 2/3 of the operating cost.

目录 | Contents

科学箴言录 | Science Maxims Book

第 1 章 | 实践是生活舞台最伟大的背景
Practice is the greatest background of life stage

（1985 年同济大学本科 Undergraduate of Tongji University）

1. 环境与本能同等重要。

   The environment is as important as instinct.

2. 一个不朽的灵魂，必定同时理解艺术、自然、哲学。

   An immortal soul must understand art, nature and philosophy at the same time.

3. 自信力就是风度。

   Self-confidence is grace.

4. 两个完美事物之选择，意味着精神的毁灭。

   The choice of two perfect things means the destruction of the spirit.

5. 数学是对现实中逻辑的抽象。

   Mathematics is an abstraction of logic in reality.

6. 我们祈求所希冀得到的，不是对宇宙的奢谈，我们甚至也不打算运用哲学的方法来论述宇宙，唯一使我们感兴趣并且去渴望追求的，是用所有的事实和纯粹的科学来论证宇宙的无限性与她的演变史，从而使广漠而浩瀚的太空中辉映起整个人类的理性。

We pray for what we want, not to talk about the universe, we do not even intend to use philosophical methods to discuss the universe, the only thing that interests us and aspires to pursue is the use of all the facts and pure science to demonstrate the infiniteness of the universe and her evolution, thus letting the vastness of space reflect the whole human reason.

7. 开放性是宇宙演变的源泉。

Openness is the source of the universe evolution.

8. 宇宙是无限性、层次性、对称性的统一体。无限性为其根本，而层次是无限中的层次，对称是同一层次的对称。

The universe is a unity of infinity, hierarchy and symmetry. Infinity is fundamental, while hierarchy is the hierarchy in infinity, and symmetry is the symmetry of the same hierarchy.

9. 事物在极端混乱中，会自发走向新的有序。

In extreme chaos, things will spontaneously move towards a new order.

10. 美，是意识透过感觉所见到的有序。

Beauty is the order that consciousness sees through the sense.

11. 美是精神界的有序，作为负熵，她从自然界走进意识。

Beauty is the order of the spiritual world, and as a negative entropy, she enters consciousness from nature.

12. 当一种现实和一个人所形成的意念吻合时，就会获得一个永不磨灭的印象；并且为这个印象而存在过的往事，将伴随他去度过漫长的一生。

When a reality coincides with a person's idea, he will get an indelible impression, and the past that exists for that impression will accompany him through a long life.

13. 如果失去故往的回忆——哪怕是懊恼，那么我们的眼前将是一片空虚。
If we lose the memories of the past—even if it is chagrin, then our eyes will be empty.

14. 任何关于“本质”的判断都应当具有深刻的内涵和广泛的外延，并且可以解释它所研究的所有现象。
Any judgment of “essence” should have profound connotation and extensive extension, and it can explain all the phenomena it studies.

15. 美是目的性与规律性的合一。
Beauty is the unity of purpose and regularity.

16. 审美不像亚里士多德的形式说那样是逻辑判断，也不像康德的先验论那样是趣味判断；而是经验判断——潜在的知识判断，其特点在于：利用经验判断却难以觉察，误以为是情感判断，而美正产生在这种错觉里。
Aesthetics is not a logical judgment as Aristotle's form says, nor is it interesting judgment as Kant's a priori theory; it is experience judgment—potential knowledge judgment, it is characterized by the use of experience judgment but difficult to detect, mistaken for emotional judgment, and beauty is produced in this illusion.

17. 美既是意识与物质相分离的产物，又是意识和物质的统一。实践的发展是意识和物质在形式上愈加分离，而实质上愈加统一的过程，并且也是丑向美转化的伟大历程。
Beauty is not only the separation product of consciousness and matter, but also the unity of consciousness and matter. The practice development is the process of increasing separation of consciousness and matter in form, and increasing unity in substance, and also the great process of the transformation of ugliness into beauty.

18. 审美作为经验判断有赖于人们的知识构成。一个越是知识渊博的人，他所认识的美也就越加有深度和广度，他就越加能在广泛的范围里发现深刻的美。

Aesthetics as an experience judgment depends on people's knowledge. The more knowledgeable a person is, the more deep and broad the beauty he knows, the more he can find profound beauty in a wide range of scope.

19. 科学发展的结果在于随机性减少和必然性增多。在这种意义上，科学的本质是优化，它应该告诉人们：如何省力地劳动并且可以获得更多果实。科学的本质体现美的本质。

The result of scientific development is the decrease of randomness and the increase of inevitability. In this sense, the essence of science is optimization, it should tell people: how to work saving of labour and get more fruit. The essence of science embodies the essence of beauty.

20. 美属于实践范畴，是人类实践发展中的肯定价值。在这种意义上，美反映人类历史发展的水平与现状。

Beauty belongs to the category of practice, and is the positive value of the development of human practice. In this sense, beauty reflects the level and present situation of the development of human history.

21. 美是现实世界发展中伴随实践而诞生意识之后的产物，是人类社会独有的历史现象，因此美的本质必然反映实践中作为目的性的人的本质。换言之，美是与人的目的性相关的产物。

Beauty is the product of the real world development after the birth of consciousness with practice, is the unique historical phenomenon of human society, so the essence of beauty must reflect the essence of the people as the purpose in practice. In other words, beauty is a product of human purpose.

22. 任何一门科学作为关于现实世界某一方面事物和现象的系统描述，产生于人类在实践中为着实现目的而寻求方法的需要，并且随着这个需要而发展。

Any science as a systematic description of things and phenomena in a certain aspect of the real world, arises from the need for human beings to seek methods in practice to achieve their purposes, and develops with this need.

23. 同一事物可能具有这种形式的美，而不具有那种形式的美；因为审美主体的目的性转向这个方面，而非那个方面。

The same thing may have this form of beauty, not that form of beauty; because the purpose of the aesthetic subject turns to this aspect, not that aspect.

24. 相对美是现实可能性的反映，是时间与空间对审美的局限，并且也是我们通常意义上所认识的真实美。

Relative beauty is a reflection of the possibility of reality, is the limitation of time and space to aesthetics, and also is the real beauty that we usually know.

25. 一个时代的特征，就以审美判断的模式为其显著标志。

The characteristics of an era are marked by the model of aesthetic judgment.

26. 体现精神和物质的紧密联系，正是美在人类发展史上的神秘性和特殊地位之所在。

The close connection between spirit and matter is precisely where the mystery and special status of beauty lie in the history of human development.

27. 对自身的理解和对自然的热爱，是驱使人类生活与思想的源泉。

The understanding of oneself and the love of nature are the source of human life and thought.

28. 任何现实真理对于未来的演化，都是一种有待证伪的谬误。

Any real truth is a fallacy to be falsified for future evolution.

29. 人类艺术的显著特征，在于忽视次要而突出主题。

The distinctive feature of human art is the neglect of secondary and prominent subjects.

30. 实践发展阶段的不同以人类在目的和经验的深度差异为标志，并且由此区分美的层次。

Differences in the stage of practical development are marked by the depth difference of human purpose and experience, and thus distinguish the level of beauty.

31. 思想的实质，是对已知事物的延续和对间断现实的填补。

The essence of thought is the continuation of the known things and the filling of the intermittent reality.

32. 艺术激发生命的活力与动机。

Art stimulates the vitality and motivation of life.

33. 每一门技艺所达到的高峰都是艺术。

The peak of every skill is art.

34. 人生的意义就在于没有具体的意义，在于生活和思想的多元化与开放性，以及由此形成丰富多彩的生活篇章；给人生规定意义是对精彩生活的亵渎。

The meaning of life lies in the absence of concrete meaning, in the diversity and openness of life and thought, and in the formation of a colorful chapter of life; it is a desecration of a wonderful life to give meaning to life.

35. 如果对生活的理解只停留在内心深处，我们将失去许多宝贵的东西。

If the understanding of life only stays deep in our hearts, we will lose many precious things.

36. 多元化与开放性是现实世界的本质所在。

Diversity and openness are the essence of the real world.

37. 对一件事物做出深刻判断的最可靠途径就是静观结局。

The surest way to make a profound judgment about something is to wait and see the ending.

38. 伟大作品犹如照耀心灵的曙光，把人们从现实的黑暗面引向光明。

Great works are like the dawn of the heart, to lead people from the dark side of reality to the light.

39. 对生活持有的态度，比对生活的认识更加重要。

The attitude to life is more important than the understanding of life.

40. 艺术是心灵的语言，传达人类的感知。

Art is the language of the mind conveying human perception.

41. 实践是驱使人类发展的洪流。

Practice is the flood that drives human development.

42. 正是曾经生活过的水土、目睹过的景色、结识过的人们、经历过的往事，换言之，正是实践的深度与广度构成现实自我的精神与血肉。

It is the water and soil that you have lived, the scenery that you have witnessed, the people that you have met, the past experience that you have gone through, in other words, it is the depth and breadth of practice that constitute the spirit and flesh of the reality of self.

43. 思想超越现实和语言。

Thought transcends reality and language.

44. 所能感知的一切，构成我们生活与思想的基础。

Everything that can be perceived forms the basis of our lives and thoughts.

45. 所谓生活，就是对现实生命的挑战。

Life is a challenge to real vitality.

46. 目的的深度和广度，是衡量人类发展的水准。

The depth and breadth of purpose are a measure of the level of human development.

47. 时间对不同的事物和不同的人来说，具有不同的价值和意义。

Time has different values and meanings for different things and different people.

48. 生活是生命展现的形式。

Life is the form of vitality.

49. 美是物质与精神的伟大融合。

Beauty is a great fusion of matter and spirit.

50. 人与人之间的仇恨以及人对自然的恐惧，来自人的目的性遭到抵触或受到局限。

The hate between people and the fear of nature come from the purpose of the people is resisted or limited.

51. 人具有目的性，因此有关人的矛盾就是目的性的矛盾。

Man has purpose, so the contradiction about human being is the contradiction of purpose.

52. 实践是生活舞台最伟大的背景。

Practice is the greatest background of life stage.

53. 自然代表吸引的力量，是人类之母；实践代表排斥的力量，是人类之父。
Nature represents the power of attraction, being the mother of mankind; and practice represents the power of exclusion, being the father of mankind.

54. 向往而不苛求完美是一种幸福。
Yearning for instead of being overcritical perfection is a kind of happiness.

55. 科学是人与自然的通信，艺术是人们传达生活经验和内心感受的精神语言，哲学是对现实世界的本质抽象。科学、艺术、哲学是人类精神文明的三大支柱。
Science is the communication between man and nature, art is the spiritual language of people to convey life experience and inner feeling, philosophy is the essence abstract of the real world. Science, art and philosophy are the three pillars of human spiritual civilization.

56. 艺术是内心感受符合形式规律的传达，是形式与内容的统一体。
Art is the transmission of inner feelings in line with the form law, and the unity of form and content.

57. 艺术以形式作为手段传达良性信息，以开拓观众的知觉与思想疆土。
Art conveys a benign message by means of form in order to open up the audience's perception and ideological frontier.

58. 由重复的感觉形成经验，从相似的经验提炼思想。
Experience is formed from repetitive feelings, and thoughts are distilled from similar experiences.

59. 实践为思想提供沃土。
Practice provides fertile ground for thought.

60. 探索就是从求实出发，抵达求是境界。

Exploration is to start from being practical-minded, to arrive at the realm of truth-seeking.

61. 教育的目的在于使我们有能力：建立正确目标、掌握科学方法、拥有系统知识。

The purpose of education is to empower us: to set the right goals, to master scientific methods, to have systematic knowledge.

62. 哲学对过去而言是本质论，对未来而言是方法论。

Philosophy is essential discuss to the past and methodology to the future.

63. 人类实践不外乎两种：对自然的超越和对自然的回归。

Human practice is no more than two kinds: the transcendence of nature and the return of nature.

64. 生活是人类的起点而非目标。

Life is the starting point, not the goal of mankind.

65. 在人类行为的背后隐藏两种动机：对本能的渴望和对理想的追求。

Behind the human act lies two motives: the desire for instinct and the pursuit of ideals.

66. 越有知识，越能感受无知的边界。

The more knowledgeable, the more you can feel the boundaries of ignorance.

67. 理想和本能的对立统一，构成人类存在与发展的矛盾机制。

The opposition unity of ideal and instinct constitutes the contradictory mechanism of human existence and development.

68. 理想控制本能则生活向前发展，本能抑制理想则生活更加丰富；因此无论如何，人类所拥有的生活都令人向往。

Ideal controls instinct life forward, instinct inhibits ideal life more rich; so in any case, the life that human beings have is desirable.

69. 没有理性思考的生活注定肤浅，哲学不仅是方法论，更是我们体验和享受生活的工具。

Life without rational thinking is doomed to superficiality, philosophy is not only methodology but also a tool for us to experience and enjoy life.

70. 气质是人的精神所放射的光芒。

Temperament is the light of the human spirit.

71. 生活是意志的诗篇。

Life is the poems of will.

72. 理性和本能的矛盾决定人类的演变。

The contradiction between reason and instinct determines the evolution of human beings.

73. 艺术丰富生活，生活丰富艺术。

Art is rich in life, life is rich in art.

74. 美是经验的比较和现实的选择。

Beauty is a comparison of experience and realistic choice.

75. 艺术所要表达的真谛，隐藏在感觉形式的背后。

The true meaning of art is hidden behind the form of feeling.

76. 气质体现心灵的力量。

Temperament embodies the power of the mind.

77. 生活的体验是内心的体验。

The experience of life is the experience of the heart.

78. 人们往往缺乏信心去充当生活的主角。

People often lack the confidence to play the main role in life.

79. 生活因为具体才显得生动和丰富。

Life is vivid and rich because of its specificity.

80. 形而上学是思考的起点，辩证法是思考的结局，并且在思维中如此周而复始；形而上学和辩证法是思维不同阶段的抽象与分离，人们在思维中交替从形而上学的表皮进入辩证法的内核。

Metaphysics is the starting point of thinking, dialectics is the end of thinking, and so much in thinking, metaphysics and dialectics are the abstraction and separation of different stages of thinking, people in thinking alternately from the metaphysical epidermis into the core of dialectics.

81. 生活是一种交替过程：首先建立并进入理性王国，其次击碎理性王国回归现实；如此这般，每一过程都在深化我们的认识。

Life is an alternating process: first to establish and enter the rational kingdom, and second to crush the rational kingdom to return to reality; so every process is deeply aware of ours.

82. 只沉湎于理性或只停留在现实，对每个人来说都是一种灾难。

It is a disaster for everyone to indulge in reason or to stay in reality.

83. 生活有着不同层次和不同方面，由此形成不同生活圈，进入上层生活圈会由于缺乏自信反而过着低级生活，人不能离其生活位置过远。

Life has different levels and different aspects, thus forming a different life circle, into the upper life circle will be due to lack of self-confidence but live a low-level life, people cannot be too far away from their living position.

84. 科学发展从来都由形而上学的猜想走向辩证法的修正。

Scientific development has always moved from metaphysics supposes to the dialectics correction.

85. 人类发展总趋势是从自然到自然，自然既是人类发展的起点也是人类发展的归宿。

The general trend of human development is from nature to nature, which is both the starting point of human development and the end of human development.

86. 深刻意味着具体和精确。

Depth means concrete and precise.

87. 迅猛的经济发展和伟大的经济规律在用金钱购买人类的灵魂和才能，在使现实世界变成滋养经济动物的草原和枯竭精神力量的沙漠。

Rapid economic development and great economic laws buy human souls and talents in the use of money, and turn the real world into grasslands that nourish economic animals and deserts that deplete spiritual strength.

88. 独立人格应当具备生活基础、经济基础、思想基础。

An independent personality shall have a living foundation, an economic foundation and an ideological foundation.

89. 生与死的对立构成人类发展低级驱动力，理性与本能的对立构成人类发展高级驱动力。

The opposition between life and death constitutes the low-level driving force of human development, and the opposition between reason and instinct constitutes the high-level driving force of human development.

90. 气质和风度是最好的容妆。

Temperament and grace are the best makeup.

91. 每一种恐惧都源自匮乏。

Every fear stems from scarcity.

92. 情感是心理结构的灰度。

Emotions are the grayscale of the structure of the heart.

93. 聪明是正确认识、迅速反应、恰当解决。

Wisdom is the right understanding, rapid response, and proper solution.

94. 实践促使精神与物质相互转化和相互提高。

Practice promotes the mutual transformation and mutual improvement of spirit and matter.

95. 不可持续的发展，导致更广泛的没落。

Unsustainable development leads to broader decline.

96. 意识的差别是人类本质的差别，不同的意识把人区分成为不同的层次并引向不同的目标。

The difference in consciousness is the difference in human essence, different consciousness divides people into different levels and leads to different goals.

97. 美属于实践、属于历史、属于人类。

Beauty belongs to practice, to history, to human beings.

98. 没有节制的贪婪，导致灭亡。

Unbridled greed leads to destruction.

99. 完美主义是禁锢思想的牢笼。

Perfectionism is a cage for the idea.

100. 欢乐基于对未来的幻想。

Joy is based on fantasies about the future.

101. 进展高于完美。

Progress is higher than perfection.

102. 孤独源自广泛的兴趣和崇高的品位。

Solitude stems from a wide range of interests and noble tastes.

103. 由感觉而思维，由思维而意识。

Thinking by feeling, consciousness by thinking.

104. 人类的胜利是意志的胜利。

The victory of man is the victory of will.

105. 人类缺少宽容而非热情。

Humans lack tolerance rather than enthusiasm.

106. 时间是最从容的批评家。

Time is the most relaxed critic.

107. 向往美在深刻影响和改变人类，美哺育一代又一代人类精英。

Longing for beauty is profoundly influencing and changing humanity, and beauty has nurtured generation after generation of human elite.

108. 精神脱离物质，又在更高层次与物质相统一，这是宇宙中一次伟大的飞跃。

The spirit is detached from matter and united with matter at a higher level, which is a great leap in the universe.

109. 一切以条件为转移。

Everything is transferred on a conditional basis.

110. 面对未来，人类所曾目睹的只是永恒宇宙的序曲。

Faced with the future what humans have witnessed is only the prelude to the eternal universe.

111. 人类最大的无知是对未来的无知。

The greatest ignorance of mankind is ignorance of the future.

112. 高速发展的科学使得：精神萎缩、艺术暗淡、环境污染、能源枯竭，以及人类有了毁灭自身的可能。长此以往，人类面临的将是一幕悲壮的结局。

The science of rapid development makes: mental atrophy, art dim, environmental pollution, energy depletion, and the possibility of human destruction of their own. In the long run mankind will face a tragic end.

113. 当人与自然所需达到的平衡遭受破坏，人类结局不堪设想；人是自然之子，不可忘乎所以。

When the balance that man and nature need to achieve are destroyed, the human end is unimaginable; man is the son of nature, so it must not be forgotten.

114. 如果科学的应用不受控制，那么科学最终给我们带来的恶果将抵消科学曾经给我们带来的一切好处。

If the application of science is uncontrolled, the evil effects of science will eventually offset all the benefits that science has brought us.

115. 必须考虑人类与自然作为总系统的优化问题，这不但是科学问题，而且是现实问题。

It is not only a scientific problem, but also a real problem to consider the optimization of human beings and nature as the general system.

116. “完美”和“终极”意味着消亡，意味着新事物的诞生。

“Perfection” and “ultimate” mean death, meaning the birth of new things.

117. 存在实践的地方便存在生机和美，由于美的存在人类树立起信仰。
Where there is practice there is vitality and beauty. Because of the existence of beauty, human beings establish faith.

118. 音乐是抽象和变幻的艺术，它在变幻艺术中最抽象，也在抽象艺术中最变幻；音乐最能反映心的概念。
Music is the art of abstraction and change. It is the most abstract in change art, but also the most variable in abstract art; music best reflects the heart concept.

119. 学习是知识的积累与经验的迭代。
Learning is the accumulation of knowledge and the iteration of experience.

120. 抽象使音乐的表现范围更宽广，从苍茫宇宙到内心世界。
Abstraction extends the range of music express, from the vast universe to the inner heart world.

121. 对人类而言，最完美的就是造就我们并为我们所感知的苍茫宇宙。
The most perfect thing for mankind is the vast universe that creates us and is perceived by us.

122. 起源于物质生活而不甘停留，立足于广袤大地而仰望苍穹，这就是觉悟者——人的特征。
Originating from material life and not willing to stay, based on the vast earth and looking up at the sky, this is the consciousness—the characteristics of people.

123. 征服现实的先决，是战胜自我。
The first thing to conquer reality is to conquer the self.

124. 对生活的渴望伴随着对美的追求。

The desire for life is accompanied by the pursuit of beauty.

125. 意志是主观对行为的控制力，是人类最高层次的意识。

Will is subjective control over behavior and is the highest level of human consciousness.

126. 信息是知识和经验的系统化有序传递。

Information is a systematic and orderly transmission of knowledge and experience.

127. 在普遍性矛盾中，统一性决定繁荣，而对立性决定发展。

In the general contradiction, unity determines prosperity and opposition determines development.

128. 量变中矛盾统一性占主导，质变中矛盾对立性占主导。

The unity of contradictions dominates in quantitative change, and the opposition of contradictions dominates in qualitative change.

129. 无限事物的本质是统一性，有限事物的本质是对立性。

The essence of infinite things is unity, and the essence of finite things is opposition.

130. 美即适度。

Beauty is moderation.

131. 外因决定发展条件，内因决定发展方向。

External causes determine the conditions for development, internal causes determine the direction of development.

132. 人类经济、政治、军事、法律、艺术等社会活动，是为满足不断增长的本能需求；与动物相比，人类把本能的发挥推进到崭新阶段。

Human economic, political, military, legal, artistic and other social activities are aimed at meeting the growing demand for instinct; compared with animals humans have advanced the development of instinct to a new stage.

133. 意识的目的，是在更高层次促进本能的发挥。

The purpose of consciousness is to promote the use of instinct at a higher level.

134. 发展以更高层次的统一性为目标。

Development is aimed at a higher level unity.

135. 正是最高层次的理性，才把人类最基本的欲望作为其宗旨。

It is the reason at the highest level that takes the most basic human desire as its purpose.

136. 没有哲学指引，人类的觉醒将是漫漫长夜。

Without philosophical guidance, the awakening of mankind would be a long night.

137. 现实世界的统一性尤为重要，任何发展都是在更高层次和更大范围促进事物间互相适应。

The unity of the real world is particularly important, and any development is to promote mutual adaptation of things at a higher level and in a wider range.

138. 艺术创作是把感觉凝结为形式，艺术欣赏则是用形式召唤感觉。

Art creation is the condensation of feelings into forms, and art appreciation is the calling for feelings with form.

139. 领悟是知识的感性延伸。

Understanding is an emotional extension of knowledge.

140. 差异是发展的动力，共性是发展的目标。

Differences are the driving force of development, and commonality is the goal of development.

141. 永恒的差异决定永恒的发展。

Eternal differences determine eternal development.

142. 共性是发展的起点和目标，差异是发展的过程和动因。

Commonality is the starting point and goal of development, and difference is the process and motivation of development.

143. 最深刻，才会最广泛。

The deepest can be the most extensive.

144. 发展以更广泛且不可逆的没落作为其代价。

Development comes at the cost of a broader and irreversible decline.

145. 没有追求与过度追求都是一种不幸。

No pursuit and excessive pursuit are both misfortunes.

146. 人类发展史是人类与自然关系的发展史。

The history of human development is the development history of human and nature relations.

147. 强者被苦难塑造。

The strong are shaped by suffering.

148. 遗传赋予我们相貌，教育赋予我们气质。

Genetics gives us looks, education gives us temperament.

149. 友谊正如血液一般注入体内，成为我们生命的一部分。

Friendship is like blood injected into the body and becomes a part of our lives.

150. 教育分为三个层次：灌输知识、教授方法、赋予信心。

Education is divided into three levels: inculcating knowledge, teaching methods, and giving confidence.

151. 科学起源于计量。

Science originated in measurement.

152. 流行是平庸的象征。

Fashion is symbols of mediocrity.

153. 通过深刻的对立，才会把我们提升到崭新高度。

We will be elevated to a new level through profound opposition.

154. 成功取决于我们在多大程度上迎接挑战。

Success depends on how well we meet the challenge.

155. 迎接挑战是我们实现价值的唯一途径。

Meeting the challenge is the only way we can realize our value.

156. 挑战预示新机遇的降临。

Challenges foreshadow the advent of new opportunities.

157. 仿真以数学再现事实。

Simulation reproduces the facts mathematically.

158. 竞争为摆脱平庸提供赛道。

Competition provides a track for getting rid of mediocrity.

159. 道德是本能与社会舆论相制衡的产物，法律是本能与社会约束相制衡的产物。

Morality is the product of the checks and balances between instinct and social public opinion, and the law is the product of the checks and balances between instinct and social constraints.

160. 苦难使我们回归现实并帮助我们获取经验。

Suffering brings us back to reality and helps us gain experience.

161. 勇气和坚毅决定人生价值。

Courage and perseverance determine the value of life.

162. 苦难是人类经验的源泉。

Suffering is the source of human experience.

163. 艺术再现心灵的力量。

Art reproduces the power of the mind.

164. 苦难使我们深刻，为我们展示生活的情节和意义。

Suffering makes us deep and shows us the plot and meaning of life.

165. 完美的艺术具备三个层次：情绪再现、经验再现、思想再现。

Perfect art has three levels: emotional reproduction, experience reproduction, and thought reproduction.

166. 苦难预示新的契机。

Suffering heralds new opportunities.

167. 艺术是情感的语言。

Art is the language of emotion.

168. 宗教是一种大众哲学。

Religion is a popular philosophy.

169. 文化是知识的共享。

Culture is the sharing of knowledge.

170. 自信是决定智力的重要因素。

Self-confidence is an important factor in determining intelligence.

171. 逻辑体现思想的连续性，是接受和传达知识的手段；想象力是创建知识的手段。

Logic embodies the continuity of thought, and it is the means of receiving and conveying knowledge; while imagination is the means of creating knowledge.

172. 一切如果不是斗争的起因，便是斗争的结果。

Everything if is not the cause of the struggle, is the result of the struggle.

173. 一个人是其历史、环境、生活、哲学。

A person is his history, environment, life, philosophy.

174. 品格是价值观的自我规定，是决定一个人发展的内在力量。

Character is the self-regulation of values and the inner strength that determines a person's development.

175. 完美的事物业已定格，不再拥有持久的未来。

The perfect thing is fixed and no longer has a lasting future.

176. 面对现实的图景，可用语言表达的信息极为有限。

In the face of reality, the information that can be expressed in words is extremely limited.

177. 美是为了生机而付出的代价。

Beauty is the price to pay for vitality.

178. 美与其说是结果，不如说是过程。

Beauty is not so much a result as a process.

179. 审美体现经验判断，是观念在心房中的映射。

Aesthetic embodies experience judgment, which is the mapping of ideas in the heart.

180. 从苦难获取经验，是每个人最深刻的记忆。

The experience gained from suffering is the deepest memory of everyone.

181. 完美的事物，缺乏个性。

Perfect things lack personality.

182. 生活方式深刻影响人的品格与思想。

The way of life has a profound influence on people's character and thought.

183. 一切在时间中展开。

Everything unfolds in time.

184. 品格取决于实践中所扮演的角色。

Character depends on the role played in practice.

185. 人类最醇厚的技术产品，最终转化为艺术。

Humans' most mellow technology products are eventually transformed into art.

186. 探索过程与探索结果拥有同等快乐。

The exploration process is as happy as the exploration results.

187. 猜测是思想的雄鹰。

Guess is the eagle of thought.

188. 美是一种深刻的理解。

Beauty is a profound understanding.

189. 圣洁意味着把平凡的事物转化为高尚。

Holyness means transforming ordinary things into nobleness.

190. 美是一种向往。

Beauty is a yearning.

191. 幸福生活意味着更多包容。

A happy life means more tolerance.

192. 浪漫是青春的幻影。

Romance is the illusion of youth.

193. 人的本质是其社会经历和社会关系的总和。

The essence of human being is the sum of his social experience and social relations.

194. 不确定性使得：生活充满期待，科学充满幻想，艺术充满激情，哲学充满启迪。

Uncertainty makes life full of expectation, science full of fantasy, art full of passion, philosophy full of enlightenment.

195. 经济建立的价值标准是获取利益，艺术建立的价值标准是形式完美，历史建立的价值标准是社会进步，科学建立的价值标准是创新意识，哲学建立的价值标准是本质再现；而每一个人的价值观则是这些具体价值标准符合社会经历的加权综合，并且价值观作为衡量的尺度，反映一个社会发展的水平与现状，以及这个社会的人们所具备的文明程度。

The value standard established by economy is to obtain benefits; the value standard established by art is the perfect form; the value standard established by history is the social progress; the value standard established by science is the consciousness of innovation, and the value standard established by philosophy is the essence of reproduction; each person's values are the weighted synthesis of these specific value standards in line with social experience, and values as a measure reflect the level and status of a social development, as well as the civilization degree of this society people.

196. 美是价值观在艺术中的体现。

Beauty is the embodiment of values in art.

197. 和平是一种智慧和价值。

Peace is a kind of wisdom and value.

198. 生活为我们的变化提供注解。

Life provides an annotation for our changes.

199. 生活的意义在于迎接各种挑战。

The meaning of life is to meet the challenges.

200. 生活改变每一个人。

Life changes everyone.

201. 理解苦难是我们走向成熟的标志。

The understanding of suffering is a sign of our maturity.

202. 我们最痛恨的对手，恰是我们最全面的教员。

Our most hated opponent is our most comprehensive faculty.

203. 没有逻辑的文字只是一种图案，具备逻辑的图案是一种艺术。

Words without logic are just a pattern, while a pattern with logic is an art.

204. 权衡舍去与获得，是我们进步的开端。

Trade paying and gaining is the beginning of our progress.

205. 经验是感性与理性的边界。

Experience is the boundary between sensibility and reason.

206. 建筑展示生活的进程与空间的逻辑。

Architecture shows the process of life and the logic of space.

207. 道德是约束本能的社会舆论。

Morality is the social opinion that constrains instinct.

208. 人的言行是环境与本能相互作用的结果。

Human words and deeds are the result of the interaction between environment and instinct.

209. 美的价值，使我们憧憬生活。

The value of beauty makes us look forward to life.

210. 价值观决定行为取向。

Values determine behavior orientation.

211. 认识体现经验的积累与迭代。

Understanding reflects the accumulation and iteration of experience.

212. 人性的弱点使我们彼此相似。

The weakness of humanity makes us look like each other.

213. 错误的引导比无知更加有害。

Wrong guidance is more harmful than ignorance.

214. 艺术展示生机。

Art shows vitality.

215. 最广博的爱意是仁慈，最广博的仁慈是和谐。

The most broad love is kindness, and the most broad kindness is harmony.

216. 能力与品格取决于社会经历中所起的作用和扮演的角色。

Competence and character depend on the action and role played in the social experience.

217. 伟大事物构建时代背景。

Great things build the background of the times.

218. 岁月如流水一般填满现实的鸿沟，在精神和岁月面前人人平等，或终究走向平等。

Years fill the real world gap like running water, everyone is equal in the face of spirit and years, or eventually toward equality.

第 2 章 | 热爱自然莫过于认识和利用自然
There is no better love for nature than to know and use it

（1994 年中国科大硕士 Master student of USTC）

1. 民主是社会利益的普及。

   Democracy is the popularization of social interests.

2. 热爱自然莫过于认识和利用自然。

   There is no better love for nature than to know and use it.

3. 体育通过体格的运动再现精神的力量。

   Sport reproduces the power of the spirit through physical movement.

4. 吸引导致事物运动，排斥是系统对运动的制约，因此运动是吸引的函数。

   Attraction leads to the movement of things, repulsion is the constraint of system on movement, so movement is a function of attraction.

5. 发展的驱动力来自事物间的千差万别和广泛联系。

   The driving force of development comes from the differences and wide connection between things.

6. 对科学发展而言，质疑众多事物与热爱众多事物同等重要。
   For scientific development, questioning many things is as important as loving many things.

7. 开放性是事物有限特性的无限组合。
   Openness is an infinite combination of the finite characteristics of things.

8. 永恒的差异决定永恒的运动。
   Eternal difference determines eternal movement.

9. 幻想是概念摆脱逻辑约束所产生的飞跃，是闪现的想象力、潜在的创造力、宝贵的思想来源。
   Fantasy is a leap of the concept from the constraints of logic, an imagination of flash, potential creativity, a valuable source of ideas.

10. 摆脱逻辑束缚，拓展幻想空间。
    Get rid of the logic and expand the fantasy space.

11. 创造力被幻想和激情所引导。
    Creativity is guided by fantasy and passion.

12. 科学的灵魂，总是在激情幻想与逻辑约束之间游荡。
    The soul of science always wanders between passionate fantasies and logical constraints.

13. 运动是吸引平衡排斥的必然结果。
    The movement is the inevitable result of attracting balanced rejection.

14. 具体和分离是科学研究的前提和特征。
    Concreteness and separation are the premise and characteristics of scientific research.

15. 吸引是驱动事物运动的因变量，排斥是制约运动轨迹的函数关系。

Attraction is the dependent variable that drives the movement of things, and repulsion is a functional relationship that restricts the trajectory of movement.

16. 规律描述吸引、排斥、运动的函数关系。

Laws describe the functional relationships of attraction, repulsion, and movement.

17. 对驱动事物运动而言，开放性和对立性同等重要。

Openness and opposition are equally important to driving the movement of things.

18. 外部吸引和排斥相互作用，决定事物运动过程；内部吸引和排斥相互作用，决定事物运动形式。

External attraction and repulsion interact to determine the process of movement of things; Internal attraction and repulsion interact to determine the form of movement of things.

19. 排斥是内部机制与外部环境相互作用。

Repulsion is the interaction of internal mechanisms with external environment.

20. 吸引通过排斥决定事物运动。

Attraction determines the movement of things through rejection.

21. 吸引作用的边界正是排斥抗衡的平衡点。

The boundary of attraction is the equilibrium of repulsion and confrontation.

22. 排斥是事物保持稳定的根源。

Repulsion is the root of the stability of things.

23. 没有排斥，现实将“沸腾”；没有吸引，现实将“死寂”。

Without repulsion, reality will “boil”; without attraction, reality will be “dead silence”.

24. 开放性体现时空联系的必然特征。

Openness embodies the inevitable characteristics of space-time connections.

25. 在传播中，梯度既是起因也是结果。

Gradients are both cause and effect in propagation.

26. 内因决定运动形式，外因决定运动过程。

Internal causes determine the form of motion, and external causes determine the process of motion.

27. 吸引和排斥的相互作用，形成运动的普遍机理。

The interaction between attraction and repulsion forms a universal mechanism of movement.

28. 运动，是吸引和排斥对立统一的结果。

Movement is the result of the unity of attraction and repulsion of opposites.

29. 运动，是吸引和排斥平衡点的前移。

Movement is the forward shift of the equilibrium of attraction and repulsion.

30. 开放性构建运动的前提。

Openness builds the premise of movement.

31. 运动由开放性和对立性驱使。

Movement is driven by openness and opposition.

32. 差异是运动的起因，和谐是运动的目标。

Difference is the cause of movement, and harmony is the goal of movement.

33. 运动由梯度驱动。

The movement is driven by gradients.

34. 运动耗散梯度，使其归零，从而支付能量代价。

The motion dissipates the gradient, zeroing it out, thus paying the energy price.

35. 开放性为有限种特性场提供无限多梯度，从而驱使事物永恒运动。

Openness provides an infinite number of gradients for finite characteristic fields, thus driving the eternal motion of things.

36. 开放性构建差异，因此而成为运动的本源。

Openness builds differences and thus becomes the source of movement.

37. 运动是系统性与对立性作用的必然结果。

Movement is the inevitable result of systemic and antagonistic effects.

38. 运动的速率变化，由特性场的空间梯度决定。

The rate change of motion is determined by the spatial gradient of the characteristic field.

39. 运动方程中吸引和排斥的相互作用，体现为空间梯度影响速率变化。

The interaction of attraction and repulsion in the equation of motion is reflected in the spatial gradient affecting the rate change.

40. 由生命力所焕发的想象力，推进人类文明。

Imagination rejuvenated by vitality advances human civilization.

第 3 章 | 生命被自然演绎的法则所缔造
Life is created by the laws of natural evolution

（1996 年中国科大博士 PhD student of USTC）

1. 思想以其质疑和批判引导人类实践。

Thought guides human practice with its questioning and criticism.

2. 经验是从失败通向成功的环节。

Experience is the link from failure to success.

3. $Q=a[x+y+z]^{[f_1(u)+f_2(v)+f_3(w)]}$

其中：Q- 成就；a- 品格；x- 知识；y- 勤奋；z- 天赋；f_1（u）- 方法；u- 哲学；f_2（v）- 创造力；v- 美学；f_3（w）- 社会性；w- 心理。

$Q=a[x+y+z]^{[f_1(u)+f_2(v)+f_3(w)]}$

Where: Q-achievement; a-character; x-knowledge; y-diligence; z-talent; $f_1(u)$-method; u-philosophy; $f_2(v)$-creativity; v-aesthetics; $f_3(w)$-social nature; w-psychology.

4. 爱情基于精神选择，离婚基于现实选择。

Love is based on spiritual choice, and divorce is based on realistic choice.

5. 挚爱源自对自然演绎的敬畏。

Love comes from awe of natural evolution.

6. 熵深具科学和哲学双重意义，描述事物发展的条件与方向。

Entropy has both scientific and philosophical meanings, describing the conditions and direction of the development of things.

7. 发明是构建一条抵达已知目标的路径，发现是在已知路径中寻找一个意外的目标。

Invention is the construction of a path to a known target, and discovery is the search for an unexpected target in a known path.

8. 科学发展基于思想、实验、仿真。

Scientific development is based on ideas, experiments, simulations.

9. 星辰和大海向寂静的沉思者传达无言的哲理。

The stars and the sea convey a wordless philosophy to the silent meditators.

10. 每一种变化都基于一种力量。

Each change is based on a force.

11. 人的力量来自社会与自然。

Human power comes from society and nature.

12. 人类只能改变事物运动的过程而非运动的机制。

Human beings can only change the movement process of things rather than the movement mechanism.

13. 偶像只是机遇，而非选择。

Idols are just opportunities, not choices.

14. 生命只被希望点燃。

Life can only be ignited by hope.

15. 故土和经验不仅充实我们的机体和血液，而且充实我们的思想和精神。

Homeland and experience not only enrich our bodies and blood, but also enrich our thoughts and spirits.

16. 精神的价值，是引导我们跨越现实的鸿沟。

The spirit value is to guide us across the reality gap.

17. 艺术让我们感受生命不可遏制的力量。

Art makes us feel the unquenchable power of life.

18. 语言是社会交流，艺术是精神交流。

Language is social communication; art is spiritual communication.

19. 驾驭命运的缰绳掌握在自己手中。

The reins of the destiny are in our own hands.

20. 忍耐显示生命的张力与高贵。

Patience shows the tension and nobility of life.

21. 真理被先知掌握，被人民共享。

The truth is held by the prophets and shared by the people.

22. 思想在质疑和批判中产生并完善。

Thoughts are generated and perfected through questioning and criticism.

23. 变化是现实世界唯一永恒、绝对的本质。

Change is the only eternal, absolute essence of the real world.

24. 科学的最高境界是真，哲学的最高境界是善，艺术的最高境界是美。

The highest realm of science is trueness; the highest realm of philosophy is kindness, and the highest realm of art is beauty.

25. 科学的价值在于修正的过程，艺术的价值在于启迪的结局。

The value of science lies in the process of revision, and the value of art lies in the enlightening ending.

26. 爱情的魅力在于重构社会、文化、品格、精神。

The charm of love lies in reconstructing society, culture, character, and spirituality.

27. 我们在每一份迟疑和犹豫中衰老，却在每一份渴望和创造中复活。

We age in every hesitation and indecision, but we are resurrected in every desire and creation.

28. 规则是行为的逻辑。

Rules are the logic of behavior.

29. 我们最深刻的感受只能用艺术而非语言表达。

Our deepest feelings can only be expressed in art, not in words.

30. 创造源自对生命的挚爱，并体现生命演绎的价值。

Creation comes from the love of life and embodies the value of life evolution.

31. 政治、经济、军事召唤对社会的适应性，科学、哲学、艺术召唤对事物的创造力。

Politics, economy, military call to the adaptability of society; science, philosophy, art call to the creativity of things.

32. 置身于辽阔的社会场景和远大的社会进程，我们会忘却自身的痛苦并获得永恒的力量。

Immersed in vast social scenes and ambitious social processes, we forget our own pain and gain eternal strength.

33. 人类文明源自对生命的挚爱。

Human civilization comes from the love of life.

34. 缺乏精神价值，生命就丧失意义。

Without spiritual values, life loses its meaning.

35. 生命的价值体现在超越极限的勇气。

The value of life is reflected in the courage to go beyond limits.

36. 探索者以坚毅开启生命历程。

Explorers begin their lives with perseverance.

37. 赞美生命不仅是艺术的永恒主题，而且是人类文明赖以建立的基础。

Praise of life is not only the eternal theme of art, but also the foundation on which human civilization is founded.

38. 负熵是对人类社会发展机会的度量，意味着差别、梯度、动力，意味着有序、活力、生命，意味着逻辑、道德、法律，意味着语言、思想、精神。

Negative entropy is a measure of the opportunities for the development of human society, meaning difference, gradient, motivation; meaning order, vitality, life; meaning logic, morality, law; meaning language, thought, spirit.

39. 荒原对于探索的价值，在于磨砺人类求知的勇气。

The value of the wasteland for exploration lies in sharpening the courage of human beings to learn.

40. 美召唤我们踏上探索的征途。

Beauty calls us on the journey of exploration.

41. 坚毅的探索者，才是伟大的征服者。

The determined seeker is the great conqueror.

42. 艺术的动人之处不仅在于我们所感知的，更在于我们所联想的。

The beauty of art lies not only in what we perceive, but also in what we think about.

43. 痛苦源自期待多于忍耐。

Pain comes from more expectation than tolerance.

44. 我们渴望机遇，期待结果。

We are eager for opportunity and expect results.

45. 偶像是自带光环的事物。

Idols are things that come with their own halos.

46. 生存是人的生理成长，意味着衣、食、住、行；生命是人的精神成长，意味着教育、文化、事业。

Survival is the physiological growth of human beings, which means clothing, food, housing and travel; and life is the spiritual growth of human beings, which means education, culture and cause.

47. 真、善、美是人类文明的最高境界。

Truth, kindness and beauty are the highest realm of human civilization.

48. 脚踏热土并仰望天空是理性的生活。

Stepping on hot soil and looking up at the sky is a rational life.

49. 生活，是生命展开的进程。

Life is the process by which life unfolds.

50. 人类只能用精神而非肉体征服世界。

Man can only conquer the world with spirit rather than body.

51. 挚爱以拥有而骄傲。

Love prides itself on having.

52. 热爱是心灵的大学。

Love is the university of the heart.

53. 热爱是智慧的源泉。

Love is the source of wisdom.

54. 希望是照耀生命的曙光。

Hope is the first light of morning that shines on life.

55. 探索的征途蕴含求知的快乐。

The journey of exploration contains the joy of pursuing knowledge.

56. 音乐展现生命的节奏。

Music shows the rhythm of life.

57. 激情和诗意是人文主义精粹。

Passion and poetry are the essence of humanism.

58. 人类以虔诚面对希祈。

Human beings face prayer with piety.

59. 如果不勇敢地面对现实、迎接挑战、捕捉机遇，从而获得自身发展的力量；无异于当我们还活着的时候，就开始掩埋自己的灵魂。

If you do not bravely face reality, meet challenges, and seize opportunities, so as to gain the power of our own development; it is tantamount to burying our souls when we are still alive.

60. 现实是力量的唯一来源。

Reality is the only source of power.

61. 生命伴随希祈而展开。

Life unfolds with prayer.

62. 以生命验证忠诚是我们缺乏信任所能产生的最大悲哀。

Proving loyalty with life is the greatest sorrow we can produce without trust.

63. 悲剧以其结局验证现实对人性的局限。

Tragedy proves the limitation of reality to humanity by its ending.

64. 没有读懂一颗心灵的独白之前，我们总是面临一副陌生的面孔。

Before we read a monologue of a heart, we always face a strange face.

65. 信仰抚慰我们所经历的苦难。

Faith soothes the suffering we experience.

66. 生命力源自内心的渴望。

The vitality comes from the desire of inner hearts.

67. 从圣洁到神明差一个理性的距离。

There is a rational distance from holiness to god.

68. 发明是以技术的逻辑实现梦想。

Invention is the realization of dreams with the logic of technology.

69. 人性的卑鄙和神圣同样超出我们的想象。

The meanness and sacredness of humanity are equally beyond our imagination.

70. 创造源自个性所带来的独特视角。

Creation comes from a unique perspective that comes from personality.

71. 完美主义者对于经典乐章怀有顶礼膜拜的激情，并且沉浸在人文主义卓越氛围中。

Perfectionists have a passion for classical music and are immersed in the atmosphere of humanism excellence.

72. 审美体验是完美主义者获取激情的唯一来源。

Aesthetic experience is the only source of passion for perfectionists.

73. 宽容是和谐的根基。

Tolerance is the foundation of harmony.

74. 我们应当对科学、哲学、美学怀有同等热忱，这不仅会加深理解科学，还会把精神基础修建在更高平台上。

We should have equal enthusiasm for science, philosophy, and aesthetics, not only to deepen our understanding of science, but also to build our spiritual foundation on a higher platform.

75. 文明应当是充满神圣理念的教堂，充满知识乐趣的讲堂，充满艺术情趣的殿堂。

Civilization should be a church full of sacred ideas, a lecture hall full of intellectual pleasures, and a temple full of artistic interest.

76. 独立性，是共同发展和相互理解的前提。
Independence is a prerequisite for common development and mutual understanding.

77. 情感是信仰的一部分，也会成为骨髓和血液的一部分，并超越生命而永存。
Emotions are part of faith, they also become part of the bone marrow and blood, and live on forever beyond life.

78. 艺术是心灵的窗口。
Art is the window to the mind.

79. 感性的艺术和理性的科学交互循环，推动文明的可持续发展。
The interaction cycle between the art of sensibility and the science of reason promotes the sustainable development of civilization.

80. 善良具有更强的可持续性。
Kindness has greater sustainability.

81. 收获是对有效付出的回报。
Harvest is a reward for effective effort.

82. 艺术赞美生机。
Art celebrates vitality.

83. 诗歌由概念勾勒意境。
Poetry outline the prospect by concepts.

84. 科学回归自然的逻辑。
Science returns to the logic of nature.

85. 创造总是被希望所引导。

Creation is always guided by hope.

86. 生命是艺术的永恒主题。

Life is the eternal theme of art.

87. 艺术由具象之手开启理性之门。

Art opens the door to reason by the figurative hand.

88. 每一种工具都体现一种方法。

Each tool embodies an approach.

89. 由科学的具体走向哲学的普遍。

From the concrete of science to the universality of philosophy.

90. 期待，是生活的理由。

Expectation is the reason for life.

91. 目标由路径连接，路径由方法实现。

Targets are connected by paths, and paths are implemented by methods.

92. 艺术赋予我们现实的渴望和理性的启迪。

Art gives us the desire for reality and the enlightenment of reason.

93. 宗教以历史引导未来。

Religion guides the future with history.

94. 希望赋予人类征服未来的勇气。

Hope gives humanity the courage to conquer the future.

95. 道德是基本的常识，法律是基本的道德。

Morality is basic common sense, and law is basic morality.

96. 每一个生命的挫折都会激荡出浪花。

Every setback in life stirs up waves.

97. 创造比分享拥有更持久的快乐。

Creating has a more lasting happiness than sharing.

98. 善意具有更普遍的传播。

Good intentions have a more general spread.

99. 生命成长不可逆转。

Life grows irreversibly.

100. 教育在不发达社会是特权，在发展中社会是机遇，只有在发达社会才会成为普遍的权利。

Education is a privilege in underdeveloped societies, an opportunity in a developing society, and only in developed societies will it become a universal right.

101. 抽象以本质还原事物。

Abstraction restores things by essence.

102. 教育使精英创造知识并拥有成就，使常人接受知识并拥有技能。

Education enables elites to create knowledge and possess achievements, and enables ordinary people to accept knowledge and possess skills.

103. 尊重历史，就是尊重生命。

To respect history is to respect life.

104. 我们从现实的转折中感知哲学的指南。

We perceive the guide of philosophy from the turning point of reality.

105. 交响乐再现一个时代的洪流。
The symphony recreates the torrent of an era.

106. 热爱总是发起并传播自信。
Love always initiates and spreads self-confidence.

107. 热爱，是思想的源泉。
Loving is the inexhaustible source of thought.

108. 思想的力量，源自现实的逻辑。
The thought power comes from the reality logic.

109. 以生命的精华创造思想的力量。
Create the power of thought with the essence of life.

110. 艺术再现生命的活力与动机。
Art reproduces the vitality and motivation of life.

111. 没有科学依据的哲学只是一种空想，没有哲学指导的科学只是一门技艺。
Philosophy without scientific basis is just a fantasy, and science without philosophical guidance is just a skill.

112. 人类由实现精神目标而改变现实世界。
Human beings change the real world by achieving spiritual goals.

113. 真、善、美的交织，引导人类进步。
The interweaving of truth, kindness and beauty guides human progress.

114. 我们热爱所理解的，惧怕所未知的，崇拜所渴望的，珍惜所仅有的。
We love what we understand, fear what we don't know, worship what we desire, and cherish what we only have.

115. 一个人所拥有的力量取决于他的社会价值。

The power that each person possesses depends on his social values.

116. 凡是生命，就是在环境变迁中能够捕捉到机遇的事物。

Any life is something that captures opportunity in the environmental change.

117. 创造是以独特的方法重构现实逻辑。

Creation is to reconstruct the reality logic by a unique way.

118. 心境不仅源自我们所拥有的，而且源自我们所展望的。

The state of mind comes not only from what we have, but also from what we look forward to.

119. 所有的善良源于真实，所有的美丽源于善良。

All kindness comes from truth, and all beauty comes from kindness.

120. 命运是性格和机遇的组合。

Destiny is a combination of character and opportunity.

121. 力量是梯度的释放和差异结果。

Force is the release of gradients and the result of differences.

122. 不会有持久的喧嚣。

There will be no lasting hustle.

123. 在随机运动中时间没有意义。

Time has no meaning in random movement.

124. 本质必然简洁。

The essence is necessarily concise.

125. 思想是把梦想转化为现实的力量。

Ideas are the power that transforms dreams into reality.

126. 目标决定方向，机制决定路径。

The goal determines the direction, and the mechanism determines the path.

127. 力量不仅是事物间的相互作用，更是事物间的相互联系。

Power is not only the interaction between things, but also the interrelation between things.

128. 生命进化就是把联系完善到更广泛的境地和更深刻的层次，也是辩证法的必然结果。

Life evolution is the perfection of connections to a wider and deeper level, and it is also the inevitable result of dialectics.

129. 仿真使科学的结果用于现实的目的，从而实现设计优化和过程控制。

Simulation puts scientific results to use for real purposes, enabling design optimization and process control.

130. 科学把更多现象从偶然转为必然。

Science turns more phenomena from chance to necessity.

131. 艺术为现实增添光彩。

Art adds brilliance to reality.

132. 哲学不仅使我们预测目标，而且使我们选择路径。

Philosophy not only makes us predict goals, but also makes us choose paths.

133. 探索使我们从现实中获取璀璨的色彩。

Exploration allows us to get brilliant colors from reality.

134. 探索的魅力在于期待的前景和未知的里程。

The charm of exploration lies in the prospect and unknown journey.

135. 目标、机制、能量决定事物发展。

Goals, mechanisms, and energies determine the development of things.

136. 只有科学能把偶然性转化为必然性。

Only science can transform contingency into necessity.

137. 形式为内容播种。

The form sows the seeds for content.

138. 艺术为思想播种。

Art sows the seeds for ideas.

139. 科学的深刻与哲学的高度为思想腾飞提供落差。

The profundity of science and the height of philosophy provide a gap for ideas to take off.

140. 每一门科学都在把一种能量转化为一种力量。

Every science transforms an energy into a power.

141. 机制和路径，决定发展的方向和速度。

Mechanisms and paths determine the direction and speed of development.

142. 方法决定效率，目标决定路径。

The method determines the efficiency, and the goal determines the path.

143. 经典是被普遍性逻辑所约束的结果。

Classics are the result of being constrained by the logic of universality.

144. 开放的尺度是发展的局限。

The scale of openness is the limitation of development.

145. 目的性、社会性、实践性，是人类区别于动物的边界。

Purposefulness, sociality, and practicality are the boundaries that distinguish humans from animals.

146. 超越人类认知，体现探索的价值。

The transcendence of human cognition embodies the value of exploration.

147. 循环是通往可持续的路径。

Circulation is the path to sustainability.

148. 生命以循环和节奏展现。

Life unfolds in cycles and rhythms.

149. 苦难让我们深刻感知规律的壁垒。

Suffering makes us deeply aware of the barriers of law.

150. 真理是美和善良的基石。

Trueness is a common source of beauty and kindness.

151. 方法是进入过程的门槛。

The method is the threshold to entry process.

152. 经验是感悟的迭代，规律是经验的迭代。

Experience is the iteration of perception, and law is the iteration of experience.

153. 变革基于重组机制。

Change is based on restructuring mechanisms.

154. 颠覆是彻底的开拓。

Disruption is radical pioneering.

155. 善良是道德的基石。

Kindness is the cornerstone of morality.

156. 现实被事物的逻辑所演绎。

Reality is deduced by the logic of things.

157. 艺术再现时代的心声。

Art reproduces the voice of the times.

158. 真是自然的规律，美是感知的形式。

Trueness is the law of nature, and beauty is the form of perception.

159. 伟大的力量注定普遍和持久。

Great power is destined to be universal and lasting.

160. 艺术不仅展示美的结果，而且述说美的起因。

Art not only shows the results of beauty, but also tells the causes of beauty.

161. 真理是被多重规律所迭代的仅有结果。

Truth is the only result of iteration by multiple laws.

162. 交响乐是感性与理性交织的界面。

The symphony is an interface between sensibility and reason.

163. 思想以概念再现逻辑。

Ideas reproduce logic with concepts.

164. 思想是概念的重组和逻辑的延伸。

Ideas are the reorganization of concepts and the extension of logic.

165. 发展就是以优化的逻辑突破未来。

Development is to break through the future with optimized logic.

166. 运动就是在时空中展开事物的逻辑。

Movement is the logic of unfolding things in time and space.

167. 发展就是优化事物演变的逻辑。

Development is to optimize the logic of the things evolution.

168. 思想以概念重现经验。

Ideas reproduce experience with concepts.

169. 理性使人类从现实中获取自由。

Reason frees human beings from reality.

170. 创造是逻辑组合的艺术。

Creation is the art of logical combination.

171. 发展以优化事物的逻辑而促进其演变。

Development promotes the evolution of things by optimizing their logic.

172. 现实的联系体现为事物的逻辑。

The connection of reality is reflected in the logic of things.

173. 真理以事物的逻辑预测现实的联系。

Truth predicts the connection of reality with the logic of things.

174. 艺术体现历史和现实的精粹。

Art embodies the essence of history and reality.

175. 印象是被希望所渲染的视角。

The impression is the perspective that is rendered by the wish.

176. 希望为人类带来变革的勇气。

Hope brings humanity the courage to change.

177. 逻辑是存在的前提，发展是存在的方式。

Logic is the premise of existence; development is the way of existence.

178. 理性是回归现实的途径。

Reason is the way back to reality.

179. 唯物论由逻辑展示现实并产生科学；唯心论由上帝展示现实并产生宗教。

Materialism presents reality by logic and produces science; Idealism presents reality by God and gives rise to religion.

180. 本质不会有原因。

The essence will not have a reason.

181. 思想以概念再现事物演变的逻辑。

Ideas reproduce the evolution logic of things with concepts.

182. 科学是分析方法的产物，技术是综合方法的产物。

Science is the product of analytical methods, and technology is the product of comprehensive methods.

183. 年轻具有期待未来的勇气和力量。

Young people have the courage and strength to look forward to the future.

184. 生命被地理赋予特征。

Life is characterized by geography.

185. 艺术在为精神升华提供通道。

Art provides a channel for spiritual sublimation.

186. 艺术对于文明的价值在于，思想只能被形式启迪。

The value of art for civilization is that ideas can only be inspired by form.

187. 普遍性与可持续性是生命的机制。

Universality and sustainability are the mechanisms of life.

188. 系统性是逻辑的必然特征。

Systematization is an inevitable feature of logic.

189. 艺术传播生命的渴望。

Art spreads the desire for life.

190. 逻辑的系统性决定逻辑的普适性。

The systematization of logic determines the universality of logic.

191. 苦难是思想诞生的洗礼。

Suffering is the baptism of thought.

192. 系统通过逻辑演变。

The system evolves through logic.

193. 语言是现实逻辑的镜像。

Language is a mirror image of the logic of reality.

194. 系统的活力源自事物演变的逻辑。

The vitality of the system comes from the evolution logic of things.

195. 逻辑是概念的脉络。

Logic is the context of concepts.

196. 种群以生态逻辑延伸至自然。

The population extends to nature through ecological logic.

197. 提升系统性是自然演化的方式。

Improving systematization is the natural evolution way.

198. 每一个概念都有它内涵演变的历史和外延罗列的版图。

Each concept has its history of intension evolution and its layout of extension list.

199. 苦难，是尚未破解的逻辑。

Suffering is an uncracked logic.

200. 思想还原事物演变的逻辑。

Thought restores the evolution logic of things.

201. 优化事物演变的逻辑是发展的首要特征。

Optimizing the evolution logic of things is the primary feature of development.

202. 发展的完整性源自事物的系统性。

The integrity of development stems from the systematicness of things.

203. 时间的完整性源自空间的整体性。

The integrity of time derives from the wholeness of space.

204. 每一个目标都在寄托希望。

Every goal is pinned on hope.

205. 雕塑是空间整体性艺术，音乐是时间完整性艺术。

Sculpture is the art of space wholeness, music is the art of time integrity.

206. 苦难与欢乐交替，由此展开生命的节奏。

Suffering and joy alternate to expand the rhythm of life.

207. 时间体现逻辑在空间演变的秩序。

Time embodies the order in which logic evolves in space.

208. 计量和仿真共同体现科学的标志：逻辑的确定性。

Metrology and simulation together embody the hallmark of science: logical certainty.

209. 艺术展示生命的闪烁点和最强音。

Art shows the flickering points and strongest sounds of life.

210. 没有黑暗就没有闪烁。

There is no flicker without darkness.

211. 生命是事物系统性高度进化的必然产物。

Life is the inevitable product of the systematization of things highly evolved.

212. 完美的艺术具有生命的特征。

Perfect art has the characteristics of life.

213. 每一种满足抑制一种能力，每一种需求促进一种能力。

Each satisfaction inhibits a capacity, and each need promotes a capacity.

214. 竞争驱动事物的演变。

Competition drives the evolution of things.

215. 根本性力量源自系统性逻辑。

Fundamental power comes from systemic logic.

216. 辩证法导演现实的演变。

Dialectics directs the evolution of reality.

217. 规律就是事物演变的逻辑。

Law is the evolution logic of things.

218. 科学探索事物的规律，哲学探索规律的本质。

Science explores the laws of things, and philosophy explores the essence of laws.

219. 艺术是现实和理想的交集。

Art is the intersection of reality and ideal.

220. 辩证法是事物演变的推手。

Dialectics is the driving hand behind the things evolution.

221. 概念是逻辑的翅膀。

Concepts are the wings of logic.

222. 历史是社会演变的逻辑。

History is the logic of social evolution.

223. 科学是事物演变的逻辑。

Science is the evolution logic of things.

224. 力量反映事物联系的方式，能量反映事物联系的程度。

Power reflects the way things are connected, and energy reflects the extent to which things are connected.

225. 文明的每一次进步，都在扩展和加深人类与自然的联系。

Every advance of civilization expands and deepens the connection between human beings and nature.

226. 探索能量转换力量的方式，构成科学的全部内容。

Exploring the ways in which energy transforms power makes up the whole of science.

227. 语言是思想的轨迹。

Language is the trajectory of thought.

228. 发展是逻辑在演变中的迭代。

Development is an iteration of logic in evolution.

229. 生命的诞生与进化是逻辑在演变中迭代的必然结果，也是逻辑从种群系统延伸至生态系统和环境系统的必然结果。

The birth and evolution of life is the inevitable result of the iteration of logic in evolution, and it is also the inevitable result of the extension of logic from population systems to ecosystems and environmental systems.

230. 顺境是收获的季节，逆境是演变的季节。

Good times are the season of harvest, and bad times are the season of evolution.

231. 艺术以深刻的抽象展示普遍的具象。

Art presents universal figurative with profound abstraction.

232. 经典具有最广泛的普遍性。

The classics have the widest universality.

233. 经典植根于普遍性的力量。

Classics are rooted in the power of universality.

234. 现实具有开放性、多元化、系统性、完整性的必然结果。

Reality is the inevitable result of openness, pluralism, systematization, and integrity.

235. 运动是逻辑的演变，发展是逻辑的迭代。

Movement is the evolution of logic, and development is the iteration of logic.

236. 事物的确定性源自平衡。

Certainty in things comes from balance.

237. 吸引驱动事物的逻辑演变。

Attraction drives the logical evolution of things.

238. 人生就是生命力的演绎。

Life is the deduction of vitality.

239. 哲学是真理的内核。

Philosophy is the core of truth.

240. 现实不过是逻辑演绎的舞台。

Reality is nothing more than a stage for logical deduction.

241. 文学揭示人性演变的逻辑。

Literature reveals the evolution logic of humanity.

242. 理性是概念的本质与逻辑的演绎。

Rationality is the essence of concepts and the deduction of logic.

243. 伟大事物都是自然的演绎。

Great things are natural deductions.

244. 善是合规律性的目的性。

Kindness is the purpose according with regularity.

245. 科学和哲学构建人类的理性。

Science and philosophy construct human reason.

246. 文学揭示人性，科学探索规律，哲学挖掘本质。

Literature reveals humanity, science explores regularity and philosophy excavates essence.

247. 我们用哲学透视现实的本质。

We use philosophy to grasp the essence of reality.

248. 善是由规律性所延伸的目的性。

Kindness is the purpose extended by regularity.

249. 能量赋予我们希望，逻辑赋予我们自由。

Energy gives us hope; logic gives us freedom.

250. 科学是自然的逻辑，哲学是逻辑的法典。

Science is the logic of nature, and philosophy is the code of logic.

251. 文学以观念揭示人性。

Literature reveals humanity with ideas.

252. 人类文明是科学的深度、哲学的高度、人文的广度。

Human civilization is the depth of science, the height of philosophy, and the breadth of humanity.

253. 道德是心灵的法典。

Morality is the code of the mind.

254. 文学在现实演绎中揭示人性。

Literature reveals humanity in the deduction of reality.

255. 艺术是形式的，科学是规律的，哲学是本质的，文学是人性的。

Art is form; science is regularity; philosophy is essence and literature is humanity.

256. 每一朵花蕾都是羞涩的。

Every bud is shy.

257. 每一种美都被现实付以代价。

Every beauty is paid for by reality.

258. 苦难能够揭示人性的动机。

Suffering can reveal the motives of humanity.

259. 苦难是人类探索现实的力量。

Suffering drives human beings to explore the power of reality.

260. 苦难使我们深刻理解可持续的价值。

Suffering makes us deeply understand the sustainable value.

261. 苦难为我们揭示现实的全景。

Suffering reveals to us the panorama of reality.

262. 苦难揭示逻辑的根源。

Suffering reveals the roots of logic.

263. 苦难开启人类探索的征程。

Suffering begins the journey of human exploration.

264. 每一种现实的局限都在孕育伟大的思想。

Every limitation of reality breeds great ideas.

265. 苦难是人性的试卷。

Suffering is a test paper of humanity.

266. 苦难迫使人类重建发展目标。

Suffering has forced humanity to rebuild its development goals.

267. 苦难折射人性的色彩。

Suffering reflects the color of humanity.

268. 逻辑演绎是系统性的结果。

Logical deduction is a systematic result.

269. 文明是人类逐步建立目标的进程。

Civilization is the process by which human beings gradually establish their goals.

270. 艺术使大众共享审美体验。

Art enables the public to share aesthetic experiences.

271. 成长就是把人性的弱点转化为人生的优势。

Growth is about turning human weaknesses into strengths in life.

272. 和谐是远大目标的必然选择。

Harmony is an inevitable choice for ambitious goals.

273. 量变是自适应过程。

Quantitative change is an adaptive process.

274. 痛苦是梦想与现实的落差。

Pain is the gap between dreams and reality.

275. 勇气使人类凝聚心灵的力量。

Courage makes human beings unite the power of the heart.

276. 逻辑是实现梦想的必由之路。

Logic is the only way to achieve dreams.

277. 逻辑的确定性使得时间不可逆转。

The certainty of logic makes time irreversible.

278. 可持续性是系统进化的目标。

Sustainability is the goal of phylogenetic evolution.

279. 希望的价值是超越现实。

The value of hope is beyond reality.

280. 突变是系统重构所引发的逻辑切换。

A mutation is a logical switchover caused by system recombination.

281. 人生是对社会逻辑的遵从。

Life is about following the logic of society.

282. 每一种现实，都有其演绎的逻辑。

Every reality has its own logic of deduction.

283. 现实逻辑的演绎决定社会的发展。

The deduction of realistic logic determines the development of society.

284. 我们由观念和经验感受现实。

We feel reality through ideas and experiences.

285. 系统性联系决定事物的发展。

Systematic linkages determine the things development.

286. 色彩是对生机的度量。

Color is a measure of vitality.

287. 审美是观念的感知。

Aesthetics is the perception of ideas.

288. 美是现实的光芒。

Beauty is the light of reality.

289. 经验是由感性通往理性的阶梯。

Experience is a ladder from sensibility to reason.

290. 科学是被计量标度和仿真预测的逻辑。

Science is the logic of measurement scales and simulation predictions.

291. 质变由外部驱动所引导，由内部机制所制约。

Qualitative change is guided by external drivers and constrained by internal mechanisms.

292. 现实在哲学的高度实现其统一性。

Reality achieves its unity at the height of philosophy.

293. 系统性是有重点的、全面的、有界限的开放。

Systematization is comprehensive with focuses, openness with boundaries.

294. 经验是通往理性的台阶。

Experience is the step to reason.

295. 概念在逻辑的构架中才会具有活力。

Concepts are only alive in the framework of logic.

296. 混沌引发社会变革。

Chaos triggers social change.

297. 混沌是系统变革的起点。

Chaos is the starting point for system change.

298. 生命是物质、能量、信息的交集。

Life is the intersection of matter, energy, and information.

299. 可持续是理性的标志。

Sustainability is a sign of rationality.

300. 逻辑是万物存在的形式。

Logic is the form in which all things exist.

301. 不确定性是邪恶的特征。

Uncertainty is a characteristic of evil.

302. 感性认知具有最大的不确定性。

Perceptual cognition has the greatest uncertainty.

303. 批判是理性之门。

Criticism is the door of reason.

304. 计算力是人类最后的战争。

Computing power is the last war of humanity.

305. 感性认知代表宽泛的逻辑。

Perceptual cognition represents broad logic.

306. 混沌源于逻辑的不确定性。

Chaos stems from logical uncertainty.

307. 可持续性蕴含生机。

Sustainability contains vitality.

308. 普遍性包含真理。

Universality contains truth.

309. 逆行者才会拯救人类。

Retrograde will save humanity.

310. 灾难为科学和资本注入新的需求和生机。

Disasters inject new needs and vitality into science and capital.

311. 美是形式主义价值观对于经验的肯定判断。

Beauty is the positive judgment of formalist values for experience.

312. 需求是逻辑演绎的目标。

Requirements are the goals on which logic deduces.

313. 人性是社会的基石。

Humanity is the cornerstone of society.

314. 成长以系统重构为特征。

Growth is characterized by system reorganization.

315. 黑暗是对文明的考验。

Darkness is a test of civilization.

316. 有待完善的事物，构成发展的接口。

Things to be perfected constitute the interface for development.

317. 普遍性是可持续的基石。

Universality is the cornerstone of the sustainability.

318. 社会交往体现人性的逻辑。

Social interaction embodies the logic of humanity.

319. 可持续性体现自然选择的智慧。

Sustainability embodies the wisdom of natural selection.

320. 真是理性的根基，善是理性的目标，美是理性的窗口。

Truth is the foundation of reason, kindness is the goal of reason, and beauty is the window of reason.

321. 信任是最大的宽容，宽容是最深的热爱。

Trust is the greatest tolerance, and tolerance is the deepest love.

322. 善良是对长远目的性的选择。

Kindness is a long-term purposeful choice.

323. 个性是社会关系的接口。

Personality is the interface of social relations.

324. 没有出海口，就只能成为湖泊。

Without access to the sea, it can only become a lake.

325. 基于现实的人性演绎，构成文学展示的主题。

The humanity deduction based on the reality constitutes the theme of literary display.

326. 智慧是可持续的充分条件，聪明是可持续的必要条件。

Wisdom is a sufficient condition for sustainability, and intelligence is a necessary condition for sustainability.

327. 科学使民主成为社会发展的趋势。

Science has made democracy a trend of social development.

328. 多元化使逻辑演绎的非线性成为必然。

Pluralism makes the nonlinearity of logical deduction inevitable.

329. 上游决定存量，下游决定导向。

The upstream determines the stock, and the downstream determines the orientation.

330. 科学逻辑是社会逻辑的内核。

Scientific logic is the core of social logic.

331. 激情是意志的放射，诗意是自然的回归。

Passion is the radiation of will; poetry is the return of nature.

332. 激情和诗意构建艺术的两种风格。

Passion and poetry make up the two styles of art.

333. 流动是另一种传播。

Flow is another kind of transmission.

334. 生态是可持续性的基石。

Ecology is the cornerstone of sustainability.

335. 激情是希望所带来的躁动。

Passion is the restlessness that comes with hope.

336. 艺术在用不确定的意念启迪确定性的概念。

Art enlightens the concept of certainty with the idea of uncertainty.

337. 艺术是以感觉为先导、以形式为手段、以含蓄为特征、以经验为内容、以生命为主题、以人性为对象、以启迪为目的、以思想为结果、以人文为精神的多元化系统。

Art is a diversification system with sense as the guide, form as the means, implicit as the characteristic, experience as the content, life as the theme, humanity as the object, enlightenment as the aim, thought as the result, humanism as the spirit.

338. 文明在真、善、美的轮回中扩展其边界。

Civilization expands its boundaries in the cycle of truth, kindness, and beauty.

339. 人性的本质是基于规律性的目的性。

The essence of humanity is the purpose based on regularity.

340. 善良以其确定性而降低社会运行成本。

Kindness reduces the cost of running society with its certainty.

341. 检测黑暗，就是标度光明。

To detect darkness is to scale light.

342. 时代在发展，实践在深化，技术在迭代，科学在证伪。

The times are developing; practice is deepening; technology is iterating, and science is falsifying.

343. 文明基于自然的规律性和人类的目的性。

Civilization is based on the nature regularity and the human beings purpose fulness.

344. 理性是认知的终点和创造的起点。

Reason is the end of cognition and the beginning of creation.

345. 艺术的价值是启迪方法论，引导目的性。

The value of art is to enlighten the methodology and guide the purpose.

346. 宗教赋予人类生命的希祈。

Religion gives human a prayer to life.

347. 解构生命，才是享受生命。

Deconstructing life is the enjoyment of life.

348. 科学和哲学构筑理性的内核。

Science and philosophy form the core of reason.

349. 艺术是召唤理性的号角。

Art is the trumpet calling for reason.

350. 实践是由自然规律性实现人类目的性。

Practice is the realization of human purpose by the laws of nature.

351. 社会命运是历史性目标。

The destiny of society is a historic goal.

352. 教育把构建目的性作为己任。

Education takes the construction of purposefulness as its own responsibility.

353. 苦难能够激发人性的光辉。

Suffering can inspire the brilliance of humanity.

354. 艺术是灵魂的传播。

Art is the transmission of the soul.

355. 科学探索理性，艺术构架感性。

Science explores rationality; art structures sensibility.

356. 宗教以其教义提升人性。

Religion elevates humanity with its doctrine.

357. 苦难还原现实逻辑而萃取人性的智慧。

Suffering restores the logic of reality and extracts the wisdom of humanity.

358. 艺术启迪探索者，鼓舞实践者。

Art enlightens explorers and inspires practitioners.

359. 探索者承担认知的使命，实践者承担变革的使命。

Explorers take on the mission of cognition, and practitioners take on the mission of change.

360. 每一种伟大都在承担历史变革的使命。

Every greatness takes on the mission of historical change.

361. 美诱导人类广泛的目的性。

Beauty induces the broad purpose of mankind.

362. 价值是结果与成本的落差。

Value is the difference between results and costs.

363. 精辟意味着表述本身就是证明。

Incisiveness means that the expression itself is proof.

364. 渴望驱使人性的演绎。

Desire drives the deduction of humanity.

365. 传播性是思想的特征。

Propagation is a characteristic of thought.

366. 感知是思想的触角。

Perception is the tentacle of thought.

367. 认知是由人类目的性构建自然规律性。

Cognition is the construction of natural laws by human purpose.

368. 热爱生命是人性的基石。

Love of life is the cornerstone of humanity.

369. 生命是意志的舞蹈。

Life is the dance of will.

370. 探索本身具有无尽前沿。

Exploration has the endless frontiers.

371. 意志导演生命的旋律。

The will directs the melody of life.

372. 意志是生命演绎的动因。

Will is the motivation of life deduction.

373. 价值是可持续性的度量。

Value is a measure of sustainability.

374. 变革是征服者的收获。

Change is the harvest of the conqueror.

375. 善是人性的度量。

Kindness is a measure of humanity.

376. 人性是历史演绎的动因。

Humanity is the motivation for historical deduction.

377. 人性是品格和欲望的落差。

Humanity is the gap between character and desire.

378. 目的性的相互指向是构建社会网络的接口。

The interdirection of purposes is the interface to construct social networks.

379. 实践展开的先决是构建目的性。

The prerequisite for practice is to construct purpose.

380. 实践以规律性展开并实现目的性。

Practice unfolds with regularity and fulfills purpose.

381. 认知是以概念所构架的逻辑，还原事物的演变。

Cognition is to restore the evolution of things with the logic framed by concepts.

382. 数学以抽象性再现普遍性。

Mathematics reproduces universality in abstraction.

383. 社会是多重目的性的协奏曲。

Society is a concerto of multi-purpose.

384. 艺术以具象性再现普遍性。

Art reproduces universality with figurativeness.

385. 戏剧总是由人性的弱点展开。

Drama is always played out by the weaknesses of humanity.

386. 知识具有自信力，未知具有吸引力。

Knowledge generates confidence, unknown generates attraction.

387. 和谐是社会发展的终极目标。

Harmony is the ultimate goal of social development.

388. 艺术以具象性扩展人类的认知。

Art expands human cognition with figurativeness.

389. 和谐是统一性的目的。

Harmony is the purpose of unity.

390. 人们以目的指向性而相互联系。

People are interconnected to each other by purpose-directed.

391. 思想体现经验的价值，经验体现岁月的价值。

Thought reflects the value of experience; experience reflects the value of years.

392. 人未必像他自信的那样伟大，却像他自卑的那样渺小。

A man may not be as great as he is self-confident, but he is as small as he is self-deprecating.

393. 弱者的耻辱正是社会的耻辱。

The shame of the weak is the shame of society.

394. 邪恶是偏离规律性的目的性。

Evil is the purpose of deviation from regularity.

395. 认知是经验萃取的过程。

Cognition is the process of experiential extraction.

396. 感性丰富理性，理性引导感性。

Sensibility enriches reason, reason guides sensibility.

397. 现象多于感知，感知多于认知。

There is more phenomenon than perception, more perception than cognition.

398. 现象是被感知的事物演绎。

Phenomena are deductions of things that are perceived.

399. 和谐是社会的同一性。

Harmony is the unity of society.

400. 被现实迭代过的思想才会具有威力。

The thought iterated by reality has the power.

401. 真实性是认知的基石。

Authenticity is the cornerstone of cognition.

402. 创新就是以科学释放现实活力。

Innovation is to release the vitality of reality with science.

403. 导向决定战略，机制决定战术。

Orientation determines strategy, mechanism determines tactics.

404. 人生轨迹由阶段性目标所连接。

The trajectory of life is connected by its phased goals.

405. 可持续性就是衡量系统构架的完善度。

Sustainability is a measure of the integrity of a system architecture.

406. 人生从美开始以善告终。

Life begins with beauty and ends with kindness.

407. 故乡是思想萌发的土壤。

Hometown is the soil for ideas to germinate.

408. 可持续性是系统高度进化的结果。

Sustainability is the result of a highly evolved system.

409. 与邪恶相比，善良具有更多不确定性。

Evil has more uncertainty than kindness.

410. 有感知的地方就会有艺术，有艺术的地方就会有思想。

Where there is perception there will be art, and where there is art there will be thought.

411. 实践所留下的遗产是文明。

The legacy of practice is civilization.

412. 普遍性具有传播的力量。

Universality has the power to spread.

413. 自由的心灵才会奔腾。

A free mind will rush.

414. 飞翔高于奔腾，萃取高于集合。

Flying is higher than gallop, extraction is higher than collection.

415. 善良是个体的协同，和谐是群体的协同。

Kindness is the coordination of individuals, and harmony is the coordination of groups.

416. 有效力量来自极简事物的无限普及。

The effective power comes from the infinite popularity of minimalist things.

417. 形式源于事物演变的逻辑。

Form derives from the evolution logic of things.

418. 均匀性具有传导的力量。

Uniformity has the power of conduction.

419. 有文明的地方，就不会有真正的黑暗。

Where there is civilization, there can be no real darkness.

420. 教育使人由向往而目标。

Education makes people aim from aspirations.

421. 理性是跨越现实和理想的桥梁。

Reason is a bridge between reality and ideals.

422. 灾难赋予人类见识和勇气。

Disasters give humanity insight and courage.

423. 理想和现实的落差驱动社会发展。

The gap between ideals and reality drives social development.

424. 文明是历史的遗产。

Civilization is a heritage of history.

425. 善良是社会化的目的性。

Kindness is the purpose fulness of socialization.

426. 文明是连接历史和未来的桥梁。

Civilization is a bridge between history and the future.

427. 目的性被生活渴望和实践需求所孕育。

Purpose fulness is bred by the desire of life and the need of practice.

428. 思想是文明的内核。

Ideas are the core of civilization.

429. 生命的可持续性展现个体成长、种群延续、环境变迁、气象演化、年代更迭、地理迁徙。

The sustainability of life shows individual growth, population continuity, environmental change, meteorological evolution, chronological change, and geographical migration.

430. 法律是社会化的规则，道德是社会化的舆论。

Law is the rule of socialization, and morality is the public opinion of socialization.

431. 诗意是激情的起点和归宿。

Poetry is the starting point and destination of passion.

432. 艺术是感知的先导和认知的曙光。

Art is the precursor of perception and the dawn of cognition.

433. 社会构成中，哲学是头脑，政治是神经，科学是步履，工业是大腿，技术是臂膀，军事是拳头，新闻是喉舌，教育是基因，经济是血液，金融是动脉，艺术是感官。

In the composition of society, philosophy is the brain; politics is the nerves, science is the steps; industry is the thigh; technology is the arm; the military is the fist; news is the mouthpiece; education is the gene; economy is the blood; finance is the artery, and art is the senses.

434. 和谐是长远计划与宏大目标的必然结果。

Harmony is the inevitable result of long-term plans and ambitious goals.

435. 希祈是生命的本意和象征。

Prayer is the intention and symbol of life.

436. 希祈源自广泛的目的性。

Prayer stems from a broad purpose fulness.

437. 艺术寄托生命的希祈。

Art sends the prayer of life.

438. 艺术传播生命的希祈。

Art spreads the prayer of life.

439. 灾难促使人类重构文明。

Disasters have prompted humanity to reconstruct civilization.

440. 反省是自律的标志。

Introspection is a sign of self-discipline.

441. 生命在适应中进化。

Life evolves through adaptation.

442. 科学以概念仿真事物演变的逻辑。

Science simulates the evolution logic of things with concepts.

443. 现实是探索者的金矿，知识是实践者的金矿。

Reality is the gold mine for explorers, and knowledge is the gold mine for practitioners.

444. 人类在生命的希祈中演绎历史。

Humans interpret history in the prayer of life.

445. 创新是历史演绎中最可持续的力量。

Innovation is the most sustainable force in the historical evolution.

446. 对于挚爱生命的人们，现实永远是最美的图景。

For those who love their lives, reality is always the most beautiful picture.

447. 思想被现实演绎的逻辑所迭代。

Ideas are iterated by the logic of reality deduction.

448. 伟大的艺术散发现实主义的光芒。

Great art radiates the light of realism.

449. 善良构建社会的向心力。

Kindness builds the centripetal force of society.

450. 思维受语言的提示和制约。

Thinking is prompted and restricted by language.

451. 伟大的艺术中折射理性的光芒。

The light of reason is refracted in great art.

452. 现象是现实的断面。

Phenomena are segments of reality.

453. 激情似瀑布，诗意如流水。

Passion is like a waterfall; poetry is like flowing water.

454. 象牙塔是哲学的殿堂、科学的坟墓。

The ivory tower is a temple of philosophy and a tomb of science.

455. 苦难是现实给我们最深刻的提问。

Suffering is the most profound question that reality gives us.

456. 文明源自生命的希祈。

Civilization comes from the prayer of life.

457. 思想是逻辑迭代的结果。

Ideas are the result of logical iteration.

458. 听见音乐未必听见旋律，看到太阳未必看到光明。

Hearing music may not hear the melody, and seeing the sun may not see the light.

459. 思想是概念的解构。

Ideas are the deconstruction of concepts.

460. 思想要还原现实。

Thoughts should restore reality.

461. 方法高于结论，形式大于内容。

The method is higher than the conclusion, the form is greater than the content.

462. 社会发展受文明的制约。

Social development is restricted by civilization.

463. 需求引导一切事物的演绎。

Demand guides the deduction of everything.

464. 艺术要重构现实。

Art reconstructs reality.

465. 演绎就是现实存在的方式。

Deduction is the way reality exists.

466. 灾难赋予人类探索的勇气。

Disasters give humanity the courage to explore.

467. 探索以重构认知边界。

Explore to reconstruct cognitive boundaries.

468. 收益取决于规模和效率。

Benefits depend on scale and efficiency.

469. 思想受实践的制约。

Thought is restricted by practice.

470. 科学是自然的逻辑。

Science is the logic of nature.

471. 宗教借助神的形象引导生命的希祈。

Religion uses the image of God to guide the prayer of life.

472. 一切都在为生存而改变。

Everything is changing for survival.

473. 吸引与排斥的对立统一驱动事物的演绎。

The opposition unity of attraction and repulsion drives the deduction of things.

474. 美是理性与感性的界面。

Beauty is the interface of reason and sensibility.

475. 吸引通过内部的需求，导入外部的资源。

Attraction is both internal demand and external resources.

476. 信仰源自生命的希祈。

Faith comes from the prayer of life.

477. 循环与节奏是生命演绎的基石。

Circulation and rhythm are the cornerstones of life evolution.

478. 文学解构人性。

Literature deconstructs humanity.

479. 表达是认知的吸引，感受是认知的排斥。

Expression is cognitive attraction, and perception is cognitive exclusion.

480. 循环与节奏是吸引和排斥相互作用的必然结果。

Circulation and rhythm are the inevitable result of the interaction of attraction and repulsion.

481. 现实属于理解并热爱它的人们。

Reality belongs to the people who understand and love it.

482. 美再现自然演绎的生机。

Beauty reproduces the vitality of natural deduction.

483. 艺术是一条无极之路。

Art is the road to infinity.

484. 灾难迫使人类重建生命的希祈。

The disaster forced humanity to rebuild its prayers for life.

485. 现象是事物演绎的形式。

Phenomena are forms of deduction of things.

486. 文明是社会共享经验。

Civilization is the shared experience of society.

487. 哲学提炼规律的本质和本质的规律。

Philosophy refines the essence of law and the law of essence.

488. 美引导生命的希祈。

Beauty guides the prayer of life.

489. 美接力生命的希祈。

Beauty relays the prayer of life.

490. 本能是根本性目的。

Instinct is the fundamental purpose.

491. 本能是生命的底色。

Instinct is the undertone of life.

492. 没有甜蜜的种子，只有甜蜜的果实。

There are no sweet seeds, only sweet fruits.

493. 节奏是演绎的形式，循环是演绎的路径。

Rhythm is the form of deduction, and circle is the path of deduction.

494. 演绎就是现实存在的逻辑。

Deduction is the logic reality exists.

495. 生机就是生命演绎的力量。

Vitality is the power of life deduction.

496. 花朵是对果实的预言。

A flower is a prophecy of the fruit.

497. 艺术的使命是再现生机。

The mission of art is to reproduce vitality.

498. 突破认知边界是探索者的使命。

Breaking through the boundaries of cognition is the mission of explorers.

499. 思想是对现实演绎的运算。

Thought is the operation on the reality deduction.

500. 认知是经验在实践中的迭代。

Cognition is an iteration of experience in practice.

501. 探索必然是漫长而孤独的使命。

Exploration must be a long and lonely mission.

502. 没有期待的生活是暗淡的，充满期待的生活是痛苦的。

Life without expectation is bleak, and life full of expectation is painful.

503. 两极、多元、开放、系统是现实演绎的本质。

Bipolarity, pluralism, openness, and system atism are the essence of reality deduction.

504. 思想是引领文明的孤雁。

Thought is the lone goose that leads civilization.

505. 生命演绎可以调节，不可逆转。

Life deduction can be regulated and irreversible.

506. 文明是社会存在的形式。

Civilization is the form of social existence.

507. 征服的本意是复活，而非毁灭。

Conquest is meant to be resurrected, not destroyed.

508. 生命的经历与感受不可复制。

The experiences and feelings of life are uncopyable.

509. 超越就是从自卑到自信的成长。

Transcendence is the growth from low self-esteem to self-confidence.

510. 发展是逻辑在演绎中迭代。

Development is logic iterating in deduction.

511. 适应就是逻辑的迭代。

Adaptation is the iteration of logic.

512. 适应就是生命的进化。

Adaptation is the evolution of life.

513. 上帝赋予我们的手，用来捕捉机遇。

God gives us the hand to capture opportunity.

514. 每一种进化都为现实带来普遍的生机。

Each evolution brings universal vitality to reality.

515. 系统的活力在边界，边界的活力在出口。

The vitality of the system is at the border, and the vitality of the border is at the outlet.

516. 恨是爱的反证。

Hate is a counter-proof of love.

517. 变革是每个时代的标志。

Change is the hallmark of every era.

518. 科学是数据实验化、经验概念化、知识系统化、设计仿真化的结果。

Science is the result of data experimentation, experience conceptualization, knowledge systematization and design simulation.

519. 探索以过程为纲领，实践以目标为纲领。

Explore takes the process as the program; practice takes the goal as the program.

520. 灾难为变革带来契机。

Disasters bring opportunities for change.

521. 哲学是规律的终结。

Philosophy is the terminator of laws.

522. 生态是文明发展的极限。

Ecology is the limit of the civilization development.

523. 科学是经验的终结者。

Science is the terminator of experience.

524. 文明使自然沦为经济循环的载具。

Civilization has reduced nature to a vehicle for economic cycles.

525. 人类未来取决于科学与人文的统一。

The future of mankind depends on the unity of science and humanities.

526. 有的大路通往小溪，有的小溪通往大海。

Some roads lead to streams, and some streams lead to the sea.

527. 逻辑是现实演绎的推手。

Logic is the driving force behind the deduction of reality.

528. 我们用概念判断，用逻辑思考。

We judge by concept and think by logic.

529. 人类一切变革都是文明与生态的妥协。

All human changes are a compromise between civilization and ecology.

530. 与现实妥协是最具智慧的适应。

Compromise with reality is the wisest adaptation.

531. 吸引是生机背后的推手。

Attraction is the driving force behind vitality.

532. 把握变革就是把握智慧。

To grasp change is to grasp wisdom.

533. 生机就是现实中的普遍机遇。

Vitality is a universal opportunity in reality.

534. 阳光是蒸发的吸引，大海是河流的吸引。

Sunlight is the attraction of evaporation, and the sea is the attraction of rivers.

535. 循环的边界，就是增长的极限。

The boundary of the cycle is the limit of growth.

536. 美是经验的判断。

Beauty is the judgment of experience.

537. 艺术以现实的生机召唤人类的憧憬。

Art summons the vision of human beings with the vitality of reality.

538. 普遍性需求引导可持续生机。

Universal needs lead to sustainable vitality.

539. 结果取决于机制、方法、时机。

The result depends on the mechanism, method, and timing.

540. 抽象注定被具象启迪。

Abstraction is destined to be enlightened by figurativeness.

541. 卓越是跨入未来的力量。

Excellence is the power to step into the future.

542. 物种由竞争而适应。

Species adapt through competition.

543. 逻辑传播现实的力量。

Logic communicates the power of reality.

544. 经验是科学的序言。

Experience is the preface to science.

545. 生机没有固定的法则。

There is no fixed law of vitality.

546. 文明被希祈所引导。

Civilization is guided by prayer.

547. 文明是人类自由的标志。

Civilization is a sign of human freedom.

548. 自由体现生命的意志。

Freedom reflects the will of life.

549. 经典以深刻性再现普遍性。

Classics reproduce universality with profundity.

550. 意志是征服的力量。

Will is the power of conquest.

551. 可持续性是理性的标志。

Sustainability is a sign of rationality.

552. 文明折射理性和感性的光辉。

Civilization reflects the brilliance of reason and sensibility.

553. 艺术启迪一个时代的梦想。

Art enlightens the dreams of an era.

554. 人类最远大的图景与既得利益无关。

The most ambitious picture of humanity has nothing to do with vested interests.

555. 哲学是历史和现实的迭代。

Philosophy is an iteration of history and reality.

556. 窗户在观察，门扉在进出。

The windows are watching, and the doors are going in and out.

557. 深入现实，才能获取真正的自由。

Only by going deep into reality can we gain true freedom.

558. 没有期待就没有悲伤和喜悦。

There is no sadness and joy without expectation.

559. 善良是对行为社会化的度量。

Kindness is a measure of the socialization of behavior.

560. 和谐是社会共享的自由。

Harmony is the freedom shared by society.

561. 灾难使人类共同面对未来。

Disasters make mankind face the future together.

562. 和谐是多重目的性的统一。

Harmony is unity of multiple purposes.

563. 进化就是生命可持续性的优化。

Evolution is the optimization of the life sustainability.

564. 灾难赋予人类变革的勇气。

Disasters give humanity the courage to change.

565. 思想，把概念的逻辑映射到现实的逻辑。

Thought maps the logic of concepts to the logic of reality.

566. 互补是力量的叠加。

Complementarity is the superposition of forces.

567. 人生是追梦的旅程。

Life is a journey to chase dreams.

568. 能量是自然赋予现实的爱意。

Energy is the love that nature gives to reality.

569. 规律是通往自由的道路。

Law is the path to freedom.

570. 如果没有规律，所有的梦想只是期待。

If there is no law, all dreams can only be expected.

571. 循环由梯度驱动。

The cycle is driven by a gradient.

572. 探索是面向未来的勇气。

Exploration is the courage to face the future.

573. 没有苦难揭示人性，文学就不会具有深度。

Without the humanity revealed by suffering literature would not have depth.

574. 探索是文明的曙光。

Exploration is the dawn of civilization.

575. 形式是事物演绎的空间逻辑。

Form is the spatial logic of the deduction of things.

576. 探索，具有无尽的前沿。

Exploration has endless frontiers.

577. 时机是现实演绎的节奏。

Timing is the rhythm of reality deduction.

578. 美是感性的自由。

Beauty is the freedom of sensibility.

579. 真是理性的自由。

Trueness is the freedom of reason.

580. 自然演绎使美的力量不可遏制。

Natural deduction makes the power of beauty unstoppable.

581. 方法不仅取决于事物的机制，而且取决于面临的时机。

Methods depend not only on the mechanism of things, but also on the timing of the challenge.

582. 伦理是人性的规则。

Ethics is the rule of humanity.

583. 没有人文指引的科学是没有灵魂的。

Science without the humanities guiding has no soul.

584. 人文是社会发展的灵魂。

Humanities are the soul of social development.

585. 美把人类从感性引入理性之门。

Beauty brings human beings from sensibility to the door of reason.

586. 规律是事物演绎的逻辑。

Laws are the logic of deduction of things.

587. 探索以概念的逻辑破解现实的逻辑。

Exploration cracks the reality logic with conceptual logic.

588. 循环是可持续的路径。

Circularity is the path to sustainability.

589. 科学是自然演绎的灵魂。

Science is the soul of natural deduction.

590. 科学被人文所引导。

Science is guided by humanities.

591. 没有牵挂的鸟儿，才能飞进天堂。

Birds without concern can fly into heaven.

592. 灵魂被科学塑造。

The soul is shaped by science.

593. 灾难是文明的转机。

Disaster is a turning point for civilization.

594. 伟大的意志必然指向和谐。

The great will necessarily points to harmony.

595. 文明承载所有的苦难和荣耀。

Civilization carries all suffering and glory.

596. 跨越是对奔跑的反思，飞翔是对跨越的反思。

Crossing is a reflection on running, and flying is a reflection on crossing.

597. 生命被自然演绎的法则所缔造。

Life is created by the laws of natural deduction.

598. 真情是永远的春风，四季为春天而存在。

Trueness feelings are the eternal spring breeze, and the four seasons exist for spring.

599. 假如没有春天，秋季就没有果园。

If there is no spring, there will be no orchards in autumn.

600. 假如没有春天，冬季就没有预言。

If there is no spring, there will be no prophecy in winter.

601. 假如没有春天，夏季就没有火焰。

If there is no spring, there will be no flames in summer.

602. 假如没有春天，人类就没有新年。

If there is no spring, there will be no New Year for mankind.

603. 所有的循环都是为了时机。

All cycles are for timing.

第 4 章 | 和谐是自然的法则
Harmony is natural law

（1997 年清华大学博士后 Postdoctor of Tsinghua University）

1. 图腾，把生命的激情寄予生命的联想。

   Totem puts the passion of life on a life association.

2. 梦想比现实美好，现实比梦想深刻。

   Dreams are better than reality, and reality is deeper than dreams.

3. 可持续性是通向和谐的路径。

   Sustainability is the path to harmony.

4. 人生没有回程。

   Life has no return trip.

5. 自由是个体发展的目的，和谐是群体发展的目标。

   Freedom is the goal of individual development, and harmony is the goal of group development.

6. 生命属于被现实约束而依然期待的人们。

Life belongs to people who are bound by reality and still look forward to.

7. 锁不住的是希望。

What cannot be locked up is hope.

8. 和谐是自然的法则。

Harmony is a natural law.

9. 不可逆转是生命的特征。

Irreversibility is a characteristic of life.

10. 思想的旷野和宇宙同等辽阔。

The wilderness of thought is as vast as the universe.

11. 战争为人性展示提供全景舞台。

War provides a panoramic stage for the display of humanity.

12. 我们从探索中获取的，多于探索所要获取的。

We gain more from exploration than what exploration wants.

13. 没有适应和竞争，就没有生命的进化。

Without adaptation and competition, there is no evolution of life.

14. 和谐是自然演绎的目标和万物共存的方式。

Harmony is the goal of natural deduction and the way in which all things coexist.

15. 需求是梦想与现实的落差。

Demand is the difference between dreams and reality.

16. 伟大的本意正如阳光：赋万物予生命，赋生命予自由。

The great intention is like sunshine: to give life to all kinds of things, to give freedom to life.

17. 黑暗的边缘被星光和思想企及。

The edges of darkness are matched by starlight and ideas.

18. 如果能力不配期望，本性将被扭曲。

If the ability does not match expectations, nature will be distorted.

19. 期待孕育所有的梦想。

Expectation is the cradle all the dreams.

20. 没有和谐所有的存在都会成为进步的枷锁。

Without harmony all existence becomes a yoke to progress.

21. 宗教以神明祈求和谐。

Religion prays for harmony with gods.

22. 没有目标就无所谓道路，没有自由就无所谓生命。

There is no road without a goal, no life without freedom.

23. 没有生命的希祈，人生就沦为本能的游戏。

Life becomes a game of instinct without the prayer of life.

24. 艺术为社会注入希望，希望为文明构建契机。

Art injects a desire into society and the hope build an opportunity for civilization.

25. 生命是自然界可持续进化的必然结果。

Life is the inevitable result of the sustainable evolution of nature.

26. 工具是手的延伸。

Tools are an extension of the hand.

27. 和谐是进化的目标。

Harmony is the goal of evolution.

28. 和谐是更广泛的自由。

Harmony is broader freedom.

29. 将灵魂献给：承受我们生命、宽容我们无知、分担我们屈辱、静候我们启迪的故土，以及故土中穿行、欢唱的河流。

Dedicate souls to: the homeland that bears our lives, tolerates our ignorance, shares our humiliations, waits for our inspiration, and the river that walks and sings in the homeland.

30. 每一颗恒星都用尽光芒指示方位。

Each star uses up its light to indicate orientation.

31. 灵魂被现实的责任所塑造。

The soul is shaped by the responsibility of reality.

32. 希望是文明的寄托。

Hope is the sustenance of civilization.

33. 实践是文明扎下的根须。

Practice is the root of civilization.

34. 每一颗星辰都有其闪烁的价值。

Every star has its value of flicker.

35. 工具再现征服者的意志。

Tools reproduce the will of the conqueror.

36. 经验是实践成长的枝干。

Experience is the branch of practice growth.

37. 意志，是要把生命的每一个位置都变成自由的支点。

Will is to turn every position of life into a fulcrum of freedom.

38. 思想是经验生成的花朵。

Thought is flower generated by experience.

39. 文明是思想预言的果实。

Civilization is the fruit of thought prophecy.

40. 诗人是心灵的国王。

The poet is the king of the heart.

41. 每一种规律开启一扇自由之门。

Each law opens a door to freedom.

42. 每一场灾难都是一种启蒙。

Every disaster is an enlightenment.

43. 节奏是自然演绎的步伐。

Rhythm is the pace of natural deduction.

44. 目标分解才有过程规划。

Break down the goals to plan the process.

45. 每一种理性都是一条自由的路径。

Every reason is a path of freedom.

46. 感性是理性的界面。

Sensibility is the interface of reason.

46. 成功的理由，就是失败的代价。

The reason for success is also the price of failure.

47. 希祈是期待的理由。

Prayer is a reason to expect.

48. 萃取的都是精华。

What is extracted is the essence.

49. 工具是器官的延伸，器官是意志的体现。

Tools are the extension of organs; organs are the embodiment of will.

50. 由竞争而迭代，由迭代而高效，由高效而活力，由活力而精彩。

Be iterated by competition, be efficient by iteration, be energetic by efficiency, be wonderful by vitality.

51. 如果历史能够重演，现实就失去精彩。

If history can repeat itself, reality will lose its excitement.

52. 仿真才能够预测。

Simulation is the only way to predict.

53. 实践是经验迭代的唯一途径。

Practice is the only way to iterate on experience.

54. 经验是理性之门。

Experience is the door to reason.

55. 工具扩展实践范围。

Tools extend the scope of practice.

56. 人性体现在手段。

Humanity is reflected in means.

57. 创造是对现实逻辑更深刻、更广泛的组合。

Creation is a deeper and broader combination of real logic.

58. 艺术感性把握形式，数学理性把握形式。

Art grasps form by sensibility; mathematics grasps form by rationality.

59. 艺术，以生命的特征唤起生命的希祈。

Art evokes the prayer of life with the characteristics of life.

60. 科学揭示现实演绎的逻辑，哲学揭示逻辑演绎的必然。

Science reveals the logic of the reality deduction, and philosophy reveals the inevitability of the logic deduction.

61. 文明是科学转变现实的遗产。

Civilization is the legacy of science transforming reality.

62. 我们保留的创造力，正是不被道义所束缚的本性。

The creativity we retain is nature in being unbound by morality.

63. 器官是本能的工具。

Organs are instinctive tools.

64. 文明以工具实现生命的希祈。

Civilization uses tools to realize the prayer of life.

65. 和谐是理性的基石。

Harmony is the cornerstone of reason.

66. 技术是科学的应用，工具是方法的结果。

Technology is the application of science, and tools are the result of methods.

67. 器官是自然演绎的工具。

Organs are tools of nature deduction.

68. 和谐产生多元化需求，需求产生多种类目标，目标产生多层次产品。

Harmony produces diversified needs; need produces multiple types goals, and goal produces multi-level products.

69. 一种器官延伸一种渴望。

Each organ extends a desire.

70. 回归现实，是文明的起点。

Returning to reality is the starting point of civilization.

71. 环境是天文、地理、气象、生态的全集。

Environment is a full set of astronomy, geography, meteorology and ecology.

72. 一种和谐产生十种需求，十种需求产生百种目标，百种目标产生千种产品，由此生生不息。

One harmony produces tens of needs; tens of needs produce hundreds of goals; hundreds of goals produce thousands of products, and thus live endlessly.

73. 和谐是现实演绎的统一性。

Harmony is the unity of the reality deduction.

74. 统一性是多元化的出发点。

Unity is the starting point of diversity.

75. 信息是系统交互的基石。

Information is the cornerstone of system interaction.

76. 文明是人类演绎的形式。

Civilization is the form of human deduction.

77. 精神是现实力量对生命力量的映射。

Spirit is the mapping of the reality force on the life force.

78. 和谐是自然演绎的必由之路。

Harmony is the only way to nature decnction.

79. 表格是数据的窗口。

A table is a window into data.

80. 创建和完善是两种节奏。

Creating and perfecting are two rhythms.

81. 实践是经验逻辑与现实逻辑的迭代。

Practice is an iteration of empirical logic and realistic logic.

82. 理想超越现实，观念滞后现实。

Ideals transcend reality, and concepts lag behind reality.

83. 和谐是文明的基石。

Harmony is the cornerstone of civilization.

84. 星辰暗淡，是因为时空遥远。

The stars are dim because time and space are far away.

85. 思想是现实的逻辑，而非语言的逻辑。

Thought is the logic of reality, not the logic of language.

86. 可持久的未必是昌盛之道，可昌盛的未必是持久之道。

Lasting may not be the way to prosperity; prosperity may not be the way to lasting.

87. 生机是系统逻辑与环境逻辑相迭代的结果。

Vitality is the iteration result between system logic and environment logic.

88. 工具是文明发展的标志。

Tools are the hallmark of the development of civilization.

89. 艺术由经验提炼出激情和诗意。

Art distills passion and poetry from experiences.

90. 艺术是科学的序章。

Art is the prologue of science.

91. 可持续性为现实带来生机。

Sustainability brings vitality to reality.

92. 天堂位于现实的最深层。

Heaven is located in the deepest part of reality.

93. 机遇是逻辑演绎的时间窗口。

Opportunity is a time window for logical deduction.

94. 选择的代价就是丧失其他。

The price of choice is the loss of others.

95. 完美是生命不可承受之重。

Perfection is the unbearable weight of life.

96. 竞争使目标复活。

Competition resurrects the goal.

97. 逻辑是确定性的基石。

Logic is the cornerstone of certainty.

98. 可持续性是逻辑迭代的结果。

Sustainability is the result of logical iterations.

99. 普遍性是个性的本质。

Universality is the essence of individuality.

100. 人类改造自然的同时，也在深刻改造自身。

While humanbeing transforms nature, also profoundly transforms itself.

101. 仿真以数学的逻辑再现事物演绎的逻辑。

Simulation reproduces the deduction logic of things with mathematical logic.

102. 现实是万物演绎的舞台。

Reality is the stage for all things to deduce.

103. 和谐是现实演绎的目标。

Harmony is the goal of reality deduction.

104. 寂静是宇宙的思索。

Silence is the contemplation of the universe.

105. 人文关注现实演绎的结局，科学关注现实演绎的过程。

Humanities concern the outcome of reality deduction, and science concerns the process of reality deduction.

106. 和谐是文明演绎的目标。

Harmony is the goal of the civilization deduction.

107. 创造是被需求所引导的逻辑迭代。

Creation is a logic iteration guided by requirements.

108. 生命是波澜壮阔的心理历程。

Life is a magnificent psychological journey.

109. 竞争是生态的选择。

Competition is an ecological choice.

110. 意志被苦难所造就。

The will is made by suffering.

111. 缺乏希望的浮标，我们就会被现实淹没。

Without hope buoy we will be drowned out by reality.

112. 诗意源自内心的宁静。

Poetry comes from inner peace.

113. 激情源自心灵的尺度。

Passion comes from the scale of the heart.

114. 诗意和激情形成生命的节奏。

Poetry and passion form the rhythm of life.

115. 均衡促发多元化的逻辑迭代。

Equilibrium promotes diversified logical iterations.

116. 激情在喷发，诗意在流淌。

Passion is erupting; poetry is flowing.

117. 遵从自然，是生存的要义。

Following nature is the essence of survival.

118. 越精简，就会越广泛。

The leaner it is, the more extensive it will be.

119. 变革是最快的适应。

Change is the fastest adaptation.

120. 没有希祈就没有灵魂。

Without prayer there is no soul.

121. 严谨，如果不是高效的起因，便是高效的结果。

Rigorousness is an efficiency result if not an efficiency cause.

122. 普遍性就是事物的本质。

Universality is the essence of things.

123. 经典是普遍性的标志。

Classics are a sign of universality.

124. 系统性是整体性和层次性的有机迭代。

Systematization is an organic iteration of integrity and hierarchy.

125. 感知是本能的测算。

Perception is an instinctive measurement.

126. 气象是天文和地理的迭代。

Meteorology is an iteration of astronomy and geography.

127. 季节是天文和地理的迭代。

Seasons are an iteration of astronomy and geography.

128. 狭隘是生命的透支。

Narrowness is an overdraft of life.

129. 生命力源自期待的勇气。

Vitality comes from the courage of expectation.

130. 变革的力量源自观念的普及。

The power of change comes from the popularization of ideas.

131. 意志传播生命力。

Will spreads life force.

132. 时节再现生命的变奏。

The seasons reproduce the variations of life.

133. 肖像反映心态而非容貌，景色反映生机而非色彩。

Portraits reflect mentality rather than look, scenery reflects vitality rather than color.

134. 风景再现自然演绎的力量。

The landscape reproduces the power of nature deduction.

135. 激情再现意志演绎的力量。

Passion reproduces the power of will deduction.

136. 憧憬是一种旋律。

Longing is a melody.

137. 没有永恒的喧嚣。

There is no eternal hustle and bustle.

138. 怀旧是一首序曲。

Nostalgia is a prelude.

139. 没有期待就没有心灵的光泽。

Without anticipation, there is no luster of the heart.

140. 每一种所得是另一种失去。

Every gain is another loss.

141. 科学思考所得，人文思考所失。

Science thinks about gains, humanism thinks about loss.

142. 诗意是灵魂的居所，激情是意志的召唤。

Poetry is the abode of the soul; passion is the call of the will.

143. 科学为技术划定边界，人文为发展划定极限。

Science sets boundaries for technology, and humanities set limits for development.

144. 演绎的进程慢于忍耐、快于担忧。

The process of deduction is slower than patience and faster than worry.

145. 季节是生态演绎的节奏。

Seasons are the rhythm of ecological deduction.

146. 生机是由生态所释放的普遍本能。

Vitality is a universal instinct released by ecology.

147. 可持续性是智慧的标志。

Sustainability is a sign of wisdom.

148. 具象承载艺术和人文，抽象承载概念和逻辑。

The image carries art and humanities, abstraction carries concept and logic.

149. 欣赏就是传播。

Appreciation is transmission.

150. 艺术赋予我们期待的勇气。

Art gives us the courage to expect.

151. 变革是现实演绎的抉择。

Change is a choice of reality deduction.

152. 探索承担未来的责任。

Exploration takes responsibilities for the future.

153. 艺术的职责是超越人类的感知。

The duty of art is to transcend human perception.

154. 心灵因艺术而澎湃。

The heart surges with art.

155. 未来总是在期待中降临。

The future always comes in anticipation.

156. 期待中感受心灵的躁动。

Feel the restlessness of the heart in anticipation.

157. 期待赋予我们生活的勇气。

Expectation gives us the courage to live.

158. 人类的每一次飞跃，都是源于梦想的非同寻常。

Every human flyby is born out of the extraordinary dream.

159. 摆脱既得利益，才会把握未来。

Only by getting rid of vested benefits can we grasp the future.

160. 美最接近逻辑演绎的本质。

Beauty is closest to the essence of logical deduction.

161. 诗意是自由的标志。

Poetry is a sign of freedom.

162. 逻辑是现实演绎的路径。

Logic is the path of reality deduction.

163. 教育是不仅是文明的传承，而且是探索的起点。

Education is not only the civilization heritage, but also the starting point of exploration.

164. 由实践而经验，由经验而思想。

Experience by practice, thought by experience.

165. 和谐是生态演绎的逻辑。

Harmony is the logic of ecological deduction.

166. 灾难是对文明的警示。

Disaster is a warning to civilization.

167. 创造被自由的渴望所驱使。

Creation is driven by the desire for freedom.

168. 诗意使美成为动机，激情使美成为目标。

Poetry makes beauty a motive; passion makes beauty a goal.

169. 经验是审美的滤镜。

Experience is an aesthetic filter.

170. 需求是行为的动机。

Needs are the motivation for behavior.

171. 目的性是社会性的基石。

Purpose is the cornerstone of sociality.

172. 每一片风景都有它的激情和诗意。

Every landscape has its passion and poetry.

173. 文学是人性的演绎。

Literature is the deduction of humanity.

174. 人类向往和谐的冲动，都在更深层次回归自然。

The human impulse to yearn for harmony is returning to nature at a deeper level.

175. 经典是人文的内核与文明的标志。

Classics are the core of humanities and the symbol of civilization.

176. 激情像瀑布，诗意如流水。

Passion is like a waterfall, poetry is like flowing water.

177. 交响乐是奔腾的理性。

The symphony is galloping reason.

178. 我们所得的一部分正是获取的报酬，那是社会对我们付出的认可；而另一部分则是无形的、存留心底的、值得咀嚼和不断品味的记忆，她是我们整个生命最终的所得，也是生命蔓延的轨迹，是对一切往事的概括，也是面对未来聊以自信的支柱；她是唯一有可能等价于我们生命，并在生命解体之后依然佐证生命含义的东西；她或许不比泪水更苦涩、不比汗水更辛酸、不比血液更炽热，却比所有这些更持久、更深刻、更能传达普遍意义；只有这样的东西在充分攫取之后，才会使我们有理由在弥留之际与死亡的恐惧相抗衡；这件东西就是“经验”。

Part of what we get is the reward, that is the social recognition of our pay; and the other part is the memory of invisible, retained, worth chewing and constant taste, which is the ultimate gain of our whole life, also is the trajectory of life spread, is a summary of all the past, also is a pillar for self-confidence in the face of the future; she is the only thing that is likely to be equal to cur lives, and still prove the meaning of life after it has disintegrated; she may not be bitterer than tears, not more sad than sweat, not hotter than blood, but more enduring, deeper, more universal meaning than all of them; only such things after sufficient seizure, will give us reason to contend with the fear of death on the occasion of death; this thing is “experience” .

179. 人生是被意志所分解的旅程。

Life is a journey broken down by wills.

180. 青春的每一刻都是播种的时机。

Every moment of youth is the time to sow seeds.

181. 创造美，是因为我们比美更高贵。

Beauty is created because we are more noble than beauty.

第 5 章 | 我们不可能飞到比勇气更高的位置
We cannot fly to a higher position than courage

（2015 年中航天鹅总工程师 Chief engineer of AVIC Swan）

1. 站位和视角决定我们的感知。

   Stations and perspectives determine our perception.

2. 探索者无疆界。

   Explorers have no boundaries.

3. 一个人所能到达的最远处，正是被他的观念所照耀的地方。

   The furthest a man can reach is where his ideas shine.

4. 目标所及限于方法，方法所及限于观念。

   Objectives are limited to methods, methods are limited to concepts.

5. 哲学源自危难中的转机。

   Philosophy comes from a turning point in distress.

6. 每一门技艺所达到的巅峰都是艺术。

   The pinnacle of every skill is art.

7. 适应的过程即为成长。
The process of adaptation is growth.

8. 思想没有标准和疆界。
Thought has no standards and boundaries.

9. 山在那里，无须赞美。
The mountains were there with no need for praise.

10. 深沉的海水聚集在我们之下，升华的彩云聚集在我们之上；被阳光照耀就升华上去，被阴影庇护就沉默下去；这不仅是海水也是人类命运之真谛。
The deep sea water gathers under us, and the sublimated clouds gather above us; it is sublimated if illuminated by the sun, and it is silent if sheltered by shadows; this is not only the sea water but also the true meaning of human destiny.

11. 被艺术征服是人类的荣耀。
To be conquered by art is the glory of mankind.

12. 接受阳光，就成为彩云。
Accept the sun and become a cloud of color.

13. 太阳通过风掀起波浪。
The sun surges waves through the wind.

14. 希祈是人性演绎的内核。
Prayer is the core of humanity deduction.

15. 工业文明承载于轴承之上。
Industrial civilization is carried on bearings.

16. 实践是思想与现实迭代的必由之路。

Practice is the only way to iterate ideas and reality.

17. 我们在多大程度改变自己，就能在多大程度适应现实。

The extent to which we change ourselves is the extent to which we can adapt to reality.

18. 我们从多样性中获得深刻的启迪。

We draw profound inspiration from diversity.

19. 现实属于实践者，知识属于探索者。

Reality belongs to practitioners and knowledge belongs to explorers.

20. 我们不可能飞到比勇气更高的位置。

We cannot fly to a higher position than courage.

21. 边界具有最大的梯度和更多的可能。

Boundaries have the largest gradient and more possibilities.

22. 孤独的缘由，体现孤独的价值。

The cause of loneliness embodies the value of loneliness.

23. 矗立巅峰，方可揽云。

Standing at the top of the sky, you can take the clouds.

24. 收获的季节最多彩。

The harvest season is the most colorful.

25. 尊重差异是理性的开端。

Respect for differences is the beginning of reason.

26. 辩证法是现实演绎的推手。

Dialectics is the driving force behind the deduction of reality.

27. 美可被感知，不可计量。

Beauty can be perceived, not measured.

28. 艺术由感知的形式传播观念。

Art transmits ideas through the form of perception.

29. 感受未必感知，感知未必感觉，感觉未必感动。

Feeling may not be perceived; perception may not be sensed, sensation may not be moving.

30. 思想，源自经历的梯度和感受的纵深。

Thought derived from the gradient of experience and the depth of feeling.

31. 艺术体现国家的力量。

Art embodies the power of the nation.

32. 艺术是形式的感知，数学是形式的逻辑。

Art is the perception of form; mathematics is the logic of form.

33. 秋更深、色更艳、情更浓。

Autumn is deeper; color is more colorful; emotion is more intense.

34. 书房是心灵的客厅。

The study is the living room of the mind.

35. 具有能量的事物，赋予我们希望。

Something with energy gives us hope.

36. 年轻，就是探索的勇气和颠覆的力量。

Being young is the courage to explore and the power of subversion.

37. 科学是自然的逻辑，哲学是规律的逻辑。

Science is the logic of nature, philosophy is the logic of laws.

38. 罪恶的本源是不受约束的权利。

The origin of sin is an unbridled right.

39. 无知会使我们面对真理时依旧茫然。

Ignorance will leave us blank in the face of truth.

40. 艺术展示心灵的力量。

Art shows the power of the mind.

41. 没有梦想就没有未来。

There is no future without dreams.

42. 产品发展取决于需求的牵引和技术的支撑。

Product development depends on the traction of need and the support of technology.

43. 使命感是贵族精神的内核。

A sense of mission is the core of the noble spirit.

44. 义无反顾，才会英勇决绝。

Proceed without hesitation will be heroic.

45. 只有驾驭翅膀，才能驾驭心灵。

Only by controlling your wings can you control your heart.

46. 文明的包容性是国家统一的基石。

The inclusiveness of civilization is the cornerstone of national unity.

第 6 章 | 现实凝聚所有的力量和时机
Reality unites all the power and timing

（2016 年汉钟精机总工程师 Chief engineer of HANBELL）

1. 燕栖枝头，雪夜盼春。

   Swallows perch branches, looking forward to spring at snow night.

2. 环保的国度离太阳最近。

   The country of environmental protection is closest to the sun.

3. 放下一切，才会赢得一切。

   Put everything down and you'll win everything.

4. 创造价值，才能体现价值。

   Create value in order to reflect the value.

5. 教育一旦虚化现实，就会成为现实的镜像。

   Once education virtualizes reality, it becomes a real mirror.

6. 放飞心态，获取心灵自由。

   Let go of your mind and get the freedom of your mind.

7. 知识在阅读中积累、思考中发酵、应用中引爆。

Knowledge accumulates in reading; ferments in thinking, and detonates in applying.

8. 科学转化为技术，才会具有现实力量。

Science translates into technology and has real power.

9. 教育应当开启心灵、引导探索。

Education should open the mind and guide exploration.

10. 开放心态，才能回归现实。

Only by being open mind can we return to reality.

11. 探索被渴望的力量所引导。

Exploration is guided by the power of desire.

12. 艺术再现一切，科学度量一切，神明保佑一切。

Art reproduces everything; science measures everything, and God blesses everything.

13. 艺术再现绝望的心声、哀婉的旋律、人性的共鸣。

Art reproduces the voice of despair, the melodies of sorrow, and the resonance of humanity.

14. 辩证思维的终点，是创造的起点。

The end of dialectical thinking is the starting point of creation.

15. 用心构筑向上的力量，才能托起人类的信仰。

Only by building upward power with heart can we hold up the human faith.

16. 淡水是文明的底线，理性是文明的上限。

Fresh water is the bottom line of civilization, and reason is the upper limit of civilization.

17. 感知是灵魂的先导。

Perception is the precursor of the soul.

18. 善良是探索的路标和变局的退路。

Kindness is the guidepost of exploration and the retreat of change.

19. 最美不过心情。

Nothing is more beautiful than mood.

20. 制胜之路隐藏最深智慧。

The road to victory hides the deepest wisdom.

21. 哲学体现思想的法则。

Philosophy embodies the laws of thought.

22. 幻想伴随需求而游荡。

Fantasy wanders with demand.

23. 雪花在飞舞，目光在期盼，时光在流逝，梦想在延续。

Snowflakes are flying; eyes are expecting; time is passing; dreams are continuing.

24. 建筑是历史给文明留下的脸面。

Architecture is the face of history to civilization.

25. 包容是统一性的基石。

Inclusion is the cornerstone of unity.

26. 诱导是科学的法则和技术的理念。

Inducing is the law of science and the philosophy of technology.

27. 高阶成长必然具有非线性特征。

High-order growth must have nonlinear characteristics.

28. 有竞争的地方就有法则。

Where there is competition, there is law.

29. 智慧使人顺势而为，聪明使人借力而为。

Wisdom makes people go with the trend, and smartness makes people do by force.

30. 创造是成长的灵魂。

Creation is the soul of growth.

31. 自由的体制，才能容纳创造的灵魂。

Only a free system can accommodate the soul of creation.

32. 由现实所反馈的才是真我。

What is reflected by reality is the true self.

33. 有责任才有担当，有梦想才有故事，有积淀才有地位，有创新才有未来。

With responsibility to assume, with dreams to have stories, with accumulation to have status, with innovation to have the future.

34. 色彩和曲线属于上帝。

Colors and curves belong to God.

35. 道德是社会的法则。

Morality is the law of society.

36. 诱导是物理进化的法则。

Induction is the law of physical evolution.

37. 探索是最远的征程，好奇是最美的风景。

Exploration is the furthest journey; curiosity is the most beautiful scenery.

38. 热爱是自然的选择。

Love is a natural choice.

39. 需求无边使幻想无边。

Boundless needs make illusions boundless.

40. 利他主义是一个民族免遭沉沦的浮标。

Altruism is a buoy for a people to save itself from sinking.

41. 精确是标准化的基石。

Precision is the cornerstone of standardization.

42. 需求多元化导致结果多样化。

Diversification of demand leads to diversification of results.

43. 热爱是进化的法则。

Love is the law of evolution.

44. 你被仰望的世界，是你所照耀的世界。

The world you are looked up to is the world you shine through.

45. 每一种伟大都承载其苦难与荣耀。

Every greatness carries its suffering and glory.

46. 浪漫被幻想驱使。

Romance is driven by fantasy.

47. 渴望是人性的力量。

Desire is a humanity force.

48. 每一种智慧都由长期目标所塑造。

Every wisdom is shaped by long-term goals.

49. 生命在现实的迭代中成长。

Life grows in an iteration of reality.

50. 企业为客户创造价值，管理要提升员工价值。

Enterprises create value for customers, and management enhances the value of employees.

51. 探索拓展认知边界、提升人类欲望、获取发展源泉、寻求心灵慰藉。

Exploration expands cognitive boundaries, enhances human desires, obtains sources of development, and seeks spiritual comfort.

52. 发展是用一份方法诱导九份努力。

Development is the use of one method to induce nine efforts.

53. 无法被艺术启迪的心灵，也无法被时间启迪。

A heart that cannot be enlightened by art cannot be enlightened by time.

54. 艺术把自然的生机映射到自由的心灵。

Art maps the vitality of nature to a free heart.

55. 心灵是设计的原点。

The heart is the origin of design.

56. 秩序是通向深刻的门槛。

Order is the threshold to profundity.

57. 创造把深刻的矛盾转化为发展的源泉。

Creation turns profound contradictions into sources of development.

58. 思想的价值：脱离困境的出路、实践修正的结果、个人奋斗的价值、文化传承的基因、人类尊严的体现。

The value of thought: the way out of the predicament, the result of practical revision, the value of personal struggle, the genes of cultural inheritance, the embodiment of human dignity.

59. 建筑体现时代的尊严。

Architecture embodies the dignity of the times.

60. 美不但体现在目标和结局，而且体现在路径和方法。

Beauty is reflected not only in goals and endings, but also in paths and methods.

61. 建筑是生命展开的路径。

Architecture is the path through which life unfolds.

62. 现实以其演绎的逻辑再现自然的智慧。

Reality reproduces the wisdom of nature with its deductive logic.

63. 最严酷才会最透彻。

The harshest is the most thorough.

64. 自由之路的起点，是从内心解放自己。

The beginning of the freedom path is to liberate yourself from the heart.

65. 阳光照进现实，知识照亮未来。

Sunlight shines into reality and knowledge illuminates the future.

66. 美是规律性和目的性的双重判断。

    Beauty is a double judgment of regularity and purpose fulness.

67. 法律应为罪恶的刹那预留善意的空间。

    The law should leave room for good will at the moment of evil.

68. 规则体现人类的社会属性。

    Rules embody the social attributes of mankind.

69. 危难背后存有生机。

    There is vitality behind the crisis.

70. 思想在认知的高度飞翔。

    Thought flys at the height of cognition.

71. 探索具有持久的感召力。

    Exploration has a lasting appeal.

72. 文化使我们共享社会生活。

    Culture enables us to share social life.

73. 思想填补梦想与现实的落差。

    Thought fills the gap between dreams and reality.

74. 唯有河流，开天辟地。

    Only the river opens up.

75. 灵魂，在现实和欲望之间游荡。

    The soul wanders between reality and desire.

76. 诗歌扇动理想主义翅膀。

    Poetry fans the wings of idealism.

77. 竞争体现智慧的法则。

Competition embodies the law of wisdom.

78. 硬件发展的极限，是人工智能的起点。

The limit of hardware development is the starting point of artificial intelligence.

79. 没有比历史更高的山峰。

There is no higher mountain than history.

80. 经验是实践的果实，科学是经验的果实。

Experience is the fruit of practice, and science is the fruit of experience.

81. 有放飞才有高度，有自由才有梦想。

There is flight to have the height; there is freedom to have the dream.

82. 道德既是社会性标尺，也是企业发展的原点。

Morality is not only a social scale, but also the origin of enterprise development.

83. 仿生再现自然演绎的智慧。

Bionics reproduces the wisdom of natural deduction.

84. 唯有思想和光芒能穿越时空。

Only thought and light can travel through time and space.

85. 如果丧失方向，速度就成为负数。

If the direction is lost, the speed becomes negative.

86. 思想体现生命的尊严。

Thought embodies the dignity of life.

87. 人文关怀、系统思维、艺术启迪，是工业文明的维生素。

Humanistic care, systematic thinking, and artistic enlightenment, is the vitamin of industrial civilization.

88. 年轻，是战胜自我的力量和改变世界的勇气。

Being young is the power to overcome myself and the courage to change the world.

89. 北京：历史的积淀、贵族的气质、童话的烂漫、空间的逻辑、光影的交织。

Beijing: the accumulation of history, the temperament of the nobles, the brilliantness of fairy tales, the logic of space, the interweaving of light and shadow.

90. 逻辑是力量的本源。

Logic is the source of power.

91. 没有比天空更高的山峰。

There is no higher mountain than the sky.

92. 社会以科学的脚步展望未来，以发明的脚步迈向未来。

Society looks to the future with the footsteps of science and moves towards the future with the footsteps of invention.

93. 方向是生命演绎的灵魂。

The direction is the soul of life deduction.

94. 创造是影响力原点，道德是影响力半径。

Creation is the origin of influence, and morality is the radius of influence.

95. 自我完善就是提升世界。

Self-improvement is to advance the world.

96. 每一场经济危机，都在引发一次能源革命。

Every economic crisis triggers an energy revolution.

97. 没有历史的传承，就没有基于经典的未来。

Without the heritage of history there is no the future based on the classics.

98. 丰富被深刻所承载。

Richness is carried by profundity.

99. 现实演绎由辩证法所导演。

The deduction of reality is directed by dialectics.

100. 所有的时机都是鲜活的。

All timing is alive.

101. 发展是诱导和带动，而非堆砌和组合。

Development is about inducing and driving, not stacking and combining.

102. 生命在运动中才会具有灵魂。

Life has a soul in motion.

103. 为生存而适应是自然的智慧，为适应而生存是人类的苟且。

Adaptation for survival is the wisdom of nature, and survival for adaptation is a muddle of human.

104. 时代召唤伟大的乐章。

The times call for great symphony.

105. 时间平复一切。

Time calms everything down.

106. 音乐再现生命的律动。

Music reproduces the rhythm of life.

107. 严谨的批判是伟大的告诫。

Rigorous criticism is a great admonition.

108. 韶华易逝，倾其所有。

Youthfulness is easy to die, do all one can.

109. 没有什么比自然更深刻，没有什么比现实更有力。

There is nothing more profound than nature, nothing more powerful than reality.

110. 方向比速度更有价值。

Direction is more valuable than speed.

111. 艺术的灵魂是形式。

The soul of art is form.

112. 见证是探索者的旅程。

Testimony is the journey of the explorer.

113. 被艺术征服的灵魂，才能征服世界。

The soul conquered by art can conquer the world.

114. 简约才会深刻。

Simplicity can be profound.

115. 敬畏是信仰的前提。

Awe is a premise for faith.

116. 有了翅膀，就不再遥远。

With wings it is no longer far away.

117. 没有希祈，就没有灵魂。

Without prayer there is no soul.

118. 经验为时间赋值。

Experience assigns a value to time.

119. 社会性体现劳动价值。

Sociality embodies labor values.

120. 我们在多样性中迎接未来。

We embrace the future in diversity.

121. 创造，是多样性的果实。

Creation is the fruit of diversity.

122. 每一枚独特的种子，都是文明进化之父。

Each unique seed is the father of the evolution of civilization.

123. 伟大的时空与我们同在。

The great time and space are with us.

124. 规律是现实演绎的逻辑。

Laws are the logic of reality deduction.

125. 在实践中迭代认知。

Iterative cognition in practice.

126. 本质是简约的结果。

The essence is the result of simplicity.

127. 竞争是最好的参照。

Competition is the best reference.

128. 寂静才能听音，孤独才能感知。

With silence can we hear, with loneliness can we perceive.

129. 艺术构建现实与理想的界面。

Art builds the interface between reality and ideals.

130. 教育应该使人回归本真以释放内心力量。

Education should bring people back to their trueness to free up their inner strength.

131. 经典再现自然的精髓。

Classic recreates the essence of nature.

132. 价值链传递可持续力量。

The value chain conveys the power of sustainability.

133. 教育应该为成长提供无限可能。

Education should offer endless possibilities for growth.

134. 探索的道路没有多余的知识。

There is no excess knowledge on the path of exploration.

135. 艺术展示文明的尊严。

Art shows the dignity of civilization.

136. 进化成雄狮，丛林就是花园。

Evolve into a lion, and the jungle is the garden.

137. 进化是自然演绎的兵法。

Evolution is the military method of natural deduction.

138. 远见照不进蒙昧。

Foresight does not shine into obscurantism.

139. 质疑是认知的步伐。

Questioning is the pace of cognition.

140. 身体强大，才会内心强大。

If the body is strong the heart will be strong.

141. 艺术承载着信仰和梦想。

Art carries the beliefs and dreams.

142. 不基于求真的道德只是伪善，不基于求真的决策只能无果。

Morality not based on truth-seeking is just hypocrisy, and dicision not based on truth-seeking are just fruitless.

143. 现实凝聚所有的力量和时机。

Reality unites all the power and timing.

144. 悲剧源自被现实所约束的人性。

Tragedy stems from a humanity bound by reality.

145. 责任是自尊的边界。

Responsibility is the boundaries of self-esteem.

146. 理性为我们开启的每一扇门，都要用观念去跨越。

Every door that reason opens for us must be crossed with ideas.

147. 设计以形式的逻辑承载现实的逻辑。

Design carries the logic of reality with formal logic.

148. 能源是一切的未来。

Energy is the future of everything.

149. 独立是自由之母。

Independence is the mother of freedom.

150. 不被知识照耀的角落，必然背负愚昧的阴影。

The corner that is not illuminated by knowledge must bear the shadow of ignorance.

151. 没有深度的广度毫无意义。

Breadth without depth is meaningless.

152. 自我强大是最佳策略。

Self-empowerment is the best strategy.

153. 真理以其必然性波及世界并穿越历史。

Truth spreaded to the world and crossed history with its inevitability.

154. 科学发现引发技术革命。

Scientific discoveries spark technological revolutions.

155. 河流发源于海拔与寒冷。

Rivers originate in altitude and cold.

156. 科学在认知的边界上证伪。

Science falsifies on the boundaries of cognition.

157. 科学阐述的形式，也是证伪的依据。

The form of scientific exposition is also the basis for falsification.

158. 现实演绎的终点成为理想腾飞的起点。

The end of reality deduction becomes the starting point of ideal take-off.

159. 不被河流接纳，就不会被大海接纳。

If you are not accepted by the river, you will not be accepted by the sea.

160. 建筑：在自然景观中展开空间逻辑，在空间逻辑中展现自然景观。

Architecture: unfolding the spatial logic in the natural landscape, displaying the natural landscape in the spatial logic.

161. 复杂多变是通向深刻的必由之路。

Complexity and changeability are the only way to profoundness.

162. 不被现实接纳，就不会被历史接纳。

If you are not accepted by reality, you will not be accepted by history.

163. 设计，是在现实演绎中开启梦想之门。

Design is to open the door of dreams in reality deduction.

164. 和谐是现实演绎的必由之路。

Harmony is the only way to reality deduction.

165. 文明在现实的迭代中穿越历史。

Civilization travels through history in an iteration of reality.

166. 经典是历史长河中闪烁的浮标。

Classics are buoys that flicker in history.

167. 地理是生态演绎的舞台，气象是生态演绎的背景。

Geography is the stage for ecological deduction, and meteorology is the background for ecological deduction.

168. 阳光以气象的方式驱使生态演绎。

Sunlight drives ecological deduction in a meteorological way.

169. 概念细分与技术集成提升系统价值。

Concept subdivision and technology integration enhance system value.

170. 生态演绎被气象变迁所迭代。

Ecological deduction is iteratively influenced by meteorological change.

171. 每一种动力都承载自由的意志。

Every power carries the free will.

172. 建筑不仅属于地区，而且属于时代。

Architecture belongs not only to the region, but also to the era.

173. 建筑是社会的舞台、家庭的背景、成长的经历、时代的见证。

Architecture is social stage, family background, growth experience, witness of the times.

174. 效率取决于在多大范围和多长时期进行逻辑迭代。

Efficiency depends on how wide and how long to iterate logic.

175. 经验限定事业范围，道德限定事业高度。

Experience limits the career scope, and ethics limits the career height.

176. 科学再现自然演绎的逻辑。

Science reproduces the logic of nature deduction.

177. 寂静是升华的时空。

Silence is a sublimated time and space.

178. 所有为梦想所进行的努力，都会带来意外的收获。

All the efforts made for the dream will bring unexpected rewards.

179. 探索被现实需求所驱使。

Exploration is driven by needs of reality.

180. 我们总是在历史投下的阴影中走向未来。

We are always heading for the future in the shadow cast by history.

181. 反思是成长之路。

Introspection is the path to growth.

182. 能源是现实演绎的推手。

Energy is the driving force behind the deduction of reality.

183. 管理应当释放员工活力。

Management should release the vitality of employees.

184. 战术精确，才会战略精准。

Tactical precision leads to strategic precision.

185. 文明在旋转和循环中演绎。

Civilization deduces out in spins and cycles.

186. 大学是文明的标志。

Universities are a sign of civilization.

187. 平衡由运动所构建和维持。

Balance is constructed and maintained by movement.

188. 拥有飞翔的能力，才有搏击的胸怀。

Only with the ability to fly can we have a fighting mind.

189. 本质是洞见真理的窗口。

The essence is a window into the truth.

190. 伟大的特质来自心灵。

Great qualities come from the heart.

191. 攀登才有远见，刻意才会卓越。

Climbing will be visionary, deliberation brings excellence.

192. 掩盖真相就无法借鉴历史的智慧。

Covering up the facts cannot draw on the wisdom of history.

193. 仿真是科学探索的结果、技术集成的起点。

Simulation is the result of scientific exploration and the starting point for technology integration.

194. 求真是文明的目标。

Seeking truth is the goal of civilization.

195. 经典是文明的坐标。

Classics are the coordinates of civilization.

196. 互补是最强大的结合。

Complementarity is the most powerful combination.

197. 专制社会中，自由是一种疾病。

Freedom is a disease in authoritarian societies.

198. 艺术由经验的滤镜还原现实。

Art restores reality through the filters of experience.

199. 实践为理性的迭代提供机遇。

Practice provides opportunities for rational iteration.

200. 思想：锐度取决于敏感，高度取决于目标，内容取决于实践。

Thought: sharpness depends on sensitivity, height depends on goals, and content depends on practice.

201. 生机是自然的智慧。

Vitality is the wisdom of nature.

202. 地理、气象、生态被水汽的演绎所承载。

Geography, meteorology, and ecology are carried by the water vapor deduction.

203. 清澈才会洞穿。

Clarity bring penetration.

204. 演绎才有逻辑，运动才有灵魂。

Deduction will have logic, movement will have soul.

205. 规则是演绎的通道。

Rules are channels of deduction.

206. 心灵只能被善良洞穿。

The heart can only be pierced by kindness.

207. 因梦想而努力，因期待而生活。

Work hard because of dreams, live because of expectations.

208. 文明在信仰中穿行。

Civilization travels through faith.

209. 开启心扉，洞见世界。

Open heart to see the world.

210. 智慧在实践中成长，在现实中迭代。

Wisdom grows in practice and iterates in reality.

211. 色彩是我们最深刻的记忆。

Color is our deepest memory.

212. 生命不息，运动不止。

Life goes on and on with more movement.

213. 沉淀心灵，聚焦现实。

Precipitate the mind and focus on reality.

214. 科学描述演绎的过程而非演绎的机理。

Science describes the process of deduction rather than the mechanism of deduction.

215. 科学是哲学的外延。

The end of science is the starting point of philosophy.

216. 艺术再现现实演绎的精髓。

Art reproduces the essence of the reality deduction.

217. 勇气与生命同在。

Courage is with life.

218. 道德是社会的心智。

Morality is the mind of society.

219. 感知而经验，经验而规律。

Perceive and experience; experience and regular.

220. 希望是期待的底色。

Hope is the background color of anticipation.

221. 景色凝聚生态演绎的精华。

The scenery embodies the essence of the deduction of ecology.

222. 社会发展被需求牵引、被能源驱动。

Social development is towed by demand and driven by energy.

223. 人类从现实的苦难中，升华到信仰的高度。

Humans have risen from the suffering of reality to the height of faith.

224. 艺术为信仰开启门扉。

Art opens the door to faith.

225. 翅膀承载梦想。

Wings carry the dream.

226. 在持续地跌落中，鸟儿进化出翅膀。

In a constant drop, the birds evolved wings.

227. 观念是一堵最厚的墙。

The idea is the thickest wall.

228. 迈出关键一步，就会轻松十步。

Take a key step and it is easy to take ten.

229. 科学挑战认知的边界，艺术挑战感知的边界。

Science challenges the boundaries of cognition; art challenges the boundaries of perception.

230. 肩上有翅膀，心中有彩云。

There are wings on the shoulders, there are clouds in the heart.

231. 创新基于价值链的重组。

Innovation is based on the recombination of the value chain.

232. 节能是现代文明的底色。

Energy saving is the undertone of modern civilization.

233. 强大自身，无须抱怨。

Strengthen itself without complaining.

234. 教育为价值链重组提供无限可能。

Education offers endless possibilities for the restructuring of the value chain.

235. 回归现实的力量驱使我们跨越真理之门。

The power of returning to reality drives us cross the door of truth.

236. 深刻感受，才能生动展现。

Feel deeply in order to vividly show.

237. 生态体现多样性的和谐。

Ecology embodies the harmony of diversity.

238. 批判的每一步都在接近真理。

Every step of criticism is approaching the truth.

239. 智慧把现实的力量转化为人类的意志。

Wisdom translates the power of reality into human will.

240. 多么超越，就多么孤独。

How transcendent, how lonely.

241. 审美是文化多样性的根基。

Aesthetics are the foundation of cultural diversity.

242. 诱导而非征服自然，是人类所能达到的最高理性。

Inducing rather than conquering nature is the highest rationality that human beings can achieve.

243. 真诚是回归理性的基础。

Sincerity is the basis for a return to reason.

244. 人类的任何意志，最终来源于现实。

Any human will ultimately comes from reality.

245. 真理体现历史发展的必然性。

Truth embodies the inevitability of historical development.

246. 蒸发与冷凝是现实演绎的背景。

Evaporation and condensation are the background for reality deduction.

247. 被认知的现实会成为趋势。

The perceived reality becomes the trend.

248. 没有比现实更大的勇气。

There is no greater courage than reality.

249. 经典是最深刻的现实。

Classics are the deepest reality.

250. 一切战争都是勇气的战争，一切胜利都是意志的胜利。

All wars are courage wars; all victories are will victories.

251. 每一场伟大的技术革命，都是在更深层次回归现实。

Every great technological revolution is a return to reality at a deeper level.

252. 罪恶是先发制人的恐惧。

Sin is pre-emptive fear.

253. 流水只为河床湍急。

The flowing water is turbulent only for the riverbed.

254. 没有比劳动更大的自信，没有比创造更大的荣耀。

There is no greater self-confidence than labor, and there is no greater glory than creation.

255. 认知最大的意义在于深刻理解现实。

The greatest significance of cognition lies in a deep understanding of reality.

256. 人性从文学的漏斗中流淌。

Humanity flows from the funnel of literature.

257. 所有的深刻都是在质疑中完成的。

All profundity is done in questioning.

258. 认知现实是救赎苦难的开始。

Recognizing reality is the beginning of redemptive suffering.

259. 提升理想的唯一方式是回归现实。

The only way to elevate ideals is to return to reality.

260. 深邃而平静，超越而孤独。

Deep and calm, transcendent and lonely.

261. 深入是提升的法则。

Depth is the law of elevation.

262. 探索现实，是人类最深刻的启蒙。

Exploring reality is the deepest enlightenment of mankind.

263. 希望是被文明萃取的欲望。

Hope is the desire to be extracted by civilization.

264. 战术上的完美无法弥补战略上的漏洞。

Tactical perfection cannot close strategic holes.

265. 伟大艺术是不可复制的灵魂。

Great art is an unrepeatable soul.

266. 感知印象，认知真理。

Perceive impressions, recognize truths.

267. 连续由离散表达，波动由粒子表达。

Continuity is expressed by discrete, and fluctuations are expressed by particles.

268. 规律是自然的逻辑，道德是行为的逻辑。

Law is the logic of nature; morality is the logic of behavior.

269. 拼搏未必成功，放弃必然失败。

Struggle may not be successful, and giving up is bound to fail.

270. 文明是基于技术的人文。

The civilization is based on technological invention.

271. 法律、宗教、资本、性爱、思维、财富，是人类文明的坐标。

Law, religion, capital, sex, thinking, wealth, are the coordinates of human civilization.

272. 车站是梦想的起点和归宿。

The station is the starting point and destination of dreams.

273. 丧失期望是人性毁灭的开始。

The loss of expectation is the beginning of the destruction of humanity.

274. 伟大的发明构建技术发展的拐点。

Great inventions build inflection points in technological development.

275. 技术创造产品的核心价值。

Technology creates the core value of products.

276. 艺术是灵魂的表达。

Art is the expression of the soul.

277. 自由是生命的表达。

Freedom is the expression of life.

278. 能源是变化之母。

Energy is the mother of change.

279. 善良的出发点，自有其结局。

The starting point of kindness has its own ending.

280. 有梦想就有活力，有信心就有经济。

There is vitality with dreams; there is economy with confidence.

281. 所有的灵魂都是独立的。

All souls are independent.

282. 敬畏自然是智慧的开始。

Reverence for nature is the beginning of wisdom.

283. 精简是理解的开始。

Streamlining is the beginning of understanding.

284. 回归现实是最好的出发。

Returning to reality is the best place to start.

285. 能源和淡水是文明发展的基石。

Energy and fresh water are the cornerstones of civilization.

286. 生存是最大的现实。

Survival is the greatest reality.

287. 救赎是把自我意识回归现实。

Salvation is the return of self-consciousness to reality.

288. 探索就是求真。

To explore is to seek truth.

289. 景色承载历史的变迁和生态的演绎。

The scenery carries history changes and ecology deductions.

290. 所有的形式都是逻辑的轨迹，所有的喧嚣都是逻辑的节奏。

All forms are logical trajectories, and all hustle and bustle are logical rhythms.

291. 求真就是回归现实。

To seek truth is to return to reality.

292. 可持续性基于开放性和系统性。

Sustainability is based on openness and systematization.

293. 大学是思想的舞者。

Universities are dancers of ideas.

294. 希望是人文之源。

Hope is the source of humanity.

295. 一切的对辩都是成长。

All arguments are growth.

296. 只有真正的对手才会使我们强大。

Only real opponents will make us strong.

297. 求真是文明的底线。

Restoring the facts is the bottom line of civilization.

298. 思想是概念的逻辑，词汇是语言的逻辑。

Ideas are the logic of concepts, and words are the logic of language.

299. 同情心不可兜售。

Compassion cannot be peddled.

300. 数学是逻辑的诗篇。

Mathematics is the psalms of logic.

301. 多元化才有可持续的未来。

Diversity is the only way to have a sustainable future.

302. 需求的演绎迭代技术的演绎。

Deduction of requirements iterates deduction of techniques.

303. 艺术是灵魂的归途。

Art is the return of the soul.

304. 每一种蒸馏都是文明的里程碑。

Every distillation is a milestone of civilization.

305. 每一种真诚的付出，都会拥有意外的收获。

Every sincere effort will have unexpected gains.

306. 现实是设计的起点和归宿。

Reality is the starting point and destination of design.

307. 历史是人性演绎和自然演绎的双重结局。

History is the double ending of humanity deduction and nature deduction.

308. 利他主义是回归现实的途径。

Altruism is the way back to reality.

309. 孤独是思想的时空。

Loneliness is the time and space of thought.

310. 发现和发明都是一种激情。

Discovery and invention are passions.

311. 好奇心使我们从挫折中提炼出美感。

Curiosity allows us to extract aesthetic value from setbacks.

312. 能量是自然赋予现实的激情。

Energy is the passion that nature gives to reality.

313. 没有比真诚更加高贵的品德。

There is no nobler character than sincerity.

314. 由灵魂创造的艺术，只能被灵魂解读。

Art created by the soul can only be interpreted by the soul.

315. 被真理照耀，就不再愚昧。

Illuminated by the truth, you will no longer be foolish.

316. 压缩驱动热泵，热泵诱导世界。

Compression drives heat pumps; heat pumps induce the world.

317. 所有的风光都在山峰。

All the scenery is on the peaks.

318. 上帝把最深刻的启示，赋予自然的转机。

God has given the deepest revelation to the turn of nature.

319. 领导力使我们从应变力提炼出创造力。

Leadership allows us to extract creativity from resilience.

320. 理性的价值是把握现实发展的趋势。

The value of rationality is to grasp the trend of realistic development.

321. 提炼逻辑的美感价值是科学的信仰。

Refining the aesthetic value of logic is the belief of science.

322. 希望是现实蕴含的转机。

Hope is a turning point in reality.

323. 回归真诚，就是回归现实的普遍性。

To return to sincerity is to return to the universality of reality.

324. 多样性是价值组合的源泉。

Diversity is the source of value mix.

325. 理性总是把现实的困境转化成发展的优势。

Reason always transforms real dilemmas into advantages for development.

326. 由人性的优势驱动经济循环。

The economic cycle is driven by the advantages of humanity.

327. 唯有理性的光芒穿透历史和未来。

Only the light of reason penetrates history and the future.

328. 诗意，在把事物的必然性回归自然。

Poetry is returning the inevitability of things to nature.

329. 逆卡诺循环提升热能价值，改造自然。

The reverse Kano Cycle increases the value of heat energy and transforms nature.

330. 审美是人类灵魂的居所。

Aesthetics is the residence of the human soul.

331. 建筑让时光在空间流淌。

Architecture lets time flow in space.

332. 创新在为多元文化提供无穷组合。

Innovation provides endless combinations of diverse cultures.

333. 道德是规则的内核。

Morality is the core of the rules.

334. 文明穿透内心，才能照亮世界。

Only when civilization penetrates the heart can the world be illuminated.

335. 技术是文明的内核。

Technology is the core of civilization.

336. 四季的轮回，是最好的再生。

The cycle of the four seasons is the best regeneration.

337. 探索的目标是为文明的发展提供多样性。

The goal of exploration is to provide diversity for the development of civilizations.

338. 创造的本质是多元文化的价值组合。

The essence of creation is the value combination of multiculturalism.

339. 每一次挫折都是一次逻辑的迭代。

Every setback is an iteration of logic.

340. 探索是理性的乐园。

Exploration is a paradise of reason.

341. 认知是最伟大的实践，实践是最伟大的认知。

Cognition is the greatest practice, and practice is the greatest cognition.

342. 深刻，把特殊性提升为普遍性。

Profound elevates the particularity to the universality.

343. 时代的艺术承载历史的责任。

The art of an era bears the responsibility of history.

344. 理性把人生的苦难转化为社会的阶梯。

Reason transforms the sufferings of life into social ladders.

345. 善良不止于退路，更是征途的指南。

Kindness is not only a retreat, but also a guide to the journey.

346. 文学把人性的经验赋予生活的勇气。

Literature endows humanity experience with the courage of life.

347. 收敛的每一步，就是发展的第一步。

Every step of convergence is the first step of development.

348. 传感是计量的先锋和意志的使者。

Sensing is the vanguard of metrology and the messenger of will.

349. 由否定实现再否定，是思想萃取的滤网。

Renegativeing by negation is the filter of thought extraction.

350. 真、善、美是折射理性的三棱镜。

Truth, kindness and beauty are the prisms that reflect reason.

351. 现实的普遍性，才会谱写历史。

The universality of reality will write history.

352. 地理和气象是生态演绎的背景。

Geography and meteorology are the background for ecological deduction.

353. 发现取决于视角。

Discovery depends on the perspective.

354. 民心就是国家的力量。

The people will is the strength of the country.

355. 沉浮取决于承载的力量。

The ups and downs depend on the carrying force.

356. 互补是最牢固的连接，连接是最牢固的构架。

Complementarity is the strongest connection, and connection is the strongest architecture.

357. 创新是方法与现实的博弈。

Innovation is the game between methods and reality.

358. 实践是最深刻的认知。

Practice is the deepest understanding.

359. 善恶的起点注定是善恶的归宿。

The beginning of good or evil is destined to be the end of good or evil.

360. 审美的人生才有光泽。

An aesthetic life will be lustrous.

361. 只有伟大才能感召伟大。

Only greatness can inspire greatness.

362. 艺术在表达，灵魂在感知。

Art is expressing; soul is perceiving.

363. 科学为现实演绎预测路径和极限。

Science predicts paths and limits for reality deduction.

364. 探索是实践的起点和归宿。

Exploration is the beginning and end of practice.

365. 科学发现决定技术，技术发明决定未来。

Scientific discoveries determine technology, and technological inventions determine the future.

366. 思想是概念的逻辑迭代现实的逻辑。

Ideas are the logic of concepts iterating on the logic of reality.

367. 智慧把特殊性提升为普遍性。

Wisdom turns personalization into universality.

368. 脱离现实，就是最大的危机。

Detachment from reality is the biggest crisis.

369. 所有偏离现实的刻意都在引发危机。

All deliberate deviations from reality are causing a crisis.

370. 道德是我们更长远、更周全、更从容的路径。

Morality is our longer-term, more thoughtful and more relaxed path.

371. 阻断循环，就是阻断活力。

To block circulation is to block vitality.

372. 心灵只为善意开启。

Hearts are opened only for goodwill.

373. 形式是逻辑演绎的路径。

Form is the path of logical deduction.

374. 由景深透视未来。

See through the future through depth of field.

375. 政治被艺术赋予色彩。

Art gives politics a color.

376. 被阳光照耀，就会背负自身的阴影。

When illuminated by the sun, you will carry your own shadow.

377. 理想是现实的光芒。

Ideals are the light of reality.

378. 缓慢的都会沉淀，湍急的都会飞逝。

Slow will settle, and turbulent will fly.

379. 心跳的节奏才有动人的乐章。

There is the moving music only with the heartbeat rhythm.

380. 危难之中自有生机。

There is vitality in the midst of distress.

381. 现实不比心胸更辽阔。

Reality is no wider than heart.

第 7 章 | 自然的节气召唤生命的节奏
Natural season calls the rhythm of life

（2017 年汉钟精机总工程师 Chief engineer of HANBELL）

1. 科学是发现自然，技术是诱导自然。
   Science is the discovery of nature, technology is the induction of nature.

2. 原因揭示现象而非本质。
   Causes reveal phenomena rather than essences.

3. 文明把现实的挑战转化为进步的阶梯。
   Civilization transforms real challenges into ladders of progress.

4. 艺术以感性启迪和召唤理性。
   Art enlightens and evokes reason with sensibility.

5. 规律是真理的内核。
   Law is the core of truth.

6. 技术随需求而变换。
   Technology changes with demand.

7. 技术以迭代需求的方式而进步。

Technology advances in the form of iterative requirements.

8. 敬畏自然的人们，才能获取心灵的力量。

People who revere nature can gain the strength of the heart.

9. 科学是文明的希望。

Science is the hope of civilization.

10. 被需求迭代的知识才会具有价值。

The knowledge that is iterated by needs can have its value.

11. 人性构成历史演绎最活跃的部分。

Humanity constitutes the most active part of historical deduction.

12. 现实以规律肯定人类。

Reality affirms human with laws.

13. 创新之门由需求开启。

The door to innovation is opened by demand.

14. 宽容的力量无可阻挡。

The power of tolerance is unstoppable.

15. 细节是深刻的结果。

Details are profound results.

16. 科学是一种描述，艺术是一种启示。

Science is a description; art is a revelation.

17. 发明把技术延伸至需求。

Invention extends technology to demand.

18. 需求作为经济发展的牵引力在逐步释放人性，因此发明家未必是一位物理学家，但他必须成为心理学家和诗人，要持续洞察并挖掘人类最深层、最普遍、最细微的内心渴望。

Demand as the traction of economic development is gradually releasing humanity, so the inventor may not be a physicist, but he must become a psychologist and poet, to continue to see and tap into the deepest, most universal, most subtle inner desires of mankind.

19. 被艺术激励的灵魂，都会探索自己的山峰。

Souls inspired by art will explore their own peaks.

20. 把科学延伸至需求，就会构建职业尊严。

Extending science to demand creates professional dignity.

21. 需求无边，幻想无边。

Demand is boundless; fantasy is boundless.

22. 文明的繁衍：希祈引导需求，需求引导技术，技术引导经济。

The reproduction of civilization: hope guides demand, demand guides technology, and technology guides economy.

23. 云在飘浮、燕在飞翔、水在流淌、心在徜徉、春日生辉。

Clouds are floating; swallows are flying; water is flowing; hearts are wandering, and spring is shining.

24. 需求和资源构建经济循环的两极。

Demand and resources build the two poles of the economic cycle.

25. 我们在感知艺术，艺术在考验我们。

We are perceiving art, and art is testing us.

26. 在时光中演绎的事物，只能在时光中感悟。
Things that deduce in time can only be understood in time.

27. 不断需求，不断探索。
Constant demand, constant exploration.

28. 有知识的地方，不再有真正的黑暗。
Where there is knowledge, there is no more real darkness.

29. 简约再现本质。
Simplicity reproduces essence.

30. 自然的节气感召生命的节奏。
Natural solar terms evoke the rhythm of life.

31. 创新是价值链的重组。
Innovation is the reorganization of value chains.

32. 所有为生存而进行的拼搏，都值得我们尊重。
All the struggle for survival deserves our respect.

33. 欲望是最深的陷阱。
Desire is the deepest trap.

34. 地理是历史演绎的舞台，气象是历史演绎的背景。
Geography is the stage for history deduction, and meteorology is the background for history deduction.

35. 所有的深邃都是因为真实，所有的善良都是因为真诚。
All depth is because of truth, and all kindness is because of sincerity.

36. 艺术是文明演绎最深刻的背景。

Art is the most profound background for the civilization deduction.

37. 被需求提升的技术才具有价值。

Technology that is boosted by demand will have value.

38. 运动才有灵魂，变化才有结果。

Only movement has a soul, and change has results.

39. 真理和战略面向未来。

Truth and strategy face the future.

40. 与现实迭代是制胜的法则。

Iteration with reality is the law of victory.

41. 文化差异体现进化的特征。

Cultural differences characterize evolution.

42. 人文是文明可持续发展的基石。

Humanities are the cornerstone of the sustainable development of civilization.

43. 与现实迭代是智慧的唯一来源。

Iteration with reality is the only source of wisdom.

44. 智慧在每一座现实的山峰与我们照会。

Wisdom meets us on every mountain of reality.

45. 每一种生机都是现实的必然性。

Every vitality is the inevitability of reality.

46. 一种孤独成就一种卓越，一种舍弃成就一种精华。

Every solitude achieves a kind of excellence, and every abandonment achieves a kind of essence.

47. 科学划定技术的边界和拐点。

Science delimits the boundaries and inflection points of technology.

48. 攀登山峰，阅尽彩云。

Climb the mountain and see the colorful clouds.

49. 简洁才会深刻。

Simplicity will be profound.

50. 逼真才会生动。

Realistic will be vivid.

51. 探索的目的是发现认知的极限。

The purpose of exploration is to discover the limits of cognition.

52. 智慧就是遵从自然演绎的必然性。

Wisdom is to follow the inevitability of natural deduction.

53. 被梦想点燃的知识，才会照亮世界。

Knowledge ignited by dreams will illuminate the world.

54. 成就自己，变革世界。

Achieve yourself and change the world.

55. 普遍性与必然性是现实演绎的伟大背景。

Universality and inevitability are the great background for the deduction of reality.

56. 所有的残荷都曾经历夏季。

All the remaining/withered lotus have experienced summer.

57. 文化的价值在于历史的传承。

The value of culture lies in the transmission of history.

58. 智慧的内核是求真。

The core of wisdom is truth-seeking.

59. 设计是科学逻辑通过技术逻辑，迭代需求逻辑。

Design is scientific logic to iterate requirements logic through technical logic.

60. 内圣才能外王。

Inner saint can be the outside king.

61. 文明是人类的勇气和智慧。

Civilization is human courage and wisdom.

62. 求真是科学和艺术的基石。

Truth-seeking is the cornerstone of science and art.

63. 艺术源自观察的视角、独特的方法、经验的滤镜。

Art comes from the perspective of observation, the unique method, the filter of experience.

64. 每一种特殊性，都是一种质感。

Every particularity is a texture.

65. 需求引导技术跨界，是科技发展的高阶形式。

Demand guides technology cross-border and is the high-level form of scientific and technological development.

66. 一切因变化而精彩，一切因改变而启迪。

Everything is wonderful because of change, and everything is inspired by change.

67. 探索被求真的灵魂所引导，实践被求是的灵魂所驱动。

Exploration is guided by a trueness-seeking soul, and practice is driven by a truth-seeking soul.

68. 每一条道路的尽头都充满期待。

The end of every road is full of anticipation.

69. 现实的断崖是梦想的起点。

The cliff of reality is the starting point of dreams.

70. 面向阳光才会使我们升华。

Facing the sun will sublimate us.

71. 人性是生活展开的推手，多元需求的原点，宗教诞生的缘由。

Humanity is the pusher behind the unfolding of life, the origin of diverse needs, the reason for the birth of religion.

72. 用心想全是希望，用眼看全是风险。

Thinking with your heart is all hope, and seeing with your eyes is all risk.

73. 人性洞察需求，科学推演技术。

Humanity insights demands, and science dednces technology.

74. 一切的创新，都是以理性诱导现实。

All innovation is to induce reality with reason.

75. 计算与检测是科学的核心价值。

Computation and detection are the core values of science.

76. 所有的创新，都在承担一种额外的责任。

All innovations are assuming an additional responsibility.

77. 财富取决于道德的范围和责任的延伸。

Wealth depends on the scope of morality and the extension of responsibility.

78. 艺术展示人文演绎的精髓。

Art shows the essence of humanistic deduction.

79. 变革赋予我们超越的时机和致命的一搏。

Change gives us the opportunity to transcend and a fatal fight.

80. 清澈的心灵才能洞穿自然和人性。

A clear mind can penetrate nature and humanity.

81. 理性的心中全是希望，教条的眼里全是风险。

The heart of reason is full of hope, and the eyes of dogma are full of risk.

82. 深入实践，才能触及灵魂。

Only by deep practice can we touch the soul.

83. 身体强大，才能内心强大。

The heart can be strong with the strong body.

84. 我们由历史的拐点透视真理。

We see truth through the inflection point of history.

85. 感知与联想是经验的源泉。

Perception and association are the source of experience.

86. 文明的前景取决于科学在多大程度上被人文照亮。

The prospects of civilization depend on the extent to which science is illuminated by humanity.

87. 充分的个性才会具有社会价值。

Sufficient individuality has social value.

88. 深刻才能广泛，提炼才能普及。

Profound can be extensive, and refining can be popularized.

89. 最耀眼的光芒才能照耀。

The brightest light can shine.

90. 善良是人性的内核。

Kindness is the core of humanity.

91. 教育的目的是通过知识传播而萃取个性。

The purpose of education is to extract individuality through the transmission of knowledge.

92. 创新是价值链的重组。

Innovation is the restructuring of value chains.

93. 建筑承载人类所有的期许。

Architecture carries all the expectations of mankind.

94. 道德具有最低的姿态、最强的引力、最大的学问、最高的威望。

Morality has the lowest posture, the strongest gravity, the greatest learning, the highest prestige.

95. 国家的差距取决于人民的差距。

The gap between countries depends on the gap between the people.

96. 科学传达自然演绎的智慧。

Science conveys the wisdom of natural deduction.

97. 建筑是生活的仪式。

Architecture is a ritual of life.

98. 唯有责任穿越生死。

Only the responsibility is to cross life and death.

99. 没有共同的敌人，就没有共同的英雄。

Without a common enemy there is no a common hero.

100. 开放与竞争带来普遍的生机。

Openness and competition bring universal vitality.

101. 社会被大众革命、被精英改良。

Society was revolutionized by the masses and improved by the elite.

102. 真诚无敌。

Sincerity is invincible.

103. 肉体强大才能灵魂强大。

A strong body makes a strong soul.

104. 数学是形式演绎的逻辑。

Mathematics is the logic of formal deduction.

105. 梦想先行，观念滞后。

Dreams come first, ideas lag behind.

106. 幸福取决于理想和现实的落差。

Happiness depends on the gap between ideals and reality.

107. 回归自我既是勇气也是智慧。

Returning to oneself is both courage and wisdom.

108. 非线性演绎源自多系统迭代。

Nonlinear deduction originates from multi-system iteration.

109. 文明是社会的交往界面。

Civilization is the interface of society interaction.

110. 自然演绎是最深的智慧。

Nature deduction is the deepest wisdom.

111. 竞争是自然演绎的选择。

Competition is a natural deduction choice.

112. 艺术反映时代的心声。

Art reflects the voice of the times.

113. 家电是时代的界面。

Home appliances are the interface of the times.

114. 对待失败的态度，反映一个民族的精神特质。

The attitude towards failure reflects the spiritual qualities of a nation.

115. 所有的绝境都在重塑自我。

All desperate situations are reinventing ourselves.

116. 伟大的理性把创新推向极致。

Great reason pushes innovation to the extreme.

117. 科学是通向真理的必由之路。

Science is the only way to truth.

118. 探索必然是逆水行舟。

Exploration is necessarily a boat against the current.

119. 探索的价值是以自然的启示拓展认知的边界。

The exploration value is to expand the cognitive boundary with natural revelation.

120. 功利主义必然错过最美的风景。

Utilitarianism must miss the most beautiful scenery.

121. 教育应当寻求思想自由与社会约束之间的理性平衡。

Education should seek a rational balance between thought freedom and social constraints.

122. 智慧揭示危难中的转机。

Wisdom reveals the turning point in distress.

123. 聪明是自然的选择，智慧是现实的选择。

Intelligence is a natural choice, and wisdom is a realistic choice.

124. 技术发展被社会需求所牵引。

Technological development is driven by social needs.

125. 知识只有在实践的迭代中才能逐步深化。

Knowledge can only be deepened progressively in an iteration of practice.

126. 信仰没有效率，是不可计量的。

Faith has no efficiency and is not quantifiable.

127. 财富规模基于普遍的价值需求。

The scale of wealth is based on universal value needs.

128. 技术创造价值，商业传递价值。

Technology creates value, and business delivers value.

129. 我们从现实演绎的转折中感受自然的智慧。

We feel the wisdom of nature in the twist of reality deduction.

130. 多元化与开放性是现实演绎和进化的根基。

Pluralism and openness are the foundation of reality deduction and evolution.

131. 思想的特质：缓慢才能深刻，寂静才能沉淀，清澈才能至远，博大才能穿越。

The characteristics of thought: slow can be profound, silence can be precipitated, clarity can go far, breadth can be crossed.

132. 如果真相可被一览无遗，真理可被感性推导，世界将没有过程和挫折，同时也将失去深度和智慧。

If the trueness can be seen at a glance, and the truth can be sensibly deduced, the world will have no processes and setbacks, and at the same time it will also lose depth and wisdom.

133. 没有感动，就无从表达。

Without touching there is no way to express it.

134. 苦难是提炼的滤网和进步的阶梯。

Suffering is filters to refine and a ladder to progress.

135. 为满足需求所做的每一项发明，都是工程师面临的责任。

Every invention made to meet the needs is the responsibility of engineers.

136. 文明的意义在于用历史的智慧传承未来。

The significance of civilization lies in passing on the future with the wisdom of history.

137. 只有思想能够穿越历史的长河。

Only thought can cross the long river of history.

138. 谎言经不起历史的审判。

Lies cannot stand judgment in history.

139. 子弹无法击落思想的尊严。

Bullets cannot shoot down the dignity of thought.

140. 由激情驱使的才能天下无双。

Passion-driven talent will be unparalleled in the world.

141. 释放本能的潜力是教育的宗旨。

Unleashing the potential of instinct is the purpose of education.

142. 道德是长远和宏大的必然选择。

Morality is an inevitable choice for the long term and vastness/grandeur.

143. 期待孕育所有的梦想。

Expectation gives birth to all dreams.

144. 自信是人性展开的基石。

Self-confidence is the cornerstone of humanity unfolding.

145. 促进文明可持续发展是人类的终极需求。

Promoting the sustainable development of civilization is the ultimate demand for human.

146. 零不可叠加，黑不可叠加。

Zero cannot be superimposed, so does black.

147. 未来是现实演绎的必然选择。

The future is an inevitable choice for the deduction of reality.

148. 工艺是制造的传承。

Craft is the inheritance of manufacturing.

149. 科学是内容的逻辑，数学是形式的逻辑。

Science is the logic of content; mathematics is the logic of form.

150. 承载者才会具有颠覆的力量。

The bearer will have the power to subvert.

151. 理性与神明只差一个道德的距离。

There is only a moral distance between reason and the gods.

152. 快乐是心灵的释放。

Happiness is the release of the mind.

153. 制造基于仿真的设计。

Manufacture is based on simulation-based designs.

154. 资源通过逻辑转变成结果。

Resources are transformed into results through logic.

155. 信心通过需求促进经济循环。

Confidence boosts economic circularity through demand.

156. 形式的张力构建艺术的精粹。

The tension of form constructs the essence of art.

157. 利他主义是和谐的基础。

Altruism is the basis of harmony.

158. 建筑寄托我们对生活的期待。

Architecture holds our expectations of life.

159. 艺术是感性形式，数学是理性形式。

Art is the sensual form, mathematics is the rational form.

160. 文字以感性符号传达理性信息。

Words convey rational information with emotional symbols.

161. 社会需求引导技术整合。

Social needs guide technology integration.

162. 温度是现实的维度。

Temperature is the dimension of reality.

163. 平衡的余量，就是现实的预警。

The balance margin is the early warning to reality.

164. 单纯才能穿透，宁静才能至远。

Simply can penetrate, quiet can go far.

165. 设计是把观念转换为形式。

Design is the transformation of ideas into form.

166. 功利主义是观念的枷锁。

Utilitarianism is the yoke of ideas.

167. 触及灵魂的苦难，才能诱发思想的升华。

Suffering that touches the soul can induce the sublimation of thought.

168. 险峰之侧，必有松鹤。

On the side of the steep peak there must be pine cranes.

169. 深刻，才能触及概念的本质。

Profound is able to touch the essence of the concept.

170. 科技时代由最具幻想的人们发起。

Technology age is initiated by the most fanciful people.

171. 文明是人类可持续发展的力量。

Civilization is a force for the sustainable development of mankind.

172. 文字是感性和理性的界面。

Text is the interface of sensibility and reason.

173. 能源同时具备经济发展的起点、过程、目标。

Energy also has the starting point, process and goal of economic development.

174. 只被利益驱使，就会把我们引入罪恶。

Being driven only by profit will lead us to sin.

175. 跨界集成就是提升逻辑迭代的可持续性。

Cross-border integration is to improve the sustainability of logic iteration.

176. 放弃责任是一种罪恶。

Abandoning responsibility is a sin.

177. 认知的价值是为需求提供方法。

The value of cognition is to provide a means for needs.

178. 跨界集成就是提升逻辑迭代的系统性。

Cross-border integration is to improve the systematization of logic iteration.

179. 能被逻辑所仿真的产业，终将被人工智能替代。

Industries that can be simulated by logic will eventually be replaced by artificial intelligence.

180. 坚毅是贯穿的力量。

Perseverance is the force that runs through.

181. 热泵开启现代文明。

Heat pumps usher in modern civilization.

182. 贪婪是罪恶的动机。

Greed is the motive of evil.

183. 科技时代以最科幻的方式拉开帷幕。

The age of technology has kicked off in the most science-fantasy way.

184. 每一种罪恶都会留下它的涟漪。

Every sin leaves its ripples.

185. 梯度中蕴含能量和动机。

There is energy and motivation in the gradient.

186. 只有激荡的心灵，才能理解澎湃的价值。

Only a stirring heart can understand the surging value.

187. 理性的付出才有灿烂的未来。

Only rational efforts can have a bright future.

188. 现实被光芒和激情照耀。

Reality is illuminated by light and passion.

189. 努力是付出的动量，成功是获取的势能。

Effort is the momentum to pay; success is the potential energy to obtain.

190. 只有真理才能展望未来。

Only truth can look to the future.

191. 生物技术和人工智能，颠覆民主赖以存在的基础。

Biotechnology and artificial intelligence subvert the very foundation on which democracy exists.

192. 景色是生态所展露的生机。

The scenery is the vitality that the ecology shows.

193. 生存就是决胜的法则。

Survival is the law to win.

194. 把利益作为单一目标，经济发展就会背离人性。

By taking profit as a single goal, economic development will deviate from humanity.

195. 经验是灵魂的内存。

Experience is the memory of the soul.

196. 没有比生机更加灿烂的艺术。

There is no more brilliant art than vitality.

197. 形式孕育内容。

Form breeds content.

198. 系统的开放性是基于多元化的组合。

The openness of the system is based on combinations of diversity.

199. 和谐以可持续性为现实演绎的目标。

Harmony takes sustainability as the goal of reality deduction.

200. 文化是民族传承的基因。

Culture is the gene of national heritage.

201. 形式是力量的标志。

Form is a sign of strength.

202. 文物以其真实性还原历史的必然性。

Cultural relics restore the inevitability of history with their authenticity.

203. 每一个时代都有属于自己的激情和革命。

Every era has its own passion and revolution.

204. 苦难是一所引导深刻的大学。

Suffering is a university that guides deepness.

205. 创新是挖掘内涵和拓展外延。

Innovation is to excavate the intension and expand the extension.

206. 每一种出色来自一种全面。

Every excellence comes from a comprehensiveness.

207. 艺术是每一个时代的激情和标志。

Art is the passion and hallmark of every era.

208. 和谐是自然演绎的智慧。

Harmony is the wisdom of natural deduction.

209. 现实的落差蕴含动机，欲望的平衡催生需求。

The difference of the reality contains motivation; the balance of desires gives birth to needs.

210. 疆域不会超越国王的雄心。

The territory does not exceed the ambitions of the king.

211. 我们用挫折收获经验。

We harvest experience with setbacks.

212. 缺乏历史见证，我们就会丧失进步的坐标。

Without historical witness, we lose the coordinates of progress.

213. 潮流无法探测内心的深度。

Currents cannot probe the depths of the hearts.

214. 风景是生态的界面。

Landscape is the interface of ecology.

215. 系统循环由多样性驱动。

System circulation is driven by diversity.

216. 精彩的道路是最崎岖的那条。

The wonderful road is the most rugged one.

217. 深秋揭示多样性的本色。

Late autumn reveals the true colors of diversity.

218. 狭隘的心胸超不过肩膀。

The narrow mindedness are not exceeding the shoulder.

219. 每一种形式预示一种结果。

Each form foreshadows a result.

220. 形式启发思想，思想回归形式。

Form inspires thought, and thought returns to form.

221. 坚毅的力量不可阻挡。

The power of perseverance is unstoppable.

222. 风景是时光的留痕。

The scenery is a trace of time.

223. 不曾迷失，就没有回归。

Without being lost, there is no return.

224. 历史在真理所预言的形式中穿行。

History travels through the forms predicted by truth.

225. 目标清晰，计划简洁，执行聚焦。

Clear goals, concise planning, and focused execution.

226. 自然演绎使生命的可持续性基于生态的普遍性。

Natural deduction makes the sustainability of life based on ecological universality.

227. 概念不断细分，逻辑不断集成。

Concepts are constantly broken down and logic is constantly integrated.

228. 每一个坎坷都是成长的故事。

Every bump is a story of growth.

229. 探索的价值是提升文明的可持续性。

The value of exploration is to enhance the sustainability of civilization.

230. 善良是人性的演绎。

Kindness is a deduction of humanity.

231. 智慧在实践中成长。

Wisdom grows in practice.

232. 美展示现实演绎的生机。

Beauty shows the vitality of reality deduction.

233. 炽热的渴望才会燃烧。

The blazing desire will burn.

234. 英雄肩负历史的责任。

Heroes bear the responsibility of history.

235. 秋色承载春夏的阳光。

Autumn colors carry the sunshine of spring and summer.

236. 有梯度就有方向。

Where there is a gradient，there will be a direction.

237. 宏大的事物才有远方。

Great things can be far away.

238. 梦想终会照进现实。

Dreams will eventually come true.

239. 发现是现实之花，发明是梦想之果。

Discovery is the flower of reality，and invention is the fruit of dreams.

240. 自由的灵魂，才能孤独地存在。

A free soul can exist alone.

241. 发明是以需求的维度解构技术的维度。

Invention deconstructs the dimension of technology with the dimension of needs.

242. 教育是用一种耐心培育一种信心。

Education is about cultivating confidence with patience.

243. 法律需要心灵的温度。

The law needs the heart temperature.

244. 发展的目标是存在的意义。

The development goal is the existence meaning.

245. 英雄主义用生命的激情跨越现实。

Heroism transcends reality with the life passion.

246. 坚毅是我们发给苦难的照会。

Perseverance is our note presented to suffering by us.

247. 真理只为理性留门。

Truth only leaves the door open for reason.

248. 多样性的均衡是自然演绎的智慧。

The balance of diversity is the wisdom of natural deduction.

249. 包容是加法，选择是减法。

Inclusion is addition; choice is subtraction.

250. 期待终会浓烈。

Expectations will eventually be strong.

第 8 章 | 可持续性是生命演绎的目标
Sustainability is the goal of life deduction

（2018 年上海柯茂总工程师 Chief engineer of Shanghai Comer）

1. 伪善比无知具有更大的欺骗。

Hypocrisy has greater deception than ignorance.

2. 自律是人性散发的光芒。

Self-discipline is the light of humanity.

3. 宗教是一条心灵归真的道路。

Religion is a path to spiritual truth.

4. 现实在能量的流转中演绎。

Reality deduces in the flow of energy.

5. 认知以感性和理性再现自然。

Cognition reproduces nature with sensibility and rationality.

6. 谎言有时比真理更具诱导性。

Lies are sometimes more seductive than truths.

7. 真相才能回归真理。

Only the facts can return to the truth.

8. 提炼自然的本质，才能把握力量的内核。

Refine the essence of nature in order to grasp the core of power.

9. 现实从不缺美，只缺提炼的眼光。

Reality is never short of beauty, only lack of refined vision.

10. 音乐是心灵的律动。

Music is the rhythm of the heart.

11. 所有的时空归于浩瀚。

All time and space return to the vastness.

12. 只从利益出发的事物必然以悲剧收场。

Things that proceed only from profit are bound to end in tragedy.

13. 把握事物之间的差异，才能获取现实的力量。

Only by grasping the differences between things can we gain the power of reality.

14. 聚焦意志才能点燃生命。

Focus on will to ignite life.

15. 抓住事物本质才能把握力量内核。

Only by grasping the essence of things can we grasp the core of power.

16. 能源开创每个时代的未来。

Energy creates the future of every age.

17. 真相是现实的归途，现实是真理的归途。

Trueness is the return to reality, and reality is the return to truth.

18. 美是理性散发的光芒。

Beauty is the light emanating from reason.

19. 美是真的形式，真是善的根基。

Beauty is the form of truth; truth is the foundation of kindness.

20. 诗和远方呈现多样性的变换。

Poems and distant places present diversity transformations.

21. 坚毅为时间赋值。

Perseverance assigns value to time.

22. 创新就是把概念扩展到现实。

Innovation is about extending concepts to reality.

23. 深刻是还原现实的力量。

Profundity is the power to restore reality.

24. 无视环境的发展，必然葬送可持续的前景。

The development ignoring the environment inevitably burys sustainable prospects.

25. 智慧基于现实可持续性的解构。

Intelligence is based on deconstruction of sustainability in reality.

26. 感知—仿真—再现—超越是人类认知的阶梯。

Perception-simulation-reproduction-transcendence is the ladder of human cognition.

27. 系统以可持续性取胜。

Systems win with sustainability.

28. 艺术是理想和现实的界面。

Art is the interface between ideal and reality.

29. 承载的力量就是颠覆的力量。

The power to carry is the power to subvert.

30. 感性文明包容理性文明，终将不可战胜。

Emotional civilization embraces rational civilization and will eventually be invincible.

31. 历史的价值是社会演绎的必然性。

The value of history is the inevitability of social deduction.

32. 无法解脱，才是真正的苦难。

The inability to get rid of it is the real suffering.

33. 苦难的轨迹，正是理性的边界。

The trajectory of suffering is precisely the boundary of reason.

34. 利润是被技术所提升的价值。

Profit is the value that is enhanced by technology.

35. 艺术以观念的光芒照耀世界。

Art shines on the world with the ideas light.

36. 买办时代行将结束，内生式发展渐成主流。

The era of compradors is coming to an end, and endogenous development is gradually becoming the mainstream.

37. 孤独为思想留下时空。

Loneliness leaves time and space for thought.

38. 实践检验真理，反思回归真我。

Practice tests the truth and reflection lets me to return to the true self.

39. 遗憾是无知的存留。

Regret is the persistence of ignorance.

40. 英雄主义肩负一个时代的未来。

Heroism carries the future of an era.

41. 每一种生命都是一种生态的主宰。

Every kind of life is the master of an ecology.

42. 最简单的规则胜过最崇高的道德。

The simplest rules trump the highest morality.

43. 建筑承载人类所有的期望。

Architecture carries all human expectations.

44. 以权力保障公平是文明的尺度。

Ensuring fairness with power is the measurement of civilization.

45. 运动中感知生命的灵魂。

The soul of life is perceived in motion.

46. 建筑要以空间逻辑迎接时光的变迁。

Architecture should meet the changes of time with spatial logic.

47. 理性是最深刻的善意。

Reason is the deepest goodwill.

48. 真诚才能洞穿文明。

Sincerity can penetrate civilization.

49. 姿态是生命力的绽放。

Posture is the bloom of vitality.

50. 回归真相就是回归历史。

To return to the truth is to return to history.

51. 以幻想解构自然演绎的逻辑。

Deconstructing the logic of natural deduction with fantasy.

52. 敬畏自然是智慧的启蒙。

Reverence for nature is the enlightenment of wisdom.

53. 需求在变换，梦想在闪烁。

Demands are changing; dreams are flickering.

54. 星空无语，启示方位。

The stars are speechless and reveal the direction.

55. 由目光探测灵魂的深度。

Probing the depth of the soul by the gaze.

56. 没有梦想就没有期待的人生。

Without dreams there is no life to look forward to.

57. 孤独源自内心的辽阔。

Loneliness comes from the vastness of the heart.

58. 实践基于方法和时机。

Practice is based on method and timing.

59. 技术发展的潮流由需求的风口引导。

The trend of technological development is guided by the demand outlet.

60. 建筑应当承载地理和季节的演绎。

Architecture should carry geographical and seasonal deduction.

61. 艺术以经验的滤镜再现世界。

Art recreates the world with the filter of experience.

62. 经典是历史对现实的穿越。

The classic is the crossing of history to reality.

63. 文学是人性的呐喊与召唤。

Literature is the cry and call of humanity.

64. 风景是季节的脉动和生态的演绎。

The scenery is the pulse of the seasons and the deduction of ecology.

65. 翅膀是最大的跨越。

Wings are the biggest leap.

66. 基础科学是文明发展的动脉。

Basic science is the artery of the civilization development.

67. 加持人文的理性才会从容发展。

Reason plus humanity will develop calmly.

68. 书法再现心灵的轨迹。

Calligraphy reproduces the trajectory of the mind.

69. 认清现实才能确定方向。

Recognize the reality to determine the direction.

70. 流体驱动传热。

Fluids drive heat transfer.

71. 科学指导实践，哲学指导文明。

Science guides practice; philosophy guides civilization.

72. 历史是现实最深刻的部分。

History is the deepest part of reality.

73. 拥有翅膀，山海就不再成为障碍。

With wings mountains and seas are no longer obstacles.

74. 财富来自需求的普遍性。

Wealth comes from the universality of demand.

75. 竞争促使能力的成长。

Competition leads to the growth of competence.

76. 现实不会为谎言而存在。

Reality does not exist for lies.

77. 科学揭示自然演绎的逻辑。

Science reveals the logic of nature deduction.

78. 科学是技术发展的支点。

Science is the fulcrum of technological development.

79. 美凝聚自然演绎的力量。

Beauty embodies the power of nature deduction.

80. 发明是科学献给人类的挚爱。

Invention is the love of science to mankind.

81. 没有向死的恳切，难知生命的厚重。

Without earnestness to death, it is hard to know the weight of life.

82. 充满期待，才会具有活力。

With full of expectations, one will have vitality.

83. 融冰的河水才会流淌。

Only when the ice melts will the river flow.

84. 批判是理性的进阶。

Criticism is the step to reason.

85. 疑惑是揭示机理的前奏。

Confusion is a prelude to revealing the mechanism.

86. 植根现实才能获取发展的力量。

Only by being rooted in reality can we gain the power of development.

87. 美是现实最深刻的启示。

Beauty is the most profound revelation of reality.

88. 孤独的脚步最绚丽。

Lonely footsteps are the most gorgeous.

89. 形式是逻辑演绎的结果。

Form is the result of logical deduction.

90. 储存平衡动力与负荷。

Storage balances power and load.

91. 战略是现实的本源。

Strategy is the source of reality.

92. 分布式能源：（1）成倍降低输送投资与输送损失；（2）精准匹配能源与负荷；（3）能源站、输送管网、用户末端的联合效率最大化。

Distributed energy: (1) doubling reduce transmission investment and transmission losses; (2) accurately match energy and load; (3) maximize the joint efficiency of energy stations, transmission networks, and user ends.

93. 权力放纵是罪恶的本源。

Power indulgence is the origin of sin.

94. 末端形式决定传热效率。

The end form determines the heat transfer efficiency.

95. 实践的深度限定灵魂的高度。

The depth of practice limits the height of the soul.

96. 圣洁是被现实苦难解构的人性。

Holiness is the humanity deconstructed by reality suffering.

97. 优秀是一种流程，品德是一种习惯。

Excellence is a process, character is a habit.

98. 生命最闪耀的部分是自由的渴望。

The brightest part of life is the desire for freedom.

99. 思想以概念的逻辑揭示自然的逻辑。

Thought reveals the logic of nature with the logic of concepts.

100. 标准化提升普遍的价值，个性化提升艺术的价值。

Standardization enhances universal value, and personalization enhances the art value.

101. 建筑使我们在地理的界面感受季节的时光。

Architecture allows us to feel the seasons time at the geographical interface.

102. 艺术使宗教富于张力。

Art enriches religion with tension.

103. 自我批判就是自我修复。

Self-criticism is self-healing.

104. 还原现实才能预测未来。

Restoring reality can predict the future.

105. 形式为内容播种。

Form sows for content.

106. 文学为人性提供路标。

Literature provides signposts for humanity.

107. 文明被和谐所引导。

Civilization is guided by harmony.

108. 灾难回归现实的价值。

Disaster returns to the reality value.

109. 需求是人文播撒的种子。

Demand is the seed sown by humanities.

110. 放空自己才能超越现实。

Empty yourself to transcend reality.

111. 由失败的轨迹划定成功的边界。

The successful boundaries are drawn by the failure trajectory.

112. 技术是连接需求与科学的途径。

Technology is the path to connect demand and science.

113. 科学为技术划定拐点和边界。

Science delineates inflection points and boundaries for technology.

114. 激流所向必有精彩。

There must be brilliance in the rapid current.

115. 发明就像阳光一样照耀我们，赋予我们光辉灿烂的自由。

Invention shines on us like sunlight, giving us a glorious freedom.

116. 河流是所有文明的希望。

Rivers are the hope of all civilizations.

117. 唯有真理穿越历史。

Only truth passes through history.

118. 具有犯错的自由，才有成功的可能。

With the freedom to make mistakes, there is a possibility of success.

119. 我们在持续的质疑中走向未来。

We are heading for the future in constant questioning.

120. 节奏是可持续的象征。

Rhythm is a symbol of sustainability.

121. 回归现实才能展望未来。

Only by returning to reality can we look to the future.

122. 把历史归纳为科学，才能深刻把握现实演绎。

Only by summarizing history as science can we profoundly grasp the reality deduction.

123. 质疑体现思想的尊严和价值。

Questioning embodies the dignity and value of ideas.

124. 真诚是通向真理的品德。

Sincerity is the virtue that leads to the truth.

125. 不去选择现实，就会被现实选择。

If you do not choose reality, you will be chosen by reality.

126. 对知识的藐视，都会自取其辱。

Disrespect for knowledge brings disgrace on their own head.

127. 知识被探索者掌握，财富被实践者掌握。

Knowledge is mastered by explorers; wealth is mastered by practitioners.

128. 实践的道路被真理照耀。

The path of practice is illuminated by truth.

129. 倾斜的地面上，皆是没有定力的倾轧。

On the sloping ground, there is pour into each other without firm force.

130. 精神独立是科学的信仰。

Spiritual independence is the scientific belief.

131. 思想被现实的质疑所修正。

Thoughts are corrected by the reality questioning.

132. 苦难使我们看清现实的全貌。

Suffering makes us see reality in its entirety.

133. 从缺陷中延伸契机。

Extend opportunities from defects.

134. 被意志点燃的知识才会发光。

Knowledge ignited by will can shine.

135. 自信是最好的上帝。

Self-confidence is the best God.

136. 灵魂不可被贫穷晒干，不可被财富淹没。

The soul shall not be sundried by poverty, nor drowned by wealth.

137. 心灵是事业的坐标。

The heart is the cause coordinates.

138. 意志扇动理想主义翅膀。

Will flaps the wings of idealism.

139. 资本是经济循环的血液，企业是社会构成的黏合剂。

Capital is the blood of the economic cycle, and enterprises are the glue of social composition.

140. 坚毅延展我们的社会属性。

Perseverance extends our social attributes.

141. 掩盖历史改变不了社会演绎的逻辑。

Covering up history does not change the logic of social deduction.

142. 形式的逻辑启示内容的逻辑。

The form logic reveals the content logic.

143. 敏锐决定感知的深度。

Acumen determines the depth of perception.

144. 智慧把现实的危机转化为持续的优势。

Wisdom turns real crises into lasting advantages.

145. 工业文明使人类社会偏平化：屏蔽感受、瓦解能力、削弱欲望、平息激情。

Industrial civilization flattens human society: shielding feelings, disintegrating abilities, weakening desires, and calming passions.

146. 发明把需求与科学的逻辑，转化为技术与经济的逻辑。

Invention transforms the logic of demand and science into the logic of technology and economy.

147. 艺术启迪思想。

Art enlightens thought.

148. 生存方式引导生命的演绎。

The way of survival guides the life deduction.

149. 思想贫乏是一个社会最深的没落。

Ideological poverty is the deepest decline of a society.

150. 纯净才会鲜艳。

Purity will be bright.

151. 思想以概念逻辑揭示现实逻辑。

Thought reveals the reality logic with conceptual logic.

152. 如果不基于独立精神，科研只是一场名利游戏。

If not based on independent spirit, scientific research is just a game of fame and fortune.

153. 知识是人类成长的阶梯，发明是文明进步的阶梯。

Knowledge is the ladder of human growth, and invention is the ladder of civilization progress.

154. 如果不在哲学高度被强权牵引，一个散漫的民族有可能依旧在沉睡。

If not to be drawn by the power at the height of philosophy, a loose nation may still be asleep.

155. 艺术以观念解构现实。

Art deconstructs reality with concept.

156. 灵魂游荡于激情和诗意。

The soul wanders between passion and poetry.

157. 工具体现方法的价值。

Tools reflect the value of methods.

158. 由深刻获取普遍性，由普遍性获取自由。

Universality is obtained from profoundness; freedom is obtained from universality.

159. 责任就是尊严。

Responsibility is dignity.

160. 基于科学的需求，开创颠覆性技术。

The needs based on science create disruptive technologies.

161. 道德基于规则，规则基于规律。

Morality is based on rules, and rules are based on laws.

162. 不深入本质，就被现象淹没。

Without going deep into essence, you will be drowned by the phenomenon.

163. 我们被经历的苦难塑造成形。

We are shaped by the suffering that we have experienced.

164. 信仰是意志的源泉。

Faith is the source of will.

165. 快乐的时间是静止的。

Happy time is static.

166. 真诚是人性的本源。

Sincerity is the source of humanity.

167. 拯救现实的力量就是上帝。

The power to save reality is God.

168. 有精尖才能引领，有刀锋才能突破，有思想才能飞翔。

Something with a sharp can lead, with a knife can break through, with a thought can fly.

169. 放弃偏见，才能把现实转化为力量。

Only by abandoning prejudice can reality be transformed into strength.

170. 科学拓展认知边界、划定技术范围、摆脱精神束缚。

Science expands cognitive boundaries; delineates the scope of technology, and gets rid of the spiritual constraints.

171. 每一种压倒性优势，都是可被膜拜的神明。

Each of the most overwhelming advantages is a god that can be worshipped.

172. 笔触是形式的滤镜。

Strokes are filters for form.

173. 视苦难为阶梯，则无可阻挡。

Seeing suffering as a ladder is unstoppable.

174. 开放性是获取现实力量的唯一途径。

Openness is the only way to gain the power of reality.

175. 迭代是成长的方式。

Iteration is the way to grow.

176. 思想的深度源自现实的落差。

The depth of thought comes from the decline of reality.

177. 生活是在持续适应的进阶中获取深度自由。

Life is to gain deep freedom in the advanced steps of continuous adaptation.

178. 没有危机感，就没有使命感。

Without a sense of crisis there is no sense of mission.

179. 产品是需求和经济双重优化的结果。

The product is the result of both demand and economy optimization.

180. 发明是以技术的逻辑满足需求的逻辑。

Invention is to meet the demand logic with technology logic.

181. 阳光之下必有法则，法则之下必有机遇。

Under the sun there will be laws, and under the laws there will be opportunities.

182. 奔腾才能跨越，跨越才能飞翔。

Galloping can cross; crossing can fly.

183. 无知带来盲目的恐惧。

Ignorance begets blind fear.

184. 个性是初心和本能的延伸。

Individuality is an extension of the initial heart and instinct.

185. 经济增长源自社会需求所牵引的技术创新。

Economic growth stems from technological innovation driven by social demand.

186. 科学是心灵自由的罗盘。

Science is the compass of mind freedom.

187. 成功基于勤奋的专注和均衡的全面。

Success is based on diligent focus and balanced comprehensiveness.

188. 平衡是可持续性所展现的形式。

Balance is the form in which sustainability plesents.

189. 公平是低成本的和谐。

Fairness is low-cost harmony.

190. 宏大孕育可持续的智慧。

Ambition breeds sustainable wisdom.

191. 技术革命决定每个时代的未来。

The technological revolution determines the future of every era.

192. 科学是承载自由与梦想的方舟。

Science is the ark that carries freedom and dreams.

193. 人在做，天在看，时间在批注。

People are doing, the sky is watching, and time is annotating.

194. 竞争的价值是迅速重合思想的逻辑。

The value of competition is to quickly overlap the logic of ideas.

195. 慈善是财富的反思，财富是道德的反思。

Charity is a reflection on wealth, wealth is a reflection on morality.

196. 计量是科学的原点。

Measurement is the origin of science.

197. 突破苦难的生机是最耀眼的光芒。

The vitality to break through suffering is the brightest light.

198. 简洁再现深刻。

Conciseness reproduce profoundness.

199. 持久的征服基于平衡，持久的平衡基于和谐。

Lasting conquest is based on balance, and lasting balance is based on harmony.

200. 穿透苦难的光芒直达心灵。

The light to penetrate suffering reaches the heart.

201. 尊重历史就是间接尊重自己。

To respect history is to respect oneself indirectly.

202. 公平是对所有人的尊重。

Fairness is respect for all.

203. 多元化与开放性是现实演绎的舞台。

Diversity and openness are the stage for reality deduction.

204. 城镇化的轮回，引发观念的轮回、资源的轮回、经济的轮回。

The cycle of urbanization leads to the cycle of ideas, resources, and economy.

205. 星空是远航的坐标。

The starry sky is the coordinates of the long voyage.

206. 暴力是隐藏的恐惧，虚荣是隐藏的怯懦。

Violence is hidden fear; vanity is hidden cowardice.

207. 每一位胜利者都有他绝地反击的一刻。

Every victor has a moment of his fightback.

208. 目标不会超越概念。

The target does not go beyond concepts.

209. 现实的力量被梦想召唤。

The power of reality is summoned by dreams.

210. 回归现实才能超越现实。

Only by returning to reality can we transcend reality.

211. 苦难解构现实演绎的逻辑。

Suffering deconstructs the logic of reality deduction.

212. 所有的简洁都是一次思想的聚焦。

All brevity is a focus of thought.

213. 还原事物的演绎才能预测事物的发展。

Only by restoring the things deduction can we predict the things development.

214. 每一次反省都会照亮自己。

Every reflection illuminates oneself.

215. 现实在多元化中演绎。

Reality deduces out in diversity.

216. 求真是道德底线。

Seeking truth is the moral bottom line.

217. 基因决定生命成长的方向和节奏。

Genes determine the direction and rhythm of life growth.

218. 经济发展基于社会信心。

Economic development is based on social confidence.

219. 经济循环由多样性需求驱动。

The economic cycle is driven by the need for diversity.

220. 发明是每个行业的曙光。

Invention is the dawn of every industry.

221. 肩有翅膀，心要飞翔。

With wings on the shoulders, the heart wants to fly.

222. 多元化和系统性是每一种文明的尊严。

Pluralism and systemization are the dignity of every civilization.

223. 由目标解构规则以应对变局。

Deconstruct rules by goals to deal with change.

224. 结构支撑建筑、热泵掌握冷暖。

Structures support buildings, the heat pump masters cold and warmth.

225. 孤独始于飞翔的一刻。

Loneliness begins from the moment of flight.

226. 自由的尽头是孤独，科学的极致是艺术。

The end of freedom is loneliness, and the ultimate of science is art.

227. 经典是历史散发的光芒。

Classics are the light of history.

228. 感知天下，临摹天下，表达天下。

Perceive the world, copy the world, express the world.

229. 以天下为怀的工匠，都会艺无止境。

Craftsmen who cherish the world will have endless art.

230. 经济循环承载社会构架。

Economic cycles carry the social framework.

231. 暴力是隐藏的恐惧，博爱是展现的胆识。

Violence is a hidden fear, and fraternity is the shown boldness.

232. 科学在发展，技术在变革，工艺在传承，文明在演绎。

Science is developing; technology is changing; craft is passing on, and civilization is deduceing.

233. 文明随河流而漫延。

Civilization spreads with the river.

234. 风情是地理的注解。

Customs are an annotation of geography.

235. 塑料是上世纪的发明、本世纪的灾难。

Plastic is the invention of the last century and the disaster of this century.

236. 苦难是我们回归现实的契机。

Suffering is our opportunity to return to reality.

237. 成功回归责任。

Success returns to responsibility.

238. 思想的逻辑回归现实的逻辑。

The thought logic returns to the reality logic.

239. 灵魂的更迭引导系统的重生。

The change of soul leads to the rebirth of the system.

240. 好奇开启探索之旅。

Curiosity begins a journey of discovery.

241. 历史是社会演绎的逻辑。

History is the logic of social deduction.

242. 使命感驱动可持续创新。

A sense of mission drives sustainable innovation.

243. 逆行者的背影为人类阻挡灾难。

The back of the retrograde is a barrier to disaster for humanity.

244. 每一次人类的变革都会留下历史的篇章。

Every mankind change leaves a chapter in history.

245. 苦难考验我们对现实的适应性。

Suffering tests our adaptability to reality.

246. 历史是一首意志征服时艰的变奏。

History is a variation of will to conquer the changes of time.

247. 勇气和智慧由理性启示。

Courage and wisdom are inspired by reason.

248. 跨界就是多元化的技术迭代。

Cross-border is a diversified technology iteration.

249. 每一位英雄都听从使命的召唤。

Every hero heeds the call of mission.

250. 恐惧是智慧的开端。

Fear is the beginning of wisdom.

251. 具有星空的视野，自有上帝的胸怀。

With the visual field of the starry sky, own the heart of God.

252. 利他主义是和谐的出发点。

Altruism is the starting point of harmony.

253. 历史时刻，就有历史担当。

At the moment of history, there is a historical responsibility.

254. 终结灾难，拯救人类。

End a disaster to save humanity.

255. 经济以其多样性循环承载文明的可持续性。

The economy carries the sustainability of civilization with its diversity cycle.

256. 基于系统性的完整性，体现知识的力量。

Based on system-based completeness, embodying the power of knowledge.

257. 反思的勇气提高文明的完整性。

The courage to reflect enhances the integrity of civilization.

258. 历史的荣耀由文明背负。

The glory of history is carried by civilization.

259. 我们在选择利益，上帝在选择我们。

We are choosing interests, and God is choosing us.

260. 只有简洁通达深刻。

Only simplicity can be profound.

261. 历史充满每个时代的必然性。

History is full of inevitabilities of every era.

262. 放下心结，不畏将来。

Put down the knot of the heart and do not fear the future.

263. 科学在集体的沉默中转向，又在集体的喧嚣中发展。

Science turns in collective silence and develops in collective noise.

264. 唯有热爱才能点亮生命。

Only love can light up life.

265. 强大不应是毁灭的巨响，而是持续向前的节奏。

Strength should not be a loud noise of destruction, but a continuous forward rhythm.

266. 音乐始终是生命演绎的节奏。

Music is always the rhythm of life deduction.

267. 好奇开启认知之旅。

Curiosity begins a cognitive journey.

268. 只有无际的黑暗包容星辰。

Only the endless darkness contains the starlight.

269. 历史的洪流交织民族的魂魄与血脉。

The torrent of history interweaves the soul and blood of the nation.

270. 还原事物演绎的逻辑，才能释放现实的力量。

Only by restoring the logic of deduction of things can the power of reality be released.

271. 艺术是现实与观念的重影。

Art is the double image of reality and ideas.

272. 产品的价值，是为客户创造的价值。

The value of the product is the value created for customers.

273. 美展露现实演绎的生机。

Beauty shows the vitality of reality deduction.

274. 理性的光芒才能照亮未来。

The light of reason can illuminate the future.

275. 苦难是变革的火种。

Suffering is the seeds of change.

276. 知识迎接变革，理性创造未来。

Knowledge greets change and reason creates the future.

277. 演绎形式的闪烁，赋予科学最强的启示。

The flicker of deductive forms gives science the strongest revelations.

278. 生态展示生命与自然的和谐。

Ecology shows the harmony between life and nature.

279. 现实的可持续性由多元化承载。

Sustainability in reality is carried by diversity.

280. 淡水不仅决定生命的起源，而且决定生命的归宿。

Fresh water determines not only the origin of life, but also the fate of life.

281. 放纵会使权力站在事物起因的对立面，从而降低公平性并丧失管理智慧。

Indulgence puts power on the opposite side of the cause of things, thereby reducing fairness and losing managerial wisdom.

282. 遏制本能就会由于缺乏进化的动力，而沦为任人宰割的羔羊。

One with instinct contained would be reduced to a lamb to slaughter due to the lack of evolutionary momentum.

283. 发自内心才能深入内心。

Only from the heart can we go deep into the heart.

284. 遏制本能就无法引导人类走出历史的困境。

Containing the instinct cannot lead humanity out of the historical dilemma.

285. 原木和皮革以生命的质感伴随我们。

Logs and leather accompany us with the texture of life.

286. 翅膀的敌人不是黑暗而是牢笼。

The enemy of wings is not darkness but cage.

287. 生存的方式就是搏斗的方式。

The way to survive is the way to fight.

288. 宏大必有天规。

Grandeur must have the rules of heaven.

289. 努力可能白费，成功不会碰巧。

Efforts may be in vain, and success will not happen by chance.

290. 变革的价值是以现实需求提升事物的系统性。

The value of change is to enhance the systematization of things with real needs.

291. 变革的价值是提升系统的可持续性。

The value of change is to enhance the sustainability of the system.

292. 恐惧源自认知的深度不及渴望的宏大。

Fear stems from the fact that the depth of cognition is less than the grandeur of desire.

293. 年轻就是敢于付出、期待收获的勇气。

Being young is the courage to dare to pay and expect to harvest.

294. 自律才能获取更广泛的自由。

Self-discipline can gain broader freedom.

295. 我们在多大程度上把心灵寄托给神明，就会在多大程度上失去自由。

To what extent we place hearts on the gods, we will lose freedom to the same extent.

296. 自由是从初心抵达梦想的轨迹。

Freedom is the trajectory from the first heart to the dream.

297. 艺术充满现实的启示和人类的梦想。

Art is full of realistic revelations and human dreams.

298. 能量为自由赋值。

Energy gives value to freedom.

299. 规则是社会的选择，道德是个人的选择。

Rules are social choices, and morality is the choice of individuals.

300. 善良是心灵的涟漪。

Kindness is the ripple of the heart.

301. 历史传承文明的可持续性。

History passed down the sustainability of civilizations.

302. 放下一切，才会赢得一切。

Put everything down and you will win everything.

303. 对自由的最大束缚就是无知。

The greatest constraint to freedom is ignorance.

304. 变革把文明推向发展的拐点。

Change pushes civilization to an inflection point in development.

305. 每一种科学思想都是对辩证法的另一种表述。

Every scientific thought is another expression of dialectics.

306. 重大的转折源自深刻的自醒。

The major turn stems from a profound self-awakening.

307. 使我们最终获益的，是能够打倒我们的力量。

What ultimately benefits us is the power that can defeat us.

308. 善与恶自有其轮回。

Good and evil have their own cycles.

309. 理性的全部价值，是基于科学的预测和基于可持续的和谐。

The full value of reason is prediction based on science and harmony based on sustainability.

310. 设计规划自由的路径。

Plan the path of freedom by design.

311. 理性的价值是由科学和人文照亮未来。

The value of reason is to illuminate the future by science and humanities.

312. 经济发展的驱动力是符合人文的需求与科学支撑的技术。

The driving force of economic development is to meet the needs of the humanities and the technology supported by science.

313. 思想的价值是为实践寻求可持续方法。

The value of ideas is to seek sustainable methods for practice.

314. 无敌的勇气来自为切身利益而战。

Invincible courage comes from fighting for the vital interests.

315. 邪恶是邪恶者的墓碑，道德是道德者的洗礼。

Evil is the tombstone of the evil, and morality is the baptism of the morality.

316. 平台为经济循环提供最广泛的市场。

The platform provides the widest range of markets for economic cycles.

317. 平等是最深刻的高贵。

Equality is the most profound nobility.

318. 信仰是人类的心理力量。

Faith is the psychological power of mankind.

319. 好奇为幻想播种。

Curiosity sows the seeds of fantasy.

320. 思想由概念绽放。

Ideas bloom by concepts.

321. 历史传承一个民族可持续的智慧。

History inherits the sustainable wisdom of a nation.

322. 思考是概念的演绎。

Thinking is the deduction of concepts.

323. 适应现实就是尊重未来。

Adapting to reality is respect for the future.

324. 每一种生机，都以它的形式绽放。

Every vitality blooms in its form.

325. 每一座山峰，都会遇见它的彩云。

Every mountain will meet its colorful clouds.

326. 批判是发展的前瞻。

Criticism is the foresight of development.

327. 发展源自事物的底层逻辑。

Development comes from the underlying logic of things.

328. 从来没有快速的精益。

Never fast perfect.

329. 平等是所有人的机会。

Equality is an opportunity for all.

330. 探索不是苦难，而是拯救苦难。

Exploration is not suffering, but saving suffering.

331. 英雄不是神明却无所畏惧。

Heroes are not gods but fearless.

332. 如何悲伤就会如何振奋。

How sad it is will be how uplifting.

333. 深刻才能持续，持续才有未来。

Only when it is profound can it last, and only after continuity can there be a future.

334. 可持续性基于现实的系统性和开放性。

Sustainability is based on the systematization and openness of reality.

335. 只有阳光能照耀，只有温暖能传播。

Only sunlight can shine; only warmth can spread.

336. 深刻才有远见。

Profoundity is visionary.

337. 气象循环就是自然界的热泵循环。

The meteorological cycle is the heat pump cycle of nature.

338. 英雄毕生实现的目标，会使一个时代难以企及。

What a hero achieves in his life will make an era out of reach.

339. 创造是精神的成长。

Creation is spiritual growth.

340. 排斥是现实可持续性的根源。

Exclusion is the root of sustainability in reality.

341. 和谐为发展预留时空。

Harmony reserves time and space for development.

342. 垄断违背现实和谐的自然机理。

Monopoly violates the natural mechanism of harmony in reality.

343. 创新是照耀实践的光辉。

Innovation is the brilliance that shines on practice.

344. 美是经验赋予现实的光辉。

Beauty is the brilliance that experience gives to reality.

345. 科学揭示自然演绎的逻辑，人文揭示需求变换的逻辑。

Science reveals the logic of nature deduction, and humanities reveal the logic of demand transformation.

346. 所有的浩瀚都没有目标和利益。

All vastness has no goals and interests.

347. 所有的梯度都由激流释放。

All gradients are released by torrents.

348. 所有的变革在为现实发展提供可持续力量。

All changes are providing sustainable power for reality development.

349. 苦难是现实与理想的界面。

Suffering is the interface between reality and ideals.

350. 探索的勇气源自生命力。

The courage to explore comes from vitality.

351. 思想是独立的视角和见解。

Ideas are independent perspectives and opinions.

352. 不以河流的长度，否定大海的深度。

Do not deny the depth of the sea by the length of the river.

353. 包容是文明迭代的力量。

Inclusion is the power of civilization iteration.

354. 探索由好奇与梦想驱使。

Exploration is driven by curiosity and dreams.

355. 数学是逻辑演绎的轨道。

Mathematics is the tracks for logical deduction.

356. 偶像是概念的价值。

Idols are the value of concepts.

357. 创新是人类实践最具活力的部分。

Innovation is the most dynamic part of human practice.

358. 实践不仅检验真理，而且塑造方法。

Practice not only tests the truth, but also shapes the method.

359. 知识承载历史变革的责任。

Knowledge carries responsibility for historical change.

360. 科学启蒙驱使人类步入近代社会。

Scientific enlightenment drove mankind into modern society.

361. 只有当和谐成为终极价值，社会才能获得普遍生机。

Only when harmony becomes the ultimate value can society gain universal vitality.

362. 实践始终是理想与现实的迭代。

Practice is always an iteration of ideals and reality.

363. 以邪恶开始，就以邪恶结束。

Start with evil, end with evil.

364. 科学迈出的每一步，都在接近民主。

Every step science takes is approaching democracy.

365. 科学是民主普及的力量。

Science is the universal force of democracy.

366. 质疑扇动思想的翅膀。

Questioning flaps the wings of thought.

367. 数学是逻辑的奇迹。

Mathematics is a miracle of logic.

368. 历史属于实践者和探索者。

History belongs to practitioners and explorers.

369. 发明为我们拓展文明的疆域。

Invention expands the boundaries of civilization for us.

370. 中国现代化是西方文明与东方文明有机迭代的结果。

Modernization of China is the result of the organic iteration of Western civilization and Eastern civilization.

371. 任何偶然性都会被必然性所修正。

Any contingency is corrected by necessity.

372. 中国激荡的四十年正是东方文明包容西方文明的四十年，也是中华文明在制度、地区、财富、技术方面层层破壁的四十年。

The 40 years of stirring in China is the 40 years of Eastern civilization tolerating Western civilization, and also the 40 years of Chinese civilization breaking down the wall in the system, region, wealth and technology.

373. 数量堆砌并非质量叠加，大而不强是一种耻辱。

Quantity stacking is not a qualitative superposition, and being large but not strong is a shame.

374. 不以沟壑的深度，否定山峰的高度。

Do not deny the height of the peak by the depth of the ravine.

375. 每一种形式都是生机的绽放。

Every form is a blossom of vitality.

376. 宗教是人性的慰藉。

Religion is the solace of humanity.

377. 所有的深刻都能被科学计量、被仿真预测。

All profundity can be measured by science and be predicted by simulation.

378. 文学用现实的苦难解构人性。

Literature deconstructs humanity from the suffering of reality.

379. 迭代是系统演绎和进化的形式。

Iteration is a form of system deduction and evolution.

380. 成功基于使命感与责任心。

Success is based on a sense of mission and responsibility.

381. 唯有科学能从现实的困境中揭示出路。

Only science can reveal a way out of the real dilemma.

382. 能被仿真的事物才能预测。

Things that can be simulated can be predicted.

383. 艺术是心灵的旅程。

Art is the journey of the heart.

384. 技术迈出的每一步都是科学。

Every step of technology is science.

385. 社会发展的拐点是历史的精华。

The inflection point of social development is the essence of history.

386. 超越的力量带来孤独的勇气。

The power of transcendence brings the courage of loneliness.

387. 权力是思想波及的范围。

Power is the scope of the thought ripple.

388. 曲线和色彩是神奇的力量。

Curves and colors are magical powers.

389. 史诗反映时代的变迁。

The epic reflects the changing times.

390. 所有因生命而悸动的心灵，都是高贵的。

All hearts that are throbbing by life are noble.

391. 对于未来的期待驱使我们从容面对现实。

Expectations for the future drive us to face reality with ease.

392. 历史的必然性体现人类的智慧。

The inevitability of history reflects human wisdom.

393. 没有力量可以战胜自然演绎的智慧。

No power can overcome the wisdom of natural deduction.

394. 所有荣耀归于责任。

All glory is attributed to responsibility.

395. 事物演绎的必然性充满智慧。

The inevitability of the deduction of things is full of wisdom.

396. 及时清空，才能快速流转。

Empty in time to quickly circulate.

397. 精简才会深刻。

Simplicity can be profound.

398. 激情是意志的节奏。

Passion is the rhythm of the will.

399. 科学起源于计量，终结于仿真。

Science originated in measurement and ended in simulation.

400. 虚伪不仅阻碍认知，而且限制智慧。

Hypocrisy not only hinders cognition, but also limits wisdom.

401. 每一种谬误都是对真理的提示。

Every fallacy is a hint of truth.

402. 云中穿行巅峰之路。

Runs through the clouds along the road to the top.

403. 唯有翅膀跨越彩云。

Only wings cross the clouds.

404. 翅膀和雄心没有疆界。

Wings and ambition know no boundaries.

405. 清澈的灵魂才能回归现实。

A clear soul can return to reality.

406. 形式是逻辑演绎的轨迹。

Form is the trajectory of logical deduction.

407. 没有现实根基的梦想就不会发芽。

Dreams without a foundation in reality do not sprout.

408. 聪明关注现实，智慧预测未来。

Smart ness pay attention to reality, wisdom predicts the future.

409. 节能是第二能源。

Energy saving is the second energy source.

410. 每一种能量转换，都释放一种现实力量。

Each energy conversion releases a reality power.

411. 每一门科学，都释放一种现实力量。

Every science unleashes a reality force.

412. 每一座山峰都有自己的灵魂。

Each mountain has its own soul.

413. 提取现实每一种力量都需要一门科学。

Extracting every reality force requires a science.

414. 使命感是面向未来所具有的忘我勇气。

A sense of mission is the selfless courage to face the future.

415. 每一种系统演绎，都植根于现实的普遍性。

Each systematic deduction is rooted in the universality of reality.

416. 创新就是重构系统最深刻的部分。

Innovation is to refactor the most profound part of the system.

417. 每一处现实的断崖，都会成为梦想的起点。

Every realistic cliff will be the starting point of dreams.

418. 每一座桥梁，都在为探索者留下遗产。

Each bridge leaves a legacy for explorers.

419. 一切都是现实演绎的结果。

Everything is the result of the reality deduction.

420. 适应是生命逻辑与现实逻辑的迭代。

Adaptation is an iteration of the life logic and the reality logic.

421. 战略是我们跨越未来所需要的定力。

Strategy is the set force we need to cross the future.

422. 音乐展示现实演绎的节奏。

Music shows the rhythm of reality deduction.

423. 商业传递需求的价值。

Business delivers the value of demand.

424. 年轻是面向未来的勇气。

Being young is the courage to face the future.

425. 每一处风景，都有其主宰的灵魂。

Every scenery has its own dominant soul.

426. 没有退路成就最强出路。

There is no retreat to achieve the strongest way out.

427. 创新闪烁智慧的光芒。

Innovation flashes the wisdom light.

428. 每一次转机，都是被真理照亮的时刻。

Every turn is a moment illuminated by the truth.

429. 每一座历史建筑，都散发时代的气息。

Each historic building exudes the atmosphere of the times.

430. 由苦难探测人性的深度。

Probe the depth of humanity through suffering.

431. 点亮黑暗只需一束光芒。

It takes only a ray of light to light up the darkness.

432. 生长是植物的灵魂。

Growth is the soul of plants.

433. 如果不以科学获取现实力量，就只能从宗教获取心灵慰藉。

If we do not obtain realistic power by science, we can only obtain spiritual solace from religion.

434. 每一种超越，都成就一种孤独。

Every transcendence achieves a loneliness.

435. 没有一种成功叫容易。

No success is easy.

436. 未知中隐藏多样性的魅力。

The charm of diversity is hidden in the unknown.

437. 具有显而易见的目标，就不再成为探索。

With obvious goals, it is no longer an exploration.

438. 蒸汽热泵引发能源革命。

Steam heat pumps spark an energy-saving revolution.

439. 思想具有最广泛和最持久的传播性。

Ideas are widely and persistently disseminated.

440. 信用是命运的出发点。

Credit is the starting point of destiny.

441. 每一种生机，都是对阳光的尊重。

Every vitality is a respect for sunlight.

442. 用知识解构现实，才会获得变革的力量。

The power of change is gained by deconstructing reality with knowledge.

443. 以道德为底线是为社会创造价值，以法律为底线是为个人谋取利益。

With morality as the bottom line is to create value for society, and with law as the bottom line is to seek personal benefits.

444. 理性在逻辑上指导感性，感性在经验上引导理性。

Reason guides sensibility in logic, and sensibility guides reason in experience.

445. 形式逻辑启示内容逻辑。

Form logic enlightens content logic.

446. 所有的苦难都是经验的序章。

All suffering is a prelude to experience.

447. 竞争为现实带来普遍的生机。

Competition brings universal vitality to reality.

448. 经典承载文明最多的梦想。

The classics carry the most dreams of civilization.

449. 战略是通向未来的定力。

Strategy is the path to the future.

450. 最伟大的探索不是突破认知边界，而是重建认知目标。

The greatest exploration is not to break through cognitive boundaries, but to reconstruct cognitive goals.

451. 聪明是以现实利益为出发点。

Cleverness is based on practical interests.

452. 智慧是我们实现长远目标所应具备的现实策略。

Wisdom is a realistic strategy for us to achieve long-term goals.

453. 由灵魂雕琢的器物，也就承载着灵魂。

Artifacts carved by the soul also carry the soul.

454. 凡是在艰难环境中拼搏的生命，都有一股朝圣般的启示和力量。

All life that struggles in difficult environments has a pilgrimage-like revelation and strength.

455. 只有宏大才能无敌。

Only grandeur can be invincible.

456. 竞争是多元化与可持续性的必然结果。

Competition is an inevitable consequence of diversity and sustainability.

457. 不同的快乐基于不同的观念。

Different pleasures are based on different concepts.

458. 每一个人的价值，都是其为社会提升的价值。

The value of each person is the value of his promotion to society.

459. 现实的生机是艺术所要展示的精髓。

The vitality of reality is the essence of art display.

460. 人类欲望驱动艺术发展，社会需求驱动技术变革。

Human desire drives artistic development, and social needs drive technological change.

461. 哲学以规律的本质解构现实。

Philosophy deconstructs reality with the essence of laws.

462. 实践是人生最伟大的舞台。

Practice is the greatest stage of life.

463. 勇气和智慧创造现实的生机。

Courage and wisdom create the vitality of reality.

464. 灾难加速文明的迭代与进化。

Disasters accelerate the iteration and evolution of civilization.

465. 每一种真诚，都是深刻的。

Every sincerity is profound.

466. 财富源自远见和担当。

Wealth comes from vision and responsibility.

467. 生命没有彩排。

Life is without rehearsal.

468. 艺术是宗教的背景。

Art is the background of religion.

469. 一种荒诞引发种种荒诞。

A kind of absurdity leads to all kinds of absurdity.

470. 可持续性是生命演绎的目标。

Sustainability is the goal of life deduction.

471. 音乐展示生命演绎的节奏。

Music shows the rhythm of life deduction.

472. 纵然不能飞翔，依然可以跨越。

Even if you cannot fly, you can still cross.

473. 科学以概念的本质重构现实。

Science reconstructs reality with the essence of concepts.

474. 胸怀世界你就是海洋，点亮黑暗你就是光明。

With the world in mind you are the ocean, and lighting up the darkness you are the light.

475. 科学性提升局部价值，系统性提升整体价值。

Science enhances the partial value and systematization enhances the overall value.

476. 宽容倍增人性的力量。

Tolerance doubles the power of humanity.

477. 有人文才有信心，有信心才有需求，有需求才有经济。

With humanities to have confidence, with confidence to have demand, with demand to have economy.

478. 节能的本质是提高能源利用的系统性。

The essence of energy saving is to improve the systematization of energy utilization.

479. 混乱的价值是暴露矛盾、推进变革；整齐的价值是展示秩序、推演逻辑。

The value of chaos is to expose contradictions and promote change; The value of neatness is to show order and deduce logic.

480. 历史不会为谎言重演。

History will not repeat itself for lies.

481. 阴影的背后就是光明。

Behind the shadows is light.

482. 信心是生命力的基石。

Faith is the cornerstone of vitality.

483. 系统性是可持续性的基石。

Systematization is the cornerstone of sustainability.

484. 历史是由朝代的掘墓者为自己刻下的墓碑。

History is the tombstones carved for themselves by the gravediggers of the dynasty.

485. 艺术为桀骜的灵魂留下归途。

Art leaves a way back for the rebellious soul.

486. 可持续性基于普遍性。

Sustainability is based on universality.

487. 英雄把社会梦想转变成时代潮流。

Heroes turn social dreams into the times trend.

488. 企业创新步骤：(1) 性质：创新意味着成为少数派，并愿意长时间接受质疑和误解。(2) 特点：必须采取非共识但正确的观点以击败竞争对手。(3) 执行：掌握一手市场信息、重组市场需求、组建技术团队、积累专业技术、进行科学仿真、实现系统整合。(4) 决策：确定商业模式、评估投资风险。

Enterprise innovation steps: (1) Nature: Innovation means being a minority and willing to accept questions and misunderstandings for a long time. (2) Features: A non-consensus but correct view must be taken to defeat the competitors. (3) Implementation: Master first-hand market information, reorganize market demand, set up technical team, accumulate professional technology, carry out scientific simulation, realize system integration. (4) Decision-making: Identify business models and assess investment risks.

489. 深度思考增强生命力。

Deep thinking strengthens vitality.

490. 审美是对现实生机的感悟。

Aesthetics is the perception of the vitality of reality.

491. 重大的现实抉择构建历史发展的拐点。

Major realistic choices constitute an inflection point in historical development.

492. 以逻辑推导为特征的产业，终将被人工智能取代。

Industries characterized by logical derivation will eventually be replaced by artificial intelligence.

493. 未来是现实可持续性演绎的必然结果。

The future is the inevitable result of the sustainable deduction of reality.

494. 自我实现作为一种超越性动机，打破工作和娱乐的界限以构建最接近成功的族群。

Self-actualization as a transcendent motivation that breaks down the boundaries of work and play to build the group closest to success.

495. 艺术把思考的起点从现实提升到多元化形式，从而为科学家和哲学家提供更深刻的启示。

Art elevates the starting point of thinking from reality to diversified forms, thus providing a more profound enlightenment for scientists and philosophers.

496. 越有知识，越感到无知。

The more knowledge you have, the more ignorant you feel.

497. 现实生机来自系统性的开放与多样性的包容。

Vitality comes from systematization openness and diversity inclusion.

498. 生物进化：越原始、越显性、越顽强，越高级、越隐性、越脆弱。

Biological evolution: the more primitive, the more dominant, the more tenacious; the more advanced, the more implicit, the more fragile.

499. 理想与现实的落差驱动文明的演绎。

The difference between ideal and reality drives the civilization deduction.

500. 地理是历史演绎的背景。

Geography is the background for historical deduction.

501. 矿山与城市留下一段文明演绎的距离。

The mine and the city leave a distance from the civilization deduction.

502. 文明为人类带来可持续的光明与温暖。

Civilization brings sustainable light and warmth to mankind.

503. 可持续性是生命和文明的精髓。

Sustainability is the essence of life and civilization.

504. 未来是可持续性的必然结果。

The future is an inevitable consequence of sustainability.

505. 提炼价格背后的价值，需要智慧的力量。

Refining the value behind the price requires the power of wisdom.

506. 每一项奇迹，都是责任的延伸。

Every miracle is an extension of responsibility.

507. 风景在地理和气象的迭代中展露生机。

The landscape shows the vitality in an iteration of geography and meteorology.

508. 均衡是多元化设计的准则。

Equilibrium is the criterion of diversified design.

509. 每一片景色都有其生机，每一种生机都有其灵魂。

Each landscape has its vitality; each vitality has its soul.

510. 科学发展已趋缓，技术整合在提速。

Scientific development has slowed down, and technological integration is accelerating.

511. 每一种形式的美，都在启示一种自然演绎的逻辑。

Every form of beauty reveals a logic of natural deduction.

512. 建立国际政治秩序与民族可持续发展的平衡点，是每个时代政治家的历史使命。

It is the historical mission of politicians of every era to establish the balance between the international political order and the sustainable development of the nation.

513. 生命力源于现实的普遍性与多元化。

Vitality comes from the universality and diversity of reality.

514. 原创性技术植根于基础科学的突变。

Original technology is rooted in mutations in basic science.

515. 系统性提升可持续性。

Systematization enhances sustainability.

516. 节奏与色彩再现生命演绎的活力。

Rhythm and color indicate the vitality of life deduction.

517. 一切都在被时间塑造。

Everything is being shaped by time.

518. 每一种传承，都延续一种历史的力量。

Each heritage continues a historical force.

519. 社会边缘揭示生存的底线。

Social fringes reveal the bottom line of survival.

520. 生命进化是从自然的普遍性中获取可持续的力量。

The life evolution is to gain sustainable power from the universality of nature.

521. 理性以现实的力量引导人类未来。

Reason guides the future of mankind with the power of reality.

522. 心理力量来自科学、艺术、信仰。

Psychological power comes from science, art, faith.

523. 节奏是生命演绎的力量。

Rhythm is the power of life deduction.

第 9 章 | 没有任何智慧能够超越历史的必然性
No wisdom can transcend the inevitability of history

（2019 年上海柯茂总工程师 Chief engineer of Shanghai Comer）

1. 站在上帝的高度，自有上帝的胸怀。

   Stand at the height of God and have the heart of God then.

2. 辩证法是自然演绎的逻辑。

   Dialectics is the logic of natural deduction.

3. 感性无法超越理性对它的吸引。

   Sensibility cannot transcend the attraction of reason to it.

4. 本质是认知回归现实的途径。

   The essence is the way for cognition to return to reality.

5. 不能萃取经验的苦难，就是一场真正的苦难。

   The suffering that cannot extract experience is a real suffering.

6. 现实的苦难在为文明进化筛选更完整的适应性。

   The suffering of reality is screening for a more complete adaptation for the civilization evolution.

7. 力量来自现实，知识来自实践。

Strength comes from reality; knowledge comes from practice.

8. 荣耀归于历史演绎的责任。

Glory is attributed to the responsibility of historical deduction.

9. 自由是灵魂闪烁的光芒。

Freedom is the shining light of the soul.

10. 秩序是社会共同的脉搏和人类自由的根基。

Order is the common pulse of society and the foundation of human freedom.

11. 智慧是文明进步的阶梯。

Wisdom is the ladder of civilization progress.

12. 实践的目标是获取现实演绎的力量。

The goal of practice is to gain the power of the reality deduction.

13. 商业的出发点是人性，企业的出发点是道德。

The starting point of business is humanity, and the starting point of enterprise is morality.

14. 每一种生命都是自然演绎的精灵。

Every life is the elf of nature deduction.

15. 建筑是城市文明的标志。

Architecture is a symbol of urban civilization.

16. 历史是现实演绎的内核。

History is the core of the reality deduction.

17. 所有的风景在于生机，所有的生机在于持续。

All scenery lies in vitality; all vitality lies in continuity.

18. 色彩是现实演绎的启示。

Color is the revelation of reality deduction.

19. 现实利益始终是人性演绎的动机。

Practical interests are always the motivation of humanity deduction.

20. 风吹灭蜡烛，却助燃烈火。

The wind blows out the candles, but fuels the fire.

21. 责任体现社会价值。

Responsibility embodies the social value.

22. 发展不会超越战略的高度。

Development does not go beyond the height of strategy.

23. 智慧的精髓是捕捉现实发展的机遇。

The essence of wisdom is to capture the opportunities of the development of reality.

24. 容忍就会放纵罪恶。

To tolerate is to indulge sin.

25. 革命是全面的扬弃而非全面的毁灭。

Revolution is a total sublation rather than a total destruction.

26. 人类是唯一灭绝同属的动物，其智力进化以残忍导致种属孤独作为代价。

Humans are the only animal that have exterminated their same species, and their intellectual evolution cames at the cost of cruelty leading to species loneliness.

27. 鸦片战争是中国迈入现代社会的门槛。

The Opium Wars were the threshold for China to enter the modern society.

28. 每一种历史的担当都在照亮未来。

Every historical responsibility illuminates the future.

29. 历史从来都是强者的借口和弱者的笑话。

History has always been an excuse for the strong and a joke for the weak.

30. 文化是一个民族传承的血脉。

Culture is the bloodline of a nation inheritance.

31. 没有感性的翅膀，理性难以腾飞。

Without emotional wings, reason is difficult to take off.

32. 没有剖析就无法理解和思考。

It is impossible to understand and think without analysis.

33. 提高组织智商：命运共同、愿景明晰、适时变革、团队协作、知识匹配、绩效传递。

Improve organizational intelligence: common destiny, clear vision, timely change, teamwork, knowledge matching, performance delivery.

34. 以科学整合技术，以技术满足需求。

Integrate technology with science and meet needs with technology.

35. 提升解析力：广泛的发现、全面的解构、深刻的变革。

Enhancing Resolution: Extensive Discovery, Total Deconstruction, Profound Change.

36. 不去引发变革就需倡导变革，不去倡导变革就需适应变革。

    It needs to advocate change without triggering change, and it needs to adapt to change without advocating change.

37. 每一种简约，都是一次解构。

    Every simplicity is a deconstruction.

38. 音乐是意志的变奏。

    Music is a variation of the will.

39. 仿真是理性的内核。

    Simulation is the core of reason.

40. 基因传承自然演绎的智慧。

    Genes are inheriting the wisdom of natural deduction.

41. 解析是批判的内核。

    Analysis is the core of criticism.

42. 现实可以追随，但无法超越。

    Reality can follow, but it cannot be surpassed.

43. 能打败我们的力量才会使我们强大。

    The power that defeats us will make us strong.

44. 每一种文明，都被其地理和时代所塑造。

    Each civilization is shaped by its geography and times.

45. 每一个时代，都有其跨越现实的勇气和方式。

    Every era has its own courage and way of crossing reality.

46. 历史被各个时代的担当和智慧所连接。

History is connected by the responsibility and wisdom of each era.

47. 每一种生机，都充满现实的期待。

Every vitality is full of realistic expectations.

48. 可持续生机源自多元化竞争。

Sustainable vitality comes from diversified competition.

49. 由解析力预测现实演绎的拐点。

The inflection point of reality deduction is predicted by analysis.

50. 生存是可持续的方式。

Survival is a sustainable way.

51. 混沌揭示重构的契机，也是变革的起点。

Chaos reveals the opportunity for reconstruction, and is also the starting point of change.

51. 所有目标在于过程，所有过程在于积累。

All goals are in the process; all processes are in the accumulation.

52. 心如大海就不再有苦难。

There is no more suffering in the heart like the sea.

53. 规范是冰冷的，设计是温暖的。

The specifications are cold and the design is warm.

54. 由利益所代表的力量驱动历史发展。

History development is driven by the power represented by interests.

55. 幻想是跨越自然的力量。

Fantasy is a force that transcends nature.

56. 平衡是宏大现实的必然趋势。

Balance is an inevitable trend of grand reality.

57. 生命是可持续的自然演绎。

Life is a sustainable natural deduction.

58. 每个时代都有其显著标志和深刻记忆。

Each era has its distinctive hallmarks and deep memories.

59. 历史源自每个时代最深刻的抉择。

History stems from the deepest choices of every era.

60. 一个民族不反省历史的罪恶，在灾难面前就会丧失免疫力。

If a nation does not reflect on the evils of history, it will lose its immunity in the face of disaster.

61. 快鱼和慢鱼各有生机。

Fast fish and slow fish have their own vitality.

62. 文化包容是一个民族不可征服的力量。

Cultural tolerance is an unconquerable force of a people.

63. 只有统一的文化，才有统一的国家。

Only with a unified culture can there be a unified country.

64. 植根利益的观念具有最大的惯性。

The concept of being rooted in interests has the greatest inertia.

65. 生活被地理和季节赋予色彩。

Life is colored by geography and seasons.

66. 可持续的文明难以征服。

Sustainable civilizations are hard to conquer.

67. 苦难是现实给我们的提示。

Suffering is a hint that reality gives us.

68. 我们脱离痛苦的喜悦，源自痛苦的真切。

The joy of our freedom from suffering comes from the reality of suffering.

69. 竞争力源自可持续机制。

Competitiveness comes from sustainable mechanisms.

70. 经济是在法律框架内由智力所带来的远见收割大众利益。

The economy is harvesting popular interests by the foresight brought about by the intelligence within the legal framework.

71. 优选的结果源自优选的方式。

The optimized result derives from the optimized way.

72. 家族是成长的心理启示。

Family is the psychological enlightenment of growth.

73. 可用眼睛观察的是假象，可用概念描述的是现象，可用理论仿真的是对象，可用实践验证的是真相。

What can be observed by the eyes is illusion; what can be described by the concepts is phenomenon; what can be simulated by the theory is object; what can be verified by the practice is the trueness.

74. 趋势源自力量的积蓄与释放。

Trends stem from the accumulation and release of power.

75. 财富是可持续的经济来源。

Wealth is a sustainable economic source.

76. 数学是形式演绎的逻辑。

Mathematics is the logic of formal deduction.

77. 现实演绎以竞争和时机筛选智慧。

Reality deduction screens wisdom by competition and timing.

78. 我们从阳光获取生命演绎的启示。

We take the revelation of life deduction from sunlight.

78. 被理性所解构的现实就不再是苦难。

The reality deconstructed by reason is no longer suffering.

79. 理性赋予我们回归现实的力量。

Reason gives us the power to return to reality.

80. 反思是现实的启示。

Reflection is a revelation of reality.

81. 智慧是可持续的力量。

Wisdom is a sustainable force.

82. 现实可以诱导却无法改变，可以退让却无法避免。

Reality can be induced but cannot be changed, and it can be retreated but cannot be avoided.

83. 时间很久远，生机只是惊艳的刹那；空间很广阔，神明只是穿透的视角。

Time is remote and vitality is only a stunning moment and space is vast and god is only a penetrating perspective.

84. 生机总会轮回、升起、照耀、闪烁、绽放。

Vitality always reincarnates, rises, shines, flickers, and blooms.

85. 所有人的底线就是霸权的坟墓。

The bottom line for all is the tomb of hegemony.

86. 不可持续就沦为平庸。

Unsustainability will be reduced to mediocre.

87. 理性是在更深层次回归现实，因而就比现实更加现实。

Reason returns to reality at a deeper level, and is therefore more realistic than reality.

88. 地理和气象是文明演绎的背景。

Geography and meteorology are the background for the deduction of civilizations.

89. 实践推动文明的演绎。

Practice drives the deduction of civilization.

90. 生命以色彩绽放。

Life blooms by color.

91. 思想由形式绽放。

Thought blooms by form.

92. 科学揭示现实演绎的逻辑。

Science reveals the logic of reality deduction.

93. 基于多元化的均衡是生命可持续性的根源。

Equilibrium based on diversity is the root of life sustainability.

94. 速度和精确是效率的精髓。

Speed and precision are the essence of efficiency.

95. 由竞争提高机制的可持续性。

The mechanism sustainability is enhanced by competition.

96. 生命基于可持续机制。

Life is based on sustainable mechanisms.

97. 由竞争而不断改进事物演绎的机制。

The mechanism of the things deduction is constantly improved by competition.

98. 品格限定员工的成长，道德限定企业的成长。

Character limits the growth of employees; morality limits the growth of enterprises.

99. 竞争的目标始终是资源。

The goal of competition is always resources.

100. 注入灵魂的艺术，也就承载着灵魂。

Art that is infused into the soul also carries the soul.

101. 观念是艺术的内核。

Concept is the core of art.

102. 每一种科学度量，都开启一个实践的维度。

Every scientific measure opens up a practical dimension.

103. 机遇是观念与现实迭代的必然结果。

Opportunity is the inevitable result of the iteration of ideas and reality.

104. 意志绽放人性的光辉。

The will blooms with the brilliance of humanity.

105. 色彩是自然的启示。

Color is a natural revelation.

106. 不以自私作为出发点，就没有可供信赖的人性基础。

Without selfishness as a starting point, there is no humanity foundation to be trusted.

107. 理性和人文是文明演绎的力量。

Reason and humanism are the forces of civilizational deduction.

108. 没有超越现实的逼真。

There is no realism beyond reality.

109. 希望是对未来的理性期待。

Hope is the rational expectation of the future.

110. 艺术以形式逻辑启迪思想逻辑。

Art enlightens the thought logic with the form logic.

111. 空灵是现实的断崖，梦想的天空。

Ethereal is the cliff of reality, the sky of dreams.

112. 占位是利益的出发点。

Placeholder is the starting point of interests.

113. 书法展示思维的轨迹。

Calligraphy shows the trajectory of thinking.

114. 道德具有社会感召力。

Morality has social appeal.

115. 美是现实最深刻的部分和最生动的时机。

Beauty is the most profound part and the most vivid timing of reality.

116. 行业先进性取决于多大程度由热泵节能。

The advanced nature of the industry depends on the extent to which heat pumps save energy.

117. 经济由艺术渲染和背书。

The economy is rendered and endorsed by art.

118. 多元化提升文明可持续性。

Diversity enhances the sustainability of civilization.

119. 人性源于自信。

Humanity comes from self-confidence.

120. 信息发展的最高境界是打破现实和虚拟的界面。

The highest state of information development is to break the interface between reality and virtuality.

121. 历史是对转折点的时间回溯。

History is a time regression on turning points.

122. 突变发生在物性的临界点。

Mutations occur at the critical point of physical properties.

123. 科学是现实演绎的逻辑。

Science is the logic of reality deduction.

124. 色彩是自然演绎的密码。

Color is the code of natural deduction.

125. 能源是文明的希望。

Energy is the hope of civilization.

126. 自由是生命的意志。

Freedom is the will to life.

127. 希望是人类面对未来所具有的全部勇气。

Hope is all the courage of mankind to face the future.

128. 一无所有是另一种所有。

Having nothing at all is another kind of having something.

129. 美以其形式启示逻辑。

Beauty enlightens logic in its form.

130. 水是构建地理循环和气象循环的载体。

Water is the vehicle that constructs the geographical and meteorological cycle.

131. 垄断是规避竞争。

Monopoly is the circumvention of competition.

132. 没有比现实更宏大的事物。

There is nothing bigger than reality.

133. 最高效的节能是闭环工艺系统。

The most efficient energy savings are closed-loop process systems.

134. 整体和谐与单体高效是现实进化的趋势。

Overall harmony and monomer efficiency are the trends of reality evolution.

135. 文明就是以心智的力量战胜臂膀的力量。

Civilization is the victory of the mind power over the arm power.

136. 历史是社会形态的演绎。

History is the deduction of social formations.

137. 由本能培育出的鲜活动机，才能建立伟大目标。

A living motive cultivated by instinct can build a great goal.

138. 由苦难探测现实的力量与转机。

Detect the power and turning point of reality through suffering.

139. 没有超越能力的慈悲。

There is no mercy beyond the ability.

140. 生命的取向决定生命的机制。

The orientation of life determines the mechanism of life.

141. 现实的苦难筛选历史的智慧。

The suffering of reality filters out the history wisdom.

142. 理解中的热爱才会深刻。

The love in understanding is profound.

143. 生命脆弱，但生命的机制是不朽的。

Life is fragile but the mechanism of life is immortal.

144. 生命固有其色彩和节奏。

Life has its color and rhythm inherently.

145. 坚持伟大目标，时间才有意义。

Time makes sense if you stick to great goals.

146. 在需求变幻的时代，技术突变来自集成和跨界。

In the era of demands changing, technological mutations come from integration and cross-border.

147. 你若不甘就点燃希望、照亮黑暗、成就人生。

If you are unwilling, you should ignite hope, illuminate darkness, and achieve life.

148. 生命是被节气所召唤的节奏。

Life is the rhythm summoned by seasons.

149. 上帝只做最后的鞭策与祈祷。

God only does the last spur and prayer.

150. 理想与现实的落差即为苦难。

The difference between ideal and reality is suffering.

151. 慈善是社会平衡的力量。

Charity is the force of social balance.

152. 生命演绎的逻辑：开放才会多元、多元才可持续、持续才能竞争、竞争才有节奏。

The logic of life deduction: openness will be diversity; diversity will be sustainability; sustainability will be competition; competition will have rhythm.

153. 历史为现实演绎提供坐标。

History provides coordinates for the reality deduction.

154. 所有的奢侈都不可持续。

All luxuries are not sustainable.

155. 年轻就是憧憬未来的勇气。

Being young is the courage to look forward to the future.

156. 竞争为现实演绎提供可持续性。

Competition provides sustainability for the reality deduction.

157. 由智慧把握现实演绎的趋势。

Grasp the trend of reality deduction by wisdom.

158. 所有的绝壁和断崖迫使我们腾飞。

All the walls and cliffs are forcing us to take off.

159. 敬畏自然是因为心中有座远山。

Reverence for nature is because there is a distant mountain in the heart.

160. 市场的选择是企业的机会。

The market choice is an opportunity for businesses.

161. 清晰才会深刻，真诚才会善良。

Clarity can be profound, sincerity can be kindness.

162. 不被智慧把握的现实都是苦难。

The reality that has not yet been grasped by wisdom is suffering.

163. 热爱是跨界的语言和光芒。

Love is cross-border language and light.

164. 审美筛选出人性和品位。

Aesthetics filter out humanity and taste.

165. 越精致，越脆弱。

The more delicate, the more fragile.

166. 企业通过资源和利益整合组织社会力量。

Enterprises organize social forces through the integration of resources and interests.

167. 善良是抑制邪恶的力量。

Kindness is the force to suppress evil.

168. 历史是社会发展最具必然性的部分。

History is the most inevitable part of social development.

169. 西方逻辑还原自然力量，东方逻辑再现人性力量。

Western logic restores the natural forces, and Eastern logic reproduces the humanity forces.

170. 师天下者无敌。

Those who learn from the world are invincible.

171. 意志谱写生命的节奏。

The will composes the rhythm of life.

172. 我们由探索和实践感知生命的价值。

We perceive the life value by exploration and practice.

173. 能改变现实的都是力量。

What can change reality is power.

174. 基于自信的谦逊是事业的起点。

Humility based on self-confidence is the beginning of a career.

175. 不植根于历史的现实不可持续。

Realities that are not rooted in history are unsustainable.

176. 遗传是生命对逻辑演绎的记忆。

Genetics is the memory for logical deduction of life.

177. 邪恶总是被时机打败。

Evil is always defeated by the timing.

178. 美是现实的精华与时机。

Beauty is the essence and timing of reality.

179. 能够撬动现实的都是智慧。

What can pry reality is wisdom.

180. 信仰是人类面向未来的勇气。

Faith is a courage for mankind to face the future.

181. 理性是引导未来的力量。

Reason is the force that guides the future.

182. 生机源自可持续机制。

Vitality comes from sustainable mechanisms.

183. 智慧需要经验与现实的迭代。

Wisdom requires iteration of experience and reality.

184. 思想的演绎揭示实践的演绎。

The deduction of ideas reveals the deduction of practice.

185. 热爱传递自然演绎的精华。

Love delivers the essence of natural deduction.

186. 思想的深度不会超越理想与现实的落差。

The depth of thought does not transcend the gap between ideals and reality.

187. 思想的深度不会超越实践的深度。

The depth of thought does not exceed the depth of practice.

188. 理性以自然演绎的逻辑与人性的和谐适应现实。

Reason adapts to reality with the nature deduction logic and humanity harmony.

189. 可持续机制通向未来。

Sustainable mechanisms lead to the future.

190. 历史体现社会演绎的必然性。

History embodies the inevitability of social deduction.

191. 山峰可与彩云共舞。

The mountain peaks can dance with the clouds.

192. 由竞争构建可持续机制。

Build sustainable mechanisms through competition.

193. 时机是生命演绎的节奏。

Timing is the rhythm of life deduction.

194. 战争加速多重文明的相互迭代。

War accelerates the iteration of multiple civilizations.

195. 进化是多重逻辑的相互迭代。

Evolution is the mutual iteration of multiple logics.

196. 不基于历史的坐标就无法掌握现实的智慧。

The reality wisdom cannot be grasped without being based on historical coordinates.

197. 系统进化由增强适应性提高可持续性。

Phyletic evolution improves sustainability by enhancing adaptability.

198. 倾注深情才能获取精华。

Pour deep feelings to get the essence.

199. 真理由实践划定边界。

Truth is bounded by practice.

200. 艺术饱含时代的激情。

Art is full of the passion of the times.

201. 和谐是多重文明共同发展的必然结果。

Harmony is the inevitable result of the common development of multiple civilizations.

202. 每一座城市，都有其灵魂闪烁的光芒。
Every city has the shining light of its soul.

203. 竞争为生命提供可持续演绎的机制。
Competition provides a mechanism for sustainable deduction of life.

204. 不会比实践更深刻，不会比现实更有力。
No more profound than practice, no more powerful than reality.

205. 阳光和彩云总是眷顾山峰。
Sunshine and clouds always favor the peaks.

206. 生机源自现实的普遍性。
Vitality comes from the universality of reality.

207. 所有的错误都在偏离现实演绎的根源，所有的罪恶都在背离现实演绎的根源。
All mistakes are drifting from the root of reality deduction, and all sins are deviating from the root of reality deduction.

208. 质疑的每一步都在逼近真理。
Every step of questioning is approaching the truth.

209. 苦难和欢乐是现实对人性的解构。
Suffering and joy are the deconstruction of humanity by reality.

210. 文明的力量来自实践的深度和广度。
The power of civilization comes from the depth and breadth of practice.

211. 苦难是规则的底线。
Suffering is the bottom line of the rules.

212. 语言的逻辑代替不了现实演绎的逻辑。

The logic of language cannot replace the logic of the reality deduction.

213. 苦难勾勒规则的底线，规则勾勒文明的底线。

Suffering outlines the bottom line of the rules, and the rules outline the bottom line of civilization.

214. 成功的法则：在勇气中希望，在希望中坚毅，在坚毅中积累，在积累中沉淀。

The law of success: hope in courage, perseverance in hope, accumulation in perseverance, sedimentary in accumulation.

215. 当你去追求价值，世界便追求你。

When you pursue value, the world pursues you.

216. 美是能量的出口和力量的支点。

Beauty is the energy exports and the power fulcrums.

217. 色彩和节奏是生命的绽放。

Color and rhythm are the bloom of life.

218. 科学划定技术的边界，技术划定实践的边界。

Science delineates the boundaries of technology; technology delineates the boundaries of practice.

219. 每一种节奏，都是一种循环的方式。

Every rhythm is a way of circle.

220. 被智慧解构的现实就不再是苦难。

The reality deconstructed by wisdom is no longer suffering.

221. 和谐是文明进化的目标。

Harmony is the goal of the civilization evolution.

222. 所有的努力都在提升希望的价值。

All efforts are increasing the value of hope.

223. 这个世界最具价值的，就是冷静的理性伴随炽热的希望。

The most valuable thing in the world is the calm reason accompanied by burning hope.

224. 由理性所延伸的梦想都有其绽放的光芒。

Dreams extended by reason have their own blossoming light.

225. 责任塑造人生。

Responsibility shapes lives.

226. 智慧是人类驾驭理性和人文的力量。

Wisdom is the power of human beings to harness reason and humanity.

227. 由梦想连接现实与未来。

Connecting reality and future by dreams.

228. 探索在为感性需求提供理性支点。

Exploration is providing a rational fulcrum for perceptual needs.

229. 播种的土地才值得期待。

The land sown is worth looking forward to.

230. 把握历史的根基，才能接纳现实。

Only by grasping the foundations of history can we accept reality.

231. 生命是仅有的机会。

Life is the only chance.

232. 如果不能深刻理解本能所求，我们就会活成另外一个人。

If we donot deeply understand what our instincts want, we will live as someone else.

233. 所有的深刻都是沉静的。

All profoundness is calm.

234. 成长是由现实的力量塑造人生。

Growth is to shape life by the reality power.

235. 只有深刻的理性才能释放现实的力量。

Only deep reason can unleash the reality power.

236. 现实由历史演变，未来由现实演绎。

Reality is developed by history, and the future is deduced by reality.

237. 现实与理想的落差把人性塑造成善良与邪恶。

The gap between reality and ideal shapes humanity into kindness and evil.

238. 太空不计深浅。

Space does not count depths.

239. 生命因梦想而闪烁。

Life flickers with dreams.

240. 每一个真相，都在佐证历史的必然性。

Every fact is evidencing to the inevitability of history.

241. 拥有伟大的对手，才有伟大的结局。

With great opponents, there is a great ending.

242. 多重苦难塑造伟大的人生。

Multiple sufferings shape great lives.

243. 我们痛苦和思考过，因此感知和生活过。

We have been painful and thinking, and therefore have felt and lived.

244. 超越必然孤独。

Transcendence necessarily leads to loneliness.

245. 繁忙不忘初心。

Be busy, do not forget the first heart.

246. 希望是人性的基石。

Hope is the cornerstone of humanity.

247. 希望是人性的光辉。

Hope is the brilliance of humanity.

248. 孤独是生命的身影。

Loneliness is the shadow of life.

249. 部分人的痛苦就是部分人的欢乐。

The pain of some is the joy of others.

250. 期望与能力的落差驱动我们成长。

The divide between expectations and capabilities drives our growth.

251. 无所期望就无所感受。

Without expectations there is nothing to feel.

252. 历史是每一位胜利者的选择。

History is the choice of every winner.

253. 没有喧嚣的智慧。

There is no wisdom of hustle and bustle.

254. 形式是逻辑的界面。

Form is a logical interface.

255. 成长被现实的苦难与欢乐所迭代。

Growth is iterated by the sufferings and joys of reality.

256. 自由是跨越现实的能力。

Freedom is the ability to transcend reality.

257. 回归现实就是回归现实演绎的逻辑。

Returning to reality is returning to the logic of reality deduction.

258. 人性具有相同的底线，不同的极限。

Humanity has the same bottom line, different limits.

259. 期望是生活的意义。

Expectation is the meaning of life.

260. 真理是现实的光辉。

Truth is the brilliance of reality.

261. 多元化没有持续的精彩。

Diversity does not have a lasting wonder.

262. 没有持久的飓风和洪流。

There are no persistent hurricanes and torrents.

263. 美是现实的变幻。

Beauty is a change in reality.

264. 智慧就是利用现实演绎的必然性。

Wisdom is the use of the inevitability of the reality deduction.

265. 和谐为文明凝聚现实的力量。

Harmony gathers the reality power for civilization.

266. 政治是利益的门面。

Politics is the facade of interests.

267. 艺术在为生命赋值。

Art is giving value to life.

268. 人性是承担责任的方式。

Humanity is the way to take responsibility.

269. 我们的力量取决于释放现实能量的方式。

Our power depends on how we release the energy of reality.

270. 聪明是以社会力量充实自己，智慧是以自己力量推动社会。

Clever is to enrich oneself by social forces, and wisdom is to promote society by its own strength.

271. 在归途中寻找自我。

Find yourself on the way home.

272. 不基于现实的内核，就没有真正的未来。

There is no real future without a reality core.

273. 苦难是被现实撕裂的灵魂。

Suffering is a soul torn apart by reality.

274. 多元化的梦想才能缔造一个时代。

The dreams of diversity can create an era.

275. 战争残忍，生命无辜。

War is cruel and lives are innocent.

276. 每一个生命，都有被理性唤醒的机会。

Every life has the opportunity to be awakened by reason.

277. 谎言就是语言的逻辑背离现实的逻辑。

Lies are the deviation of language logic from reality logic.

278. 期望赋予我们探索的勇气。

Expectations give us the courage to explore.

279. 科学是现实演绎的精髓。

Science is the essence of reality deduction.

280. 不要用语言的逻辑替代现实的逻辑。

Donot replace the reality logic with the language logic.

281. 理性是照亮未来的光芒。

Reason is the light to illuminate the future.

282. 腾飞的翅膀才有远望的心胸。

Only the soaring wings have a heart to look far away.

283. 故土是人性演绎的原点。

The homeland is the origin of the humanity deduction.

284. 多赢是和谐的路径。

Multi-win is the path of harmony.

285. 自信是思想的定力。

Self-confidence is the determination strength of thought.

286. 坚毅是成功的法则。

Perseverance is the law of success.

287. 期望是人性演绎的开端。

Expectation is the beginning of humanity.

288. 现实演绎就是现实的波折。

The reality deduction is twists and turns in the reality.

289. 理性为释放现实力量提供支点。

Reason provides the fulcrum for unleashing the reality power.

290. 节奏是现实演绎的逻辑。

Rhythm is the logic of reality deduction.

291. 行为是人性演绎的轨迹。

Behavior is the trajectory of humanity.

292. 梦想为生命赋值。

Dreams give value to life.

293. 由竞争带来的差异，驱使机制升级。

Competition gives us diverse expectations.

294. 时尚因需求变换。

Fashion changes as needed.

295. 没有任何智慧能够超越历史的必然性。

No wisdom can transcend historical inevitability.

296. 每一场变革，都在为历史演绎提供转折点。

Each change provides a turning point for the history deduction.

297. 道德是人性的砝码。

Morality is the weight of humanity.

298. 历史是现实演绎的出发点。

History is the starting point for the reality deduction.

299. 没有超越环境的现实。

There is no reality beyond the environment.

300. 保持现实与环境的和谐是科学应用的原则。

Maintaining harmony between reality and the environment is a principle of science application.

301. 探索与实践是对智慧的考验。

Exploration and practice are tests of wisdom.

302. 聪明以过程为导向，智慧以结果为导向。

Smart ness is process-oriented and wisdom is result-oriented.

303. 感情代替不了思考。

Feelings cannot replace thinking.

304. 探索就是以辩证的逻辑回归现实的逻辑。

Exploration is returning to reality logic with dialectical logic.

305. 我们的收获取决于我们的付出。

What we gain depends on what we give.

306. 和谐是文明的要义。

Harmony is the essence of civilization.

307. 理性在为现实发展构建可持续机制。

Reason is building sustainable mechanisms for the reality development.

308. 理性和人文是文明可持续发展的必然结果。

Reason and humanism are the inevitable results of the sustainable development of civilization.

309. 责任和使命是伟大的动机。

Responsibility and mission are great motivations.

310. 责任和利益是文明发展的驱动力。

Responsibility and interests are the driving force behind the civilization development.

311. 使命感是探索者初心。

A sense of mission is the original intention of explorers.

312. 梦想被勇气支撑。

Dreams are supported by courage.

313. 智慧确保制度的逻辑符合现实的逻辑。

Wisdom ensures that the system logic conforms to the reality logic.

314. 科学揭示现实演绎的必然性。

Science reveals the inevitability of the reality deduction.

315. 经营确保现实与利益的和谐。

Management ensures the harmony between reality and profit.

316. 仿真以科学的逻辑揭示现实的逻辑。

Simulation reveals the reality logic with scientific logic.

317. 经典是植根于历史的观念。

Classics are ideas rooted in history.

318. 和谐是可持续的基石。

Harmony is the cornerstone of sustainability.

319. 没有勇气就不会有持久的希望，没有希望就不会有内心的快乐。

There can be no lasting hope without courage, and there can be no inner happiness without hope.

320. 规则确保社会演绎的可持续性。

Rules ensure the sustainability of social deduction.

321. 人生最可贵的就是改变命运的勇气。

The most precious thing in life is the courage to change fate.

322. 文明的边界由勇气划定。

The boundaries of civilization are drawn by courage.

323. 节奏是力量的喘息。

Rhythm is a breather of strength.

324. 美是现实力量的展现。

Beauty is the display of the reality power.

325. 竞争的意义不仅是力量的博弈，而且是机制的改良。

The significance of competition is not only the game of power, but also the improvement of mechanism.

326. 攀登是提升自我的勇气。

Climbing is the courage to improve oneself.

327. 预言是由理性重构现实。

Prophecy is a reconstruction of reality by reason.

328. 和谐是文明的出路。

Harmony is the way out for civilization.

329. 掌控不确定性就是掌控现实发展的节奏。

To control uncertainty is to control the rhythm of reality development.

330. 选择是自由的标志。

Choices is marked by freedom.

331. 道德的感召力转化为商业的吸引力。

Moral appeal translates into business attraction.

332. 艺术赋予人类探索的激情和勇气。

Art gives human beings the passion and courage to explore.

333. 现实总是朝着和谐的方向演变。

Reality always evolves toward harmony.

334. 艺术重构心灵的力量。

Art reconstructs the power of the mind.

335. 和谐是利益可持续的方向。

Harmony is the direction of sustainable interests.

336. 探索被梦想感召，实践被责任感召。

Exploration is inspired by dreams; practice is inspired by responsibility.

337. 由梦想期待未来。

Look forward to the future from dreams.

338. 由系统性实现可持续性。

Realize sustainability through a systematization.

339. 概念的本质是哲学的外延。

The essence of concepts is an extension of philosophy.

340. 技术革命是文明发展的转折点。

The technological revolution is a turning point in the civilization development.

341. 能源是文明的原点。

Energy is the origin of civilization.

342. 文明由和谐守护。

Civilization is guarded by harmony.

343. 人生是生命与现实逐步和谐的进程。

Life is a process of gradual harmony between life and reality.

344. 由竞争获取的优势演变为现实的生机。

The advantages gained by competition evolve into reality vitality.

345. 和谐的力量转变成智慧。

The power of harmony is transformed into wisdom.

346. 多元化是现实演绎的背景。

Diversity is the background to the reality deduction.

347. 智慧是理想回归现实的路径。

Wisdom is the path of ideals back to reality.

348. 利益是构建文明的动机。

Interests are the motivation to constrnct civilizations.

349. 智慧把现实的苦难转化为发展的机遇。

Wisdom transforms the reality suffering into opportunities for development.

350. 没有核心，就不会有结果。

There will be no fruits without the core.

351. 热爱和兴趣是伟大的导师。

Love and interest are great mentors.

352. 以坚毅和智慧跨越现实。

Cross reality with perseverance and wisdom.

353. 最高的自律获取最大的自由。

The highest self-discipline obtains the greatest freedom.

354. 承载者就是颠覆者。

The bearer is the disruptor.

355. 地理和气象承载历史的脉动。

Geography and meteorology carry the pulse of history.

356. 和谐是理性的核心价值。

Harmony is the core value of reason.

357. 地理和气象承载生物的多样性。

Geography and meteorology carry biological diversity.

358. 基于和谐的发展是理性的目标。

The development based on harmony is the goal of reason.

359. 最好的情况所失即所得，最坏的情况所得即所失。

In the best case what is lost is gain, and in the worst case, what is gained is lost.

360. 没有道德就无所谓智慧。

Without morality there is no wisdom.

361. 和谐赋予文明可持续的力量。

Harmony gives a sustainable power to civilization.

362. 历史是现实演绎的根基和未来发展的起点。

History is the foundation of the reality deduction and the beginning of future development.

363. 普遍性承载可持续性。

Universality carries sustainability.

364. 事物的充分条件是其反向事物的必要条件，事物的必要条件是其反向事物的充分条件。

The sufficient condition of things is the necessary condition for its reverse things, and the necessary condition of things is the sufficient condition for its reverse things.

365. 现实的必然性具有科学的启示。

The inevitability of reality has scientific implications.

366. 概念的内涵是形式的框架，概念的外延是形式的变换。

The connotation of a concept is the form framework, and the extension of a concept is the form transformation.

367. 纯粹中方见本质，本质中方见精简，精简中方见快乐。

See essence in the pureness, see simplicity in the essence, see happiness in the simplicity.

368. 占位决定视野。

The placeholder determines the view field.

369. 透过眼睛看见树木，透过内心看见风景。

See the trees through the eyes, see the scenery through the heart.

370. 梦想是勇气呈现的形式。

Dreams are the form of courage.

371. 抓住现实力量的内核，才能抓住变革的时机。

Only by grasping the core of the reality power can we seize the opportunity for change.

372. 风景是生态的语言。

Landscape is an ecological language.

373. 多元化才有可持续未来。

Diversity has a sustainable future.

374. 需求由希望所承载。

Demand is carried by hope.

375. 不同的山峰，预见不同的未来。

Different peaks foresee different futures.

376. 所有的回忆都在感慨时光。

All memories are lamenting time.

377. 有阳光就有斑斓和阴影。

Where there is sunlight, there are colors and shadows.

378. 不断质疑，才能不断完善。

Only by constantly questioning can we continue to improve.

379. 所有的偏见都被历史抛弃。

All prejudices will be abandoned by history.

380. 飘扬只是被风吹拂。

Fluttering is just blown by the wind.

381. 回归现实，才能展望未来。

Only by restoring reality can we look to the future.

382. 概念是思考的代码。

Concepts are thinking code.

383. 审美就是感知形式中的必然性。

Aesthetics is to perceive the inevitability in the form.

384. 每一种美，都在呈现一种必然性。

Every beauty presents an inevitability.

385. 每一种理性，都是其观念在闪烁。

Every reason is flickered by its ideas.

386. 理性与人文是真理的基石。

Reason and humanity are the cornerstones of truth.

387. 历史总是呈现人民的意志。

History always presents the will of the people.

388. 所有的本质都是哲学的外延。

All essence is an extension of philosophy.

389. 真理连接现实和未来。

Truth connects reality and the future.

390. 体育是精神的标志。

Sport is the symbol of spirit.

391. 神明以信仰昭示真理。

God declares the truth with faith.

392. 人类只能以理性诱导现实。

Human beings can only induce reality with reason.

393. 伟大的人生推动历史发展的必然性。

The great life drives the inevitability of history.

394. 文明的夜空是被闪烁的个性所照耀。

The night sky of civilization is illuminated by shimmering personalities.

395. 永远感动，就会永远年轻。

Always moved, we will always be young.

396. 苦难的缘由，就是幸福的边界。

The cause of suffering is the boundary of happiness.

397. 一切灾难源自违背现实演绎的必然性。

All disasters arise from the defiance of reality deduction inevitability.

398. 现实的必然性就是现实演绎逻辑的必然性。

The reality inevitability is the logic inevitability of reality deduction.

399. 现实演绎充满逻辑的力量。

Reality deduction is full of the logic power.

400. 回归真相才能回归现实演绎的逻辑。

Only by returning to facts can we return to the logic of reality deduction.

401. 每个人的成就不会超越他的使命感。

It is impossible for every person to achieve more than his sense of mission.

402. 历史充满英雄的智慧，现实充满逻辑的力量，心灵充满期待的激情。

History is full of heroic wisdom; reality is full of logical power; the hearts are full of passion for expectation.

403. 科学是释放现实力量的密码。

Science is the code to release the reality power.

404. 深刻感知现实的力量，才能感知未来。

Only by deeply perceiving the reality power can we perceive the future.

405. 最深刻的现实，才会有最灿烂的未来。

The deepest reality will lead to the brightest future.

406. 可持续性决定现实演绎的方向。

Sustainability determines the direction of reality deduction.

407. 安全是智慧的开端。

Safety is the beginning of wisdom.

408. 伪造历史就会切断现实演绎的根源。

Falsifying history cuts off the roots of the reality deduction.

409. 历史总是选择最可持续的力量。

History always chooses the most sustainable forces.

410. 敬畏上帝是因为我们仍在现实中摇摆。

Regard God with reverence because we are still swinging in reality.

411. 每一种强大，都由可持续性转化。

Every power is transformed by sustainability.

412. 有梯度的地方就有能量和动机。

Where there is a gradient, there is energy and motivation.

413. 科学是现实演绎的逻辑，数学是形式演绎的逻辑。

Science is the logic of reality deduction; mathematics is the logic of formal deduction.

414. 健康是维持生命演绎的可持续机制。

Health is a sustainable mechanism for maintaining life deduction.

415. 方法高于结果，形式大于内容。

Method over result, form over content.

416. 在质疑中包容，在包容中质疑。

Inclusion in question, question in inclusion.

417. 现实的力量来自人文、理性、自然。

The power of reality comes from humanity, reason, and nature.

418. 离别是为更好的重逢。

Departure is for a better reunion.

419. 探索的精华是突破现实的焦点。

The essence of exploration is breaking through the focus of reality.

420. 实践是以人文、理性、自然的力量构筑文明。

Practice is the construction of civilization with the forces of humanism, reason and nature.

421. 伪证无法追溯历史的演绎。

Perjury cannot trace the history deduction.

422. 历史的河道中流淌着人文、理性、自然的力量。

The river of history flows the forces of humanity, reason and nature.

423. 偏见只是现实的影子。

Prejudice is only a shadow of reality.

424. 坚毅是成长的价值。

Perseverance is the value of growth.

425. 我们只能从高度中获得远见。

We can only gain foresight from heights.

426. 成长从独立的那一刻真正开始。

Growth really starts from the moment of independence.

427. 只有灵性才能寄托灵性。

Only spirituality can hold spirituality.

428. 我们无法从偏见中回归现实。

We cannot return to reality from prejudice.

429. 所有人的活路就是自己的归途。

The way for all to live is their own way back.

430. 欲望是本能所在。

Desire is instinctive.

431. 探索自然的同时，也在为灵魂定位。

While exploring nature it is also positioning the soul.

432. 我们在充满疑惑的阵痛中获得现实的启蒙。

We gain realistic enlightenment in the throes of doubt.

433. 持久的跌落迫使我们飞翔。

The persistent fall forces us to fly.

434. 演绎的是速度，发展的是增速。

The deduction is speed; the development is the growth rate.

435. 和谐是文明基于环境的妥协。

Harmony is a compromise of civilization based on the environment.

436. 文明总是在科学和人文的约束中演变。

Civilization always evolves within the constraints of science and humanity.

437. 吸引 / 改变的力量（F）等于（=）事物状态的改变（a）乘于（×）排斥 / 事物的惯性（m）。

Attraction / the force of change (F) is equal to (=) the change in the state of things (a) multiplied by (×) exclusion / the inertia of things (m).

438. 思想被现实演绎的逻辑启蒙。

Thought is enlightened by the logic of reality deduction.

439. 和谐是多元化演绎的必然结果。

Harmony is the inevitable result of diverse deduction.

440. 我们在现实的宽度中转折。

We turn in the breadth of reality.

441. 自由是力量的尺度。

Freedom is a measure of strength.

442. 竞争创造可持续价值。

Competition creates sustainable value.

443. 战略是由全局导向未来。

Strategy is to orient the future from the big picture

444. 温度是现实的标尺。

Temperature is the scaleplate of reality.

445. 知识经过心灵的传递照亮世界。

Knowledge illuminates the world through the transmission of the heart.

446. 现实演绎：形式不同、逻辑相似、本质归一。

Reality deduction: different forms, similar logic, and one essence.

447. 边界层最活跃，出入口最关键。

The boundary layer is the most active, and the entrance and exit are the most critical.

448. 利益的边界由责任划分。

The boundaries of interests are divided by responsibility.

449. 跨越和飞翔是一颗灵魂。

Crossing and flying is a soul.

450. 生命被希望照耀，被欲望拉伸。

Life is illuminated by hope and stretched by desire.

451. 只有温暖可以传递。

Only warmth can be transmitted.

452. 在回暖中播种，在渐冷中收获。

Sow in warmth and harvest in getting cold.

453. 时机是现实的馈赠。

Timing is a gift of reality.

454. 理性是文明的基因。

Reason is the gene of civilization.

455. 善良是人性的逻辑。

Kindness is the logic of humanity.

456. 好奇是探索的原点。

Curiosity is the origin of exploration.

457. 科学是现实的浓缩。

Science is a condensation of reality.

458. 变化是最好的感知。

Change is the best perception.

459. 力量是能量释放的形式，逻辑是力量释放的形式。

Power is the form of energy release, and logic is the form of power release.

460. 所有的质疑都通往真理。

All questioning leads to truth.

461. 科学是能量的出口和力量的支点。

Science is energy exports and power fulcrum.

462. 质疑就是聚焦现实。

To question is to focus on reality.

463. 实践激发活力，变革把握生机。

Practice stimulates vitality, and change grasps vitality.

464. 敬畏学生就是敬畏未来，敬畏知识就是敬畏历史。

Awe of students is awe of the future, and awe of knowledge is awe of history.

465. 坚毅不仅连接梦想和现实，而且也连接现实和未来。

Perseverance connects not only dreams and reality, but also reality and the future.

466. 景色是现实与梦想的界面。

The scenery is the interface between reality and dreams.

467. 历史承载着每个时代的梦想。

History carries the dreams of every era.

468. 车轮承载自由的意志。

Wheels carry freedom will.

469. 勇气是欲望与恐惧的落差。

Courage is the gap between desire and fear.

470. 黑暗才会星光灿烂。

Darkness can be a starry light.

471. 孤独才会感知，感知才会丰富。

Loneliness will perceive, and perception will be rich.

472. 从深刻的反省中萃取智慧。

Wisdom is extracted from deep introspection.

473. 人民的意识就是国家的力量。

The consciousness of the people is the power of the state.

474. 车站是地理和历史的双重界面。

The station is a dual interface of geography and history.

475. 翅膀强大，才会心胸强大。

When the wings are strong, the heart will be strong.

476. 可持续性是每一种自然演绎的未来。

Sustainability is the future of every natural deduction.

477. 水的温度取决于井的深度。

The water temperature depends on the well depth.

478. 未来是现实和谐的必然结果。

The future is the inevitable result of the reality harmony.

479. 力量源自包容异见，卓识源自质疑己见。

Power comes from inclusion of dissent; insight comes from questioning self opinions.

480. 现实是一切的出发点。

Reality is the starting point of everything.

481. 忽略现实必败，违背和谐必亡。

Ignoring reality leads to decay; violating harmony leads to perishment.

482. 流体是循环的承载者。

Fluid is the cycle bearer.

483. 内心空洞导致行为激愤。

Hollowness in the heart leads to anger in behavior.

484. 成长被内心期待、被现实约束。

Growth is expected by the heart, and is constrained by reality.

485. 节奏是生态赋予我们的时机。

Rhythm is the timing that ecology gives us.

486. 掌控时机和节奏就是掌控生命。

To control the timing and rhythm is to control life.

487. 因复杂而神秘，因简洁而本质。

Mystery because of complexity, essence because of simplicity.

488. 生命的勇气来自未来的期望。

The courage of life comes from the expectations of the future.

489. 循环是现实演绎的灵魂。

The cycle is the soul of reality deduction.

490. 实践是最好的导师，天下是最好的课堂。

Practice is the best tutor, the world is the best classroom.

491. 我们在具象中寻找时机，在抽象中寻找路径。

We look for opportunity in the concrete and the path in the abstract.

492. 我们在理想到现实的落差中获取灵感。

We get inspired by the gap between ideal to reality.

493. 没有超越规则的道德。

There is no morality beyond the rules.

494. 时机凝聚生命演绎的力量。

Timing condenses the power of life deduction.

495. 和谐是人类的终极智慧。

Harmony is the ultimate wisdom of mankind.

496. 历史凝聚人民的智慧。

History unites the wisdom of the people.

497. 偶然性迟早消亡，必然性终会延续。

Contingency will die sooner or later; inevitability will eventually continue.

498. 没有警示的危机才是真正的危机。

A crisis without warning is a real crisis.

499. 孤独是个性之母，个性是多样性之母。

Loneliness is the mother of individuality; individuality is the mother of diversity.

500. 可持续性是通往和谐的路径。

Sustainability is the path to harmony.

501. 文明是探索者的遗产。

Civilization is the legacy of explorers.

502. 节奏的频率就是循环的周期。

The rhythm frequency is the cycle period.

503. 自由是能量的尺度。

Freedom is the measure of energy.

504. 历史是社会变革所留下的轨迹。

History is the trajectory left by social change.

505. 社会变革被人文和理性的力量所引导。

Social change is guided by the forces of humanity and reason.

506. 英雄是历史的选择，神明是信仰的选择。

Heroes are the choice of history; gods are the choice of faith.

507. 历史的征服者就是人民的守护者。

The conqueror of history is the guardian of the people.

508. 只有科学才能使技术贯穿需求。

Only science can make technology run through demand.

509. 天文塑造气象，气象塑造地理，地理塑造历史。

Astronomy shapes meteorology; meteorology shapes geography; geography shapes history.

510. 必然性来自现实演绎的逻辑。

Inevitability comes from the logic of reality deduction.

511. 每一种狭隘，都在割裂自我发展的途径。

Each narrowness is cutting off the path of self-development.

512. 和谐是多样性与可持续性迭代的必然结果。

Harmony is the inevitable result of iteration of diversity and sustainability.

513. 和谐是现实多元化发展的必然法则。

Harmony is an inevitable law of diversified development of reality.

514. 毁灭来自否决的力量。

Destruction comes from the power of the veto.

515. 完整是发展的纵深。

Integrity is the depth of development.

516. 所有的创新都在实现更广泛的和谐。

All innovations are achieving broader harmony.

517. 和谐是万物共存的法则。

Harmony is the law by which all things coexist.

518. 现实的力量植根于演绎的逻辑。

The reality power is rooted in the deduction logic.

519. 包容是开放的形式。

Inclusion is a form of openness.

520. 聚焦本身就是精简。

Focus itself is simplicity.

521. 战略是可持续的路径。

Strategy is a sustainable path.

522. 成长就是以梦想和现实重构自己。

Growth is to reconstruct oneself with dreams and reality.

523. 生命是梦想的绽放。

Life is the bloom of dreams.

524. 保持快乐，就是在任何情况下守护你的希望。

To be happy is to protect your hopes in any situation.

525. 信仰神灵，就是放弃自我救赎的勇气和责任。

To believe in the gods is to give up the courage and responsibility of self-rescue.

第 10 章 | 我们从现实的需求中把握未来
We grasp the future from the reality needs

（2020 年浙江柯茂总工程师 Chief engineer of Zhejiang Comer）

1. 精准理解，才能深刻把握。

   Accurate understanding can lead to a profound grasp.

2. 简化事物才能看清本质。

   Simplify things to see the essence.

3. 你可以严谨古板，也可以放浪形骸，然而生命终究还是关于时机选择的伟大变奏。

   You can be rigid or debauched, but life is eventually a great variation on timing.

4. 每一次绽放，都在宣告生命的时机。

   Each bloom is to declare the life timing.

5. 以可持续为目标的变革是一种远见。

   Change with sustainability as the goal is a vision.

6. 让凡人做非凡之事，是管理的责任。

It is the responsibility of management to let mortals do extraordinary things.

7. 不经历绝望，就不会产生信仰。

Without experiencing despair, faith is not born.

8. 信仰是人性的力量。

Faith is the strength of humanity.

9. 道德维持社会行为的可持续性。

Ethics sustains the sustainability of social behavior.

10. 简单才能归真，正直才有方向，无私才会凝聚，坚毅才能持久。

Simplicity can lead to truth; integrity can have direction; selflessness can be condensed, and perseverance can endure.

11. 普度众生得的事物即为神明。

The things that are attained by all beings are gods.

12. 苦难为思想播种。

Suffering sows the seeds of thought.

13. 真相会被利益掩盖。

The trueness will be covered up by interest.

14. 智慧是可持续的方法。

Wisdom is a sustainable method.

15. 智慧是长远利益的结果。

Wisdom is the result of long-term interests.

16. 内心越孤独，思想越深邃。

The lonelier the heart is, the deeper the mind is.

17. 竞争为现实带来普遍的生机。

Competition brings universal vitality to reality.

18. 期望是心灵的曙光。

Expectation is the dawn of the heart.

19. 我们总是在生机中展望未来。

We always look to the future in vitality.

20. 历史的经验启示未来。

The experience of history inspires the future.

21. 只有善良的人才会具有智慧。

Only good-hearted people will have wisdom.

22. 伟大的英雄为人类带来勇气。

Great hero brings courage to mankind.

23. 我们犯下的每一个错误，都在为生命留痕。

Every mistake we make is leaving a mark on our lives.

24. 由寂静听见心声，由黑暗看见星空。

To hear the heart voice from silence, to see the starry sky from darkness.

25. 黑夜是宇宙的背景。

The night sky is the background of the universe.

26. 所有的和谐都在启示未来。

All harmony is revealing the future.

27. 史诗最闪耀的部分是抗争苦难。

The most shining part of an epic is the struggle against suffering.

28. 方法预示结果。

Methods predict results.

29. 可持续性赢得未来。

Sustainability wins the future.

30. 每一种生命，都有它致命的一击。

Every life has its fatal blow.

31. 可持续性是智慧的内核。

Sustainability is the core of wisdom.

32. 创新是文明演绎的步伐。

Innovation is the pace of civilization deduction.

33. 只有规则能让人性闪光。

Only rules can make humanity shine.

34. 选择时机是最好的方法。

Timing is the best way to do it.

35. 科学、哲学、艺术、人性、认知、经济，是人类理性的六维坐标。

Science, philosophy, art, humanity, cognition, economy are the six-dimensional coordinates of human reason.

36. 和谐是自然演绎的目标。

Harmony is the goal of natural deduction.

37. 自然进化以更广泛的和谐为目标。

Natural evolution aims for broader harmony.

38. 和谐在更广泛的基础上提高事物的系统性。

Harmony improves the systematization of things on a broader basis.

39. 现实的力量来自其演绎的逻辑。

The power of reality comes from the logic of its deduction.

40. 本质是深刻的结果。

The essence is a profound result.

41. 放弃一切，才能跨越一切。

Give up everything in order to cross everything.

42. 变革启示新的生机。

Change inspires new vitality.

43. 混沌中的变幻是现实给我们的深刻启示。

The vagaries in chaos are the profound revelations that reality gives us.

44. 混沌是变革的启示。

Chaos is the revelation of change.

45. 和谐是万物演绎的目标。

Harmony is the goal of the deduction of all things.

46. 每一种生机，都是生命与生态的和谐。

Every kind of vitality is a harmony between life and ecology.

47. 每一片土地，都有她的生机和灵魂。

Every piece of land has her vitality and soul.

48. 逻辑是必然性之母。

Logic is the mother of necessity.

49. 我们总是以远见收割未来。

We always harvest the future with vision.

50. 智慧是理性和人文所具有的远见。

Wisdom is the foresight of reason and humanity.

51. 每一次民族复兴都始于文化复兴。

Every national revival begins with a cultural revival.

52. 人文以和谐为系统演绎的目标。

Humanism takes harmony as the goal of system deduction.

53. 远见就是理性和人文的预见。

Foresight is rational and humanistic prevision.

54. 飞翔就是把自己提升到自由的高度。

To fly is to elevate yourself to the heights of freedom.

55. 科学以效率为系统演绎的目标。

Science takes efficiency as the goal of system deduction.

56. 智慧以结果为导向，聪明以过程为导向。

Wisdom is result-oriented; cleverness is process-oriented.

57. 启蒙的年代充满启示。

The Age of Enlightenment is full of revelations.

58. 从苦难中崛起才是真正的崛起。

Rising from suffering is the real rise.

59. 飞翔是自由的标志。

Flying is a sign of freedom.

60. 科学是具象的，人文是抽象的。

Science is concrete; humanities are abstract.

61. 历史总是被文明的光芒照耀。

History is always illuminated by the light of civilization.

62. 和谐是文明的宗旨。

Harmony is the tenet of civilization.

63. 可持续性是未来的标志。

Sustainability is the hallmark of the future.

64. 探索是播种的人生。

Exploration is a life of sowing.

65. 和谐是文明发展的指南。

Harmony is the guide to the civilization development.

66. 历史是城市演绎的灵魂。

History is the soul of the city deduction.

67. 生物进化就是生命机制与环境生态的有机迭代。

Biological evolution is the organic iteration of life mechanisms and environmental ecology.

68. 规则是人性的逻辑。

Rules are the logic of humanity.

69. 美是真理的门面。

Beauty is the facade of truth.

70. 发明是以科学的维度整合技术和需求。

Invention is the integration of technology and needs in a scientific dimension.

71. 实践是收获的人生。

Practice is a life of harvest.

72. 人生的价值取决于回归现实的途径。

The value of life depends on the way back to reality.

73. 光明与温暖，是文明的标尺。

Light and warmth are the yardsticks of civilization.

74. 每一种景色，都是自然演绎的舞台。

Every scenery is a stage for natural deduction.

75. 意志是自由的舞蹈。

The will is a dance of freedom.

76. 具有远见的灵魂必然承受孤独。

A visionary soul necessarily bears loneliness.

77. 智慧就是回归现实的必然性。

Wisdom is the inevitability returning to of reality.

78. 只有可持续性才能通往未来。

Only sustainability can lead to the future.

79. 逻辑由形式绽放。

Logic blooms by form.

80. 教育通过知识组合塑造人性。

Education shapes the humanity through a combination of knowledge.

81. 权力为利益选择提供门面。

Power provides a facade for profit choices.

82. 形式是空间的逻辑，节奏是时间的逻辑。

Form is the space logic, rhythm is the time logic.

83. 信仰是文明的信心。

Faith is the confidence of civilization.

84. 生命的精华在于她演绎的时机。

The essence of life lies in the timing of her deduction.

85. 形式和色彩预示着生机。

Form and color indicate vitality.

86. 历史把她的精华留给现实，现实把她的精华留给未来。

History leaves her essence to reality, and reality leaves her essence to the future.

87. 逻辑体现事物之间的必然联系。

Logic embodies the inevitable connection between things.

88. 生命是被阳光赋予的节奏。

Life is the rhythm given by the sunshine.

89. 生物进化就是机制与生态的有机迭代。

Biological evolution is the organic iteration of mechanisms and ecology.

90. 由探索而认知，由逻辑而预言。

Cognition by exploration, prediction by logic.

91. 成功取决于回归现实的方法与时机。

Success depends on how and when you get back to reality.

92. 每一种生命，都是生态的精灵。

Every life is an elf in the ecology.

93. 所有伟大事物都是和谐与远见使然。

All great things are the result of harmony and vision.

94. 不被实践所见证，就不会具有深刻的灵魂。

Without being witnessed by practice, there will be no deep soul.

95. 人文应当成为科学的灵魂。

The humanities should become the soul of science.

96. 理性是科学与人文的合集。

Reason is a collection of science and humanities.

97. 经济通过基于人文的需求，引导基于科学的生产。

Economy guides science-based production through humanity-based needs.

98. 宗教是人性的逻辑。

Religion is the humanity logic.

99. 自由是创造的灵魂。

Freedom is the soul of creation.

100. 探索应当赋予人类可持续的勇气。

Exploration should give humanity sustainable courage.

101. 苦难就是没有被理性照耀的地方。

Suffering is where reason is not illuminated.

102. 伟大的和谐都是平静的。

Great harmony is calm.

103. 人类以勇气和智慧诱导自然。

Humans induce nature with courage and wisdom.

104. 和谐是自然最神秘的力量。

Harmony is the most mysterious force of nature.

105. 艺术应当成为回归现实的力量。

Art should be a force for returning to reality.

106. 阳光饱含光明、能量、启示。

Sunlight is full of light, energy, and revelation.

107. 和谐创造普遍的生机。

Harmony creates universal vitality.

108. 探索是文明的轨迹。

Exploration is the trajectory of civilization.

109. 美是生机赋予我们的启迪。

Beauty is the inspiration that vitality gives us.

110. 心之向往必有生机。

The yearning of the heart must be alive.

111. 教育应该点燃对未来的渴望。

Education should ignite a desire for the future.

112. 渴望是我们面向未来所具有的动机。

Desire is motivation for us to look to the future.

113. 所有的陷阱都以人性为目标。

All traps are aimed at humanity.

114. 由关注而向往，由向往而创造。

From attention to yearning, from yearning to creation.

115. 艺术应当充满生机和希望。

Art should be full of vitality and hope.

116. 建筑是文明的载体。

Architecture is the carrier of civilization.

117. 历史由真实性回归社会演绎的逻辑。

History returns from authenticity to the logic of social deduction.

118. 和谐是生态的价值，可持续性是生命的价值。

Harmony is the value of ecology; sustainability is the value of life.

119. 风景是现实和历史的界面。

The landscape is the interface between reality and history.

120. 每一片风景，都有她承载的灵魂。

Every landscape has a soul she carries.

121. 期待植根于现实最深刻的部分。

Expectations rooted in the most profound part of reality.

122. 市场需求是经济循环的灵魂。

Market demand is the soul of the economic cycle.

123. 每一种生机，都是闪光的时刻。

Every vitality is a moment of flash.

124. 阳光为生命赋值。

Sunlight assigns value to life.

125. 所有的生命都为季节喝彩。

All life celebrates the seasons.

126. 实践塑造灵魂。

Practice shapes souls.

127. 风景是现实的生机。

Landscapes are the vitality of reality.

128. 实践是每个时代最深的期望。

Practice is the deepest expectation of every era.

129. 数学是形式展现的逻辑。

Mathematics is the logic of form presentation.

130. 忍耐不是懦弱，而是等待时机。

Patience is not cowardice, but waiting for the opportunity.

131. 价值被需求所赋予。

Value is given by demand.

132. 孤独是探索者的领地。

Solitude is the territory of explorers.

133. 艺术在用色彩的灰度表达心灵的热度。

Art is expressing the heart heat with the color gray scale.

134. 文明的能源由正循环驱动，消费的繁荣由逆循环驱动。

The energy of civilization is driven by a positive cycle, and the prosperity of consumption is driven by a reverse cycle.

135. 如果不能回归现实的和谐，就会引发灾难。

If we fail to return to the reality harmony, disaster will result.

136. 适时变革为我们带来现实的力量。

Change at the right time gives us the power of reality.

137. 规律设定事物演绎的路径和极限。

Laws set the path and limit of the things deduction.

138. 我们从探索的过程中获取心灵的自由。

We gain the mind freedom from the process of exploration.

139. 征服是获取自由的方式。

Conquest is the way to gain freedom.

140. 所有的谎言都需要刻意的铺垫。

All lies need deliberate foreshadowing.

141. 具象承载着情感和回忆。

Figuration carries emotions and memories.

142. 所谓创新，就是承担失败的勇气。

Innovation is the courage to take on failure.

143. 生命短暂，不负春光。

Life is short, to live up to the spring light.

144. 谎言没有现实的归途。

There is no realistic return for lies.

145. 信仰是对自然心怀敬畏。

Faith is reverence for nature.

146. 理性为文明带来普遍的生机。

Reason brings universal vitality to civilization.

147. 我们从现实的需求中把握未来。

We grasp the future from the reality needs.

148. 普遍性是可持续的基础。

Universality is the foundation of sustainability.

149. 跨越伟大需求的同时，也就跨越了未来。

Crossing great needs, it also crosses the future.

150. 创新就是在必然性中构建可持续性。

Innovation is about building sustainability out of necessity.

151. 大学是筑梦之地方。

Universities are places where dreams are built.

152. 疫情迫使人类重新审视以回风为基础的空调技术，并倡导以回热为基础的新风技术。

The epidemic has forced humans to re-examine air conditioning technology based on return air and to advocate for fresh air technology based on heat return.

153. 理性是预见未来的途径。

Reason is the way of foreseeing the future.

154. 喧嚣是观念的共鸣。

The hustle and bustle is the resonance of ideas.

155. 最深刻的逻辑来自普遍性。

The deepest logic comes from universality.

156. 色彩穿透生命。

Color penetrates lives.

157. 想象力就是回归现实的能力。

Imagination is the ability to return to reality.

158. 我们因回归现实而变得强大。

We are made strong by returning to reality.

159. 伟大的文明来自伟大的期待。

Great civilization comes from great expectations.

160. 创新是在更大范围实现和谐。

Innovation is about achieving harmony on a larger scale.

161. 探索是用已知的逻辑迭代未知的逻辑。

Exploration is iterating over unknown logic with known logic.

162. 科学是成功的必由之路。

Science is the only way to success.

163. 一切因阳光而变得璀璨。

Everything is shining brightly because of sun shine.

164. 阳光和时间造就一切。

Sunshine and time make everything.

165. 机会是现实留给我们的时间窗口。

Opportunity is a time window that reality leaves us.

165. 经济就是对和谐所引导的未来持有信心。

Economy is all about having faith in the future guided by harmony.

165. 日月同辉，山河有情。

The sun and the moon shine together, mountains and rivers have sentiments.

165. 感知伟大，就是感知普遍的必然性。

To perceive greatness is to perceive universal inevitability.

165. 与趋势为敌，才是真正的危机。

Enemy of the trend is the real crisis.

166. 我们从细节获得深刻。

We gain profundity from the details.

167. 跨界是创新的勇气。

Crossing borders is the courage to innovate.

168. 阳光之下，皆是灵魂。

Under the sun is the soul.

169. 黎明不是强大，而是时机。

The dawn is not powerful, but timing.

170. 有希望就会有活力。

With hope there can be vitality.

171. 变革来自深刻的危机感。

Change comes from a deep sense of crisis.

172. 和谐是每一个生态和社会的宗旨。

Harmony is the tenet of every ecology and society.

173. 伟大的征服者是历史的趋势。

The great conquerors are the trend of history.

174. 年轻就是不畏将来的勇气。

Being young is the courage to defy the future.

175. 创新体现自由的意志。

Innovation embodies free will.

176. 科学是回归现实的路径。

Science is the path back to reality.

177. 没有梦想，就辜负了年华。

Without dreams, you have failed to live up to the years.

178. 行动的自由来自思想的深刻。

Freedom to act comes from the thought profundity.

179. 需求开启未来之门。

Demand opens the door to the future.

180. 趋势中含有能量，时机中含有力量。

There is energy in the trend and power in the timing.

181. 经典体现时间的价值。

Classics embody the value of time.

182. 历史是城市留下的灵魂。

History is the soul of a city.

183. 现象是力量的演绎。

Phenomena are the power deduction.

184. 险峰之侧必有彩云。

There must be colorful clouds on the side of the dangerous peak.

185. 历史是国家记忆。

History is a national memory.

186. 真理是没有色彩的。

Truth has no color.

187. 我们从变幻与闪烁中获得现实的启蒙。

We gain the enlightenment of reality from change and flickering.

188. 变革是生存的法则。

Change is the law of survival.

189. 时机是趋势的窗口。

Timing is a window to the trend.

190. 真正的超越都是勇气将自身投入到黑暗。

True transcendence is the courage to plunge oneself into darkness.

191. 只有真诚，才能治愈。

Only sincerity can heal.

192. 历史被地理和气象所塑造。

History is shaped by geography and meteorology.

193. 历史总是选择可持续性。

History has always chosen sustainability.

194. 能量是发展的源泉。

Energy is the source of development.

195. 和谐是多元化发展的必然结果。

Harmony is the inevitable result of diversity development.

196. 开放性是多元化的源泉。

Openness is a source of diversity.

197. 多元化和完整性是历史演绎的力量。

Diversity and integrity are the power of historical deduction.

198. 创造源于自由的灵魂。

Creation comes from a free soul.

199. 风景是被阳光演绎的生态。

The landscape is an ecology deduced by sunlight.

200. 每一片土地都被阳光普照、被雨水滋润。

Every land is drenched in the sun and moisturized by rain.

201. 历史是每一座伟大城市的根基。

History is the foundation of every great city.

202. 所有的感动，都被人性照耀。

All touches are illuminated by humanity.

203. 时机是现实赋予我们能量。

Timing is when reality gives us energy.

204. 每一种高耸的山峰，都在承受冷酷。

Every kind of towering mountain is suffering from the cold.

205. 向水而生，是一种智慧。

Coming to water is a kind of wisdom.

206. 没有一种力量能超越阳光。

No force can transcend sunlight.

207. 生机就是变换中的出路。

Vitality is the way out in change.

208. 所有的相知都是奇迹。

All acquaintances are miracles.

209. 经济性是产品可持续性的度量。

Economy is a sustainability measure of a product.

210. 现实的本色是被阳光照耀。

The nature of reality is to be illuminated by the sun.

211. 多元化使夜景繁华、星空灿烂。

Diversification makes the night scene prosperous and the starry sky brilliant.

212. 每一种沧桑，都是浓缩的时机。

Every vicissitudes is a time to concentrate.

213. 形式呈现逻辑演绎的轨迹。

Form presents the trajectory of logical deduction.

214. 勇气构建生命的边界。

Courage builds the boundaries of life.

215. 真理如同阳光，从不陨落。

Truth is like sunshine that never falls.

216. 趋势具有力量，力量并非趋势。

Trends have power, and power is not a trend.

217. 美呈现自然演绎的必然性。

Beauty embodies the inevitability of reality deduction.

218. 形式背后的逻辑，正是现实的力量。

The logic behind form is the reality power.

219. 实践赋予文明最深的激情。

Practice gives civilization its deepest passion.

220. 黑暗是对光明的度量。

Darkness is a measure of light.

221. 空间是节奏的延伸。

Space is an extension of rhythm.

222. 只有英雄，能把现实的危难转化成历史的机遇。

Only heroes can turn real dangers into historical opportunities.

223. 道德为社会提供可持续的机遇。

Ethics provides sustainable opportunities for society.

224. 数学是逻辑代码。

Mathematics is logical code.

225. 飞翔是最深刻的跨越。

Flying is the most profound leap.

226. 形式和色彩是多元化的标志。

Form and color are hallmarks of diversity.

227. 俯瞰是一种预言。

Overlook is a prophecy.

228. 生命是一种深刻的动机，春天是一种深刻的时机。

Life is a profound motivation; spring is a profound moment.

229. 科学是逻辑的内容。

Science is logical content.

230. 勇气是文明的边界和未来的桥梁。

Courage is the border of civilization and the bridge of the future.

231. 勇气是生命的终极价值。

Courage is the ultimate value of life.

232. 生命被憧憬的勇气所延续。

Life is sustained by the courage of longing.

233. 只有理性的光芒，才能照亮未来。

Only the light of reason can illuminate the future.

234. 理性的心灵随时代而跳动。

The rational hearts beat with the times.

235. 自然总是呈现演绎的时机。

Nature always presents its timing of deduction.

236. 色彩是变换中的灵魂。

Color is the soul in change.

237. 基于系统性的完整性就是伟大的开端。

System-based integrity is a great start.

238. 印象是色彩的初心。

Impression is the original intention of color.

239. 深刻的跌落，才有伟大的崛起。

A deep fall leads to a great rise.

240. 热泵是人工诱导自然的典范。

Heat pumps are an example of artificially induced nature.

241. 多元化集成使技术承载文明进化的使命。

Diversified integration enables technology to carry the mission of civilization evolution.

242. 倾注深情的事物，就是灵魂的收获。

The things that pour deep feelings are the harvest of the soul.

243. 优化基于多样性的平衡。

Optimization is based on the balance of diversity.

244. 生机是审美的法则。

Vitality is the law of aesthetics.

245. 多元化构建的循环是创造生机的源泉。

Ciranlations constructed by diversity are the source of life creation.

246. 战略塑造每个民族的未来。

Strategies shape the future of every people.

247. 建筑是生存的形式。

Architecture determines the form in which we live.

248. 远见才是真正的自由。

Vision is truly free.

249. 未来是完整性的延伸。

The future is an extension of integrity.

250. 系统性和开放性代表真正的未来。

Systemicity and openness represent the real future.

251. 系统性和开放性创造出完整性。

Systemicity and openness create integrity.

252. 现象是逻辑的木偶。

Phenomena are puppets of logic.

253. 逻辑是所有的远见。

Logic is all foresight.

254. 审美是现实中最具启示的部分。

Aesthetics is the most revealing part of reality.

255. 逻辑是必然性的基石。

Logic is the cornerstone of necessity.

256. 灵魂就是心中所念。

The soul is what the heart thinks.

257. 阴影是光明的遗落。

Shadows are the legacy of light.

258. 变换与闪烁赋予我们启示。

Transformation and flickering give us revelation.

259. 翅膀的价值，是翱翔而非遮雨。

The value of wings is to soar, not to cover the rain.

260. 需求是经济循环的动机。

Demand is the motivation for the economic cycle.

261. 缺乏系统性的利益会阻断现实的可持续性。

The benefits lack of systematization blocks the sustainability of reality.

262. 创新的目标是在更大范围内回归现实。

The goal of innovation is to return to reality on a larger scale.

263. 因强大而孤独，就会因孤独而强大。

Lonely because of strength, thus to be strong because of loneliness.

264. 科学是最具现实意义的底层逻辑。

Science is the most realistic underlying logic.

265. 竞争带来所有的变革。

Competition brings all the change.

266. 一切的变革源于意志。

All change comes from will.

267. 文明，因持久和深刻而变得伟大。

Civilization becomes great by endurance and profoundity.

268. 颠覆式创新与革命性转型，是由掌握需求意义和科学价值的通才实现。

Disruptive innovation and revolutionary transformation are realized by generalists who master the meaning of demand and scientific value.

269. 一切在流淌中变换。

Everything changes in the flow.

270. 所有的美，都是深刻的时机。

All beauty is a profound moment.

271. 扼杀真实性，就会丧失逻辑推演的根基。

Killing authenticity loses the foundation of logical deduction.

272. 现实主义是深刻的缘由。

Realism is the profound reason.

273. 艺术的激情源自生命的渴望。

The passion of art stems from the desire for life.

274. 成长是对时间赋值。

Growth is the assignment of time.

275. 形式是现实的光芒。

Form is the light of reality.

276. 每一次结束，都是另一种开始。

Every end is another beginning.

277. 数学是逻辑的根源。

Mathematics is the root of logic.

278. 每一段历史，都有地理的烙印。

Every piece of history has a geographical imprint.

279. 忘记历史就难以重生。

Forgetting history is difficult to be reborn.

280. 内心丰富才会外表从容。

Inner richness will make the appearance calm.

281. 成功就是回归现实的逻辑。

Success is returning to the logic of reality.

282. 目的决定逻辑，逻辑决定法则。

Purpose determines logic, logic determines the law.

283. 云水相望是最善的结局。

That clouds and water look at each other is the best ending.

284. 变革源于激情，激情源于意志。

Change comes from passion, and passion comes from will.

285. 自由是探索的价值。

Freedom is the value of exploration.

286. 成长是照耀的价值，生机是成长的价值。

Growth is the value of shining, and vitality is the value of growth.

287. 开放性决定发展的程度。

Openness determines the degree of development.

288. 收获是成长的结果，成长是照耀的结果。

Harvest is the result of growth, and growth is the result of shining.

289. 灰度是观察的标尺。

Grayscale is the ruler of observation.

290. 变革是社会的进化。

Change is the evolution of society.

291. 艺术是现实的光辉。

Art is the glory of reality.

292. 自由的灵魂，才会感受光芒的启迪。

Only a free soul can feel the enlightenment of the light.

293. 教育的宗旨，是为社会培养能被光明启迪的灵魂。

The purpose of education is to cultivate a soul that can be inspired by light for society.

294. 艺术被期待充满。

Art is filled with anticipation.

295. 逻辑是必然性的演绎。

Logic is the deduction of necessity.

296. 光芒和彩云都在山峰。

The light and colorful clouds are on the mountain peaks.

297. 力量为自由提供支点。

Power provides a fulcrum for freedom.

298. 我们总是被现实塑造，被理想升华。

We are always shaped by reality and sublimated by ideals.

299. 我们被阳光普照，被阴影遮蔽。

We are drenched in the sun and obscured by shadows.

300. 人民的利益是革命的焦点。

The interests of the people are the focus of the revolution.

301. 照进现实的理想，才会灿烂。

The ideal that shines into reality can be brilliant.

302. 每一种守恒，都是现实的因果。

Every conservation is the cause and effect of reality.

303. 与现实相融，就难以战胜。

It is difficult to overcome when you integrate with reality.

304. 播撒的都是种子，收获的都是果实。

what is sown is seed; what is harvested is fruit.

305. 拥抱不确定性，就是拥抱未来。

To embrace uncertainty is to embrace the future.

306. 灰度是现实的投影。

Grayscale is a projection of reality.

307. 错过了播种，就错过了收获。

If you miss the seed, you will miss the harvest.

308. 我们从色彩与灰度中把握现实。

We grasp reality from color and grayscale.

309. 现实最多变，人性最深刻。

Reality is the most changeable, and humanity is the most profound.

310. 现实在必然性的轮回中演绎。

Reality deduces in the cycle of necessity.

311. 自由是被能力所跨越的时空。

Freedom is a time and space that can be crossed by power.

312. 有信仰就有方向，有希望就有动机。

Where there is faith there will be direction; where there is hope there will be motivation.

313. 有梦想，才有时机。

When there is a dream, there is an opportunity.

314. 回归现实，把握时机。

Get back to reality and seize the moment.

315. 美是现实演绎的时机。

Beauty is the moment for reality to deduce.

316. 不是每一座暗礁都有浮标，不是每一座港口都有灯塔。

Not every reef has buoys; not every port has a lighthouse.

317. 深刻就是跨界的视角。

Profoundity is a cross-border perspective.

318. 绝望是生活不可承受之重。

Despair is an unbearable burden of life.

319. 诗意就是回归自然的必然性。

Poetry is returning to the inevitability of nature.

320. 色彩总在启示，形式总在引导，光芒总在穿越。

Color is always revealing, form is always leading, light is always crossing.

321. 成长是自由的维度。

Growth is a dimension of freedom.

322. 哲学是生存的法则。

Philosophy is the law of survival.

323. 热力学第二定律的植物学表述：种子不会自发转化为果实，阳光则是成长的代价。

The botanical formulation of the second law of thermodynamics: seeds do not spontaneously transform into fruits, and sunlight is the price of growth.

324. 我们从色彩中感受现实演绎和万物成长。

We feel the reality deduction and the everything growth from color.

325. 进化是生命演绎的旋律。

Evolution is the melody of life deduction.

326. 飞越是为迁徙，跨界是为重组。

Overflight is for migration; cross-border is for reorganization.

327. 艺术总在启示，思想总在穿越，科学总在引导。

Art is always enlightening, thought is always traversing, science is always leading.

328. 可持续性是生物进化的目标。

Sustainability is the goal of biological evolution.

329. 建筑寄托人类的梦想。

Architecture holds the dreams of mankind.

330. 历史和地理是现实的根源。

History and geography are the roots of reality.

331. 同理心是人性的根源。

Empathy is the root of humanity.

332. 利益越清晰，愿景就越渺茫。

The clearer the benefits, the smaller the vision.

333. 回归现实，才会拥有未来。

Return to reality to have the future.

334. 独立性是灵魂的标志。

Independence is a sign of the soul.

335. 无端约束是一种罪恶。

Unwarranted restraint is a sin.

336. 忘我者才能飞翔。

Only those who forget themselves can fly.

337. 探索使人类扩展认知的边界。

Exploration allows humans to expand the boundaries of cognition.

338. 进化是生物演绎的自我变革。

Evolution is the self-transformation of biological deduction.

339. 一切因成长而灿烂。

Everything shines because of growth.

340. 色彩是现实演绎的标志。

Color is a sign of the reality deduction.

341. 遗传是生物可持续的形式。

Heredity is a biologically sustainable form.

342. 控制灰度，就是控制现实的深度。

To control grayscale is to control the depth of reality.

343. 怎样的河床，就会掀起怎样的浪花。

What kind of riverbed will set off what kind of waves.

344. 生命在于我们对现实的敬畏与热爱。

Life lies in our awe and love of reality.

345. 文明是人类可持续的形式。

Civilization is a sustainable form for humanity.

346. 敬畏自然，才会热爱自然。

Only in awe of nature will you love nature.

347. 所谓进化就是逆向成长。

Evolution is reverse growth.

348. 每一处风景，都能开启心灵的殿堂。

Every scenery can open the temple of the heart.

349. 进化是现实的出路。

Evolution is the way out for reality.

350. 基于现实的变革与创新是生命的智慧。

The change and innovation based on reality is the wisdom of life.

351. 时机的价值，在于能量的转换和力量的凝聚。

The value of timing lies in the energy transformation and the power cohesion.

352. 拯救是进化的意义。

Salvation is the meaning of evolution.

353. 创造和传播价值在深刻地影响未来。

Creating and disseminating value is profoundly influencing the future.

354. 自由是意志的光辉。

Freedom is the brilliance of the will.

355. 统一的文化、完整的工业、规模的市场，是经济可持续的底气。

A unified culture, a complete industry, a large-scale market are the foundation for economic sustainability.

356. 时机和未来属于梦想者。

The timing and the future belong to dreamers.

357. 探索是一次逆向旅程。

Exploration is a reverse journey.

358. 生命的精华在于节奏和时机。

The essence of life lies in rhythm and timing.

359. 空间感和立体感由灰度塑造。

The sense of space and three-dimensionality is shaped by grayscale.

360. 文明由梦想孕育。

Civilization is born of dreams.

361. 自由是跨入新的维度和境界。

Freedom is stepping into new dimensions and realms.

362. 敬畏与热爱是伟大的征服。

Awe and love are great conquests.

363. 时机是趋势的窗口。

Timing is a window to the trend.

364. 每一位英雄，都属于它的时代。

Every hero belongs to its time.

365. 每一种文明，都有它的光谱。

Every civilization has its own spectrum.

366. 实践是文明演绎的舞台，现实是文明演绎的背景。

Practice is the stage for the civilization deduction, and reality is the background of the civilization deduction.

367. 审美是由形式感知逻辑推演的必然性。

Aesthetics is to perceive the inevitability of the logic deduction by form.

368. 哲学体现逻辑推演的必然性。

Philosophy embodies the inevitability of logical deduction.

369. 逻辑体现形式推演的必然性。

Logic embodies the inevitability of formal deduction.

第 11 章 | 季节是被阳光赋予的节奏
The seasons are rhythms given by the sun

（2021 年浙江柯茂总工程师 Chief engineer of Zhejiang Comer）

1. 每一次能量转化的拐点都是时机的窗口。
   The inflection point of each energy conversion is a window of timing.

2. 音乐，反映人类的心声与时代的节奏。
   Music reflects the human voice and the rhythm of the times.

3. 我们通过灰度把握现实的深度。
   We grasp the depth of reality through grayscale.

4. 由忍耐而适应、由适应而持久，是生物进化的动力与人类智慧的根源。
   Adaption from patience and lasting from adaptation are the driving force of biological evolution and the root of human wisdom.

5. 更好的梦想总是在路上。
   A better dream is always on the way.

6. 坚毅不是一种选择，而且是一种成长。

Perseverance is not a choice, but a growth.

7. 没有什么能超越生物成长的效率和力量。

Nothing surpasses the efficiency and power of biological growth.

8. 每一次变革，都能带来一种自由的延伸。

Every change brings an extension of freedom.

9. 审美具有进化的意义，本质上都是一种能量的积蓄或者力量的释放。

Aesthetics has evolutionary significance, which is essentially a kind of energy accumulation or the release of power.

10. 自由的心灵，注定要飞翔。

The free mind is destined to fly.

11. 季节是被阳光赋予的节奏。

The seasons are rhythms given by the sun.

12. 历史在为成长提供缘由。

History is providing reasons for growth.

13. 自然以色彩宣告一切。

Nature announces everything in color.

14. 道德拥有最广的境界和最远的未来。

Morality has the broadest realm and the farthest future.

15. 音乐交织着现实的洪流与人类的渴望。

Music intertwined with the torrent of reality and human longing.

16. 每一座桥梁都在跨越历史与现实。

Every bridge straddles history and reality.

17. 独立是成长的标志。

Independence is a sign of growth.

18. 现实总是被艺术最先感知。

Reality is always perceived first by art.

19. 感知是智慧的启蒙。

Perception is the enlightenment of wisdom.

20. 每一个时节，都是被阳光所带的节奏。

Every season is the rhythm brought by the sun.

21. 每一种喧嚣，都有现实的逻辑。

Every hustle and bustle has a realistic logic.

22. 我们只是因为勇气而年轻。

We are only young because of courage.

23. 历史的神奇，在于只有原因没有如果。

The magic of history lies in the fact that there are only reasons and no ifs.

24. 设计是灵魂的表述。

Design is the expression of the soul.

25. 节奏是能量转换和力量释放的进程。

Rhythm is the process of energy conversion and power release.

26. 艺术是发自内心的形式。

Art is a form that comes from the heart.

27. 有目标才有期待。

Where there is a goal, there is an expectation.

28. 所有的进化都被现实的代价所支撑。

All evolution is underpinned by realistic costs.

29. 贫穷不是善良，富裕并非罪恶。

Poverty is not good; wealth is not evil.

30. 艺术要使我们从现实的脉搏中感知未来。

Art wants us to perceive the future from the pulse of reality.

31. 翅膀追逐环境，资本追逐利益。

Wings chase the environment; capital chases interests.

32. 战略是把持久性寓于普遍性。

Strategy is to put persistence in universality.

33. 智慧是自由的法则。

Wisdom is the law of freedom.

34. 艺术是每个时代的记忆和共情。

Art is the memory and empathy of every era.

35. 生命是运动的平衡。

Life is the balance of movement.

36. 色彩是现实多元化的刻度。

Color is a scale of reality diversity.

37. 色彩是生命成长的气息。

Color is the breath of life growth.

38. 掌握真理也就间接掌握了未来。

To grasp the truth is to indirectly grasp the future.

39. 改变认知而适应现实。

Change perception and adapt to reality.

40. 光芒是最好的色彩。

Light is the best color.

41. 图腾反映生存的方式。

Totems reflect ways to survive.

42. 物理的逻辑由数学描述。

The logic of physics is described by mathematics.

43. 智慧是回归现实的可持续性。

Wisdom is back to the reality sustainability.

44. 持久性就是从现实演绎的轮回与节奏中获取力量。

Persistence is to draw strength from the rotation and rhythm of reality deduction.

45. 历史是现实发展的根源。

History is the root of the reality development.

46. 趋势是伟大力量的节奏。

Trends are the rhythm of great forces.

47. 生命从现实的节奏中获得可持续力量。

Life derives its sustainable power from the reality rhythm.

48. 建筑是历史遗留的文化代码。

Architecture is a cultural code left over from history.

49. 色彩是多元化的符号。

Colors are symbols of diversity.

50. 勇气与青春同在。

Courage goes with youth.

51. 缺少真相就没有现实的价值。

There is no reality value without the facts.

52. 每一种现实演绎的逻辑，都是一种深刻的灵魂。

Every logic of reality deduction is a deep soul.

53. 真善美正是回归现实的路径。

Truth, kindness and beauty are the path back to reality.

54. 现实最深沉的力量在于它始终是自洽的。

The deepest power of reality is that it is always self-consistent.

55. 音乐是心灵的脉动。

Music is the pulse of the heart.

56. 回归现实的路径具有唯一性。

The path back to reality is unique.

57. 探索的魅力在于释放未知的力量。

The charm of exploration lies in unleashing the power of the unknown.

58. 生存逻辑决定生命的法则。

The logic of survival determines the law of life.

59. 回归现实是发展的原点。

A return to reality is the origin of development.

60. 文明是理性演绎的结果，理性是科学与人文和谐的结果。

Civilization is the result of rationality deduction; rationality is the result of the harmony between science and humanities.

61. 贪婪是罪恶的本源。

Greed is the source of sin.

62. 批判是文明进化的驱动力。

Criticism is the driving force of civilization evolution.

63. 温度是现实演绎的标志。

Temperature is a sign of reality deduction.

64. 失去多样性，就会失去现实的根基。

Without diversity, we lose the foundation of reality.

65. 征服者的光辉，掩盖历史的真相。

The brilliance of the conquerors cover up the truth of history.

66. 唯有宏大才能崇高。

Only grandeur can be sublime.

67. 每一种强大，都是因为回归理性。

Every kind of strength is due to a return to reason.

68. 灵魂是生命的特征。

The soul is a characteristic of life.

69. 成长是对时间赋值。

Growth is the assignment of time.

70. 现实呈现多样性的和谐。

Reality presents a harmony of diversity.

71. 梦想在为生命注入勇气。

Dreams are injecting courage into life.

72. 节奏是可持续的方式。

Rhythm is the way to be sustainable.

73. 个性是灵魂的标志。

Personality is the mark of the soul.

74. 使我们保持探索的动机是质疑而非生存。

The motivation to keep us exploratory is questioning rather than survival.

75. 生存是现实演绎的动机。

Survival is the motivation for the reality deduction.

76. 教育的宗旨是培育渴望的能力。

The purpose of education is to cultivate the ability to aspire.

77. 自然的逻辑并非人文的逻辑，科学的逻辑并非历史的逻辑。

The logic of nature is not the logic of humanity; the logic of science is not the logic of history.

78. 勇气源自深刻的希祈。

Courage comes from deep hope.

79. 生存是回归现实的途径。

Survival is the way back to reality.

80. 竞争是回归现实的途径。

Competition is the way back to reality.

81. 节奏是生命成长的形式。

Rhythm is the form of life growth.

82. 差异是一切变革的动机。

Difference is the motivation for all change.

83. 节奏是可持续的力量。

Rhythm is a sustainable force.

84. 节奏是生命成长的力量。

Rhythm is the force of life growth.

85. 责任就是力量。

Responsibility is power.

86. 色彩是流淌的时光。

Color is the time that flows.

87. 生命是成长的精灵。

Life is a growing elf.

88. 实践是文明进步的承载者。

Practice is the bearer of civilization progress.

89. 能量由逻辑转化为力量。

Energy is transformed into power by logic.

90. 人文是科学的灵魂。

Humanities are the soul of science.

91. 强大事物的节奏，正是弱小事物的趋势。

The rhythm of strong things is the trend of weak things.

92. 主要的节奏正是次要的趋势。

The main rhythm is precisely the secondary trend.

93. 生命是生态逻辑和自然算法的产物。

Life is the product of ecological logic and natural algorithms.

94. 文明在历史的演绎中成长。

Civilization grows through the deduction of history.

95. 实践赋予我们最深刻的启示。

Practice has given us the deepest inspiration.

96. 智慧，就是从主流事物的节奏中把握历史发展的趋势。

Wisdom is to grasp the trend of historical development from the rhythm of mainstream things.

97. 诗意就是回归自然的必然性。

Poetry is returning to the inevitability of nature.

98. 计算力就是通过逻辑释放现实的力量。

Computing power is the unleashing of the power of reality through logic.

99. 人文是社会发展的命脉。

Humanities are the lifeblood of social development.

100. 有目标才有路径。

Where there is a goal, there is a path.

101. 教育应当为本能播种。

Education should sow the seeds of instinct.

102. 痛苦是被格局限定的欲望。

Pain is the desire to be defined by patterns.

103. 远见是最美的风景。

Vision is the most beautiful scenery.

104. 没有力量能够超越人民。

No power can surpass the people.

105. 只有责任能被传承。

Only responsibility can be passed on.

106. 所有的责任都会自带光芒。

All responsibilities shine with their own light.

107. 只有阳光能够带来普遍的成长。

Only sunlight can bring about universal growth.

108. 美是生机的启示。

Beauty is the inspiration of vitality.

109. 阳光的价值不止于报晓，而是开启新的一天。

The value of sunshine is not just about announcing the arrival of dawn, while it is about starting a new day.

110. 美是感知的曙光。

Beauty is the dawn of perception.

111. 生命在被趋势引向未来。

Life is being led by trends into the future.

112. 视角和时机都是一次探索。

Both perspective and timing are an exploration.

113. 渴望转化为成长的目标。

Desire translates into a goal of growth.

114. 敬畏自然是人类的美德。

Reverence for nature is a human virtue.

115. 历史承载现实发展的必然性。

History carries the inevitability of the reality development.

116. 每一条道路，都有它蜿蜒的节奏和迎面的风景。

Each road has its winding rhythm and oncoming scenery.

117. 有进程才有节奏。

There is a process to have a rhythm.

118. 每一种无穷，都是循环的开端。

Every infinity is the beginning of a cycle.

119. 任何以进化为目标的思维都是一种智慧。

Any thinking that aims at evolution is a form of wisdom.

120. 趋势使期待成为一种快乐。

Trends make anticipation a joy.

121. 节奏使持久成为一种快乐。

Rhythm makes persistence a joy.

122. 不是节奏缓慢，而是成长需要时间。

It is not that the pace is slow, but that growth takes time.

123. 事物发展的可持续性寓于现实的普遍性中。

The sustainability of the development of things lies in the universality of reality.

124. 选择路径就是选择事物发展的节奏。

To choose a path is to choose the rhythm of the development of things.

125. 每一扇窗户，都在见证时节的演变。

Every window bears witness to the evolution of the seasons.

126. 成长是可被期待的未来。

Growth is a future to look forward to.

127. 趋势创造成长的价值。

Trends create value for growth.

128. 教育应当由内在的个性点燃持久的希望。

Education should ignite lasting hope from inner individuality.

129. 只有希望能把距离转化为目标。

Only hope can turn distance into a goal.

130. 每一次危难，都是最好的时机。

Every crisis is the best time.

131. 目标是最具可能性的希望。

The goal is the most possible hope.

132. 国家的力量来自人民的意志。

The power of the state comes from the will of the people.

133. 实践是教育绽放的契机。

Practice is an opportunity for education to bloom.

134. 艺术是心灵的载体。

Art is the carrier of the mind.

135. 每一片土地，都被星云启示。

Every land is inspired by nebulae.

136. 每一片土地，都被阳光照耀。

Every piece of land is illuminated by the sun.

137. 偏见不仅错失机会而且错失目标。

Prejudice not only misses opportunities, but also misses goals.

138. 文明演绎是由人文逻辑引导科学逻辑。

Civilization deduction is that the logic of humanities guides the logic of science.

139. 和谐是多元化的自由。

Harmony is the freedom of pluralism.

140. 每一种投机，都在与趋势为敌。

Every speculation is against the trend.

141. 自由的渴望才能焕发生命力。

The desire for freedom is the only way to rejuvenate.

142. 时间的价值，是见证现实演绎的每一种节奏和每一次趋势。

The value of time is to witness every rhythm and every trend of reality deduction.

143. 黑暗与寒冷见证文明的璀璨。

Darkness and cold bear witness to the brilliance of civilization.

144. 阳光的节奏就是生命的趋势。

The rhythm of sunlight is the trend of life.

145. 道德基于逻辑，逻辑基于真相。

Morality is based on logic; logic is based on truth.

146. 承载的力量就是颠覆的力量。

The power to carry is the power of subversion.

147. 不啻向往，造炬如阳。

Do not just yearn for; create torches like the sun.

148. 每一种维度，都是科学的标尺。

Each dimension is a ruler for science.

149. 时间见证所有的节奏和趋势。

Time witnesses all the rhythms and trends.

150. 文化在为经济发展注入激情。

Culture is injecting passion into economic development.

151. 花朵不会错过绽放的季节。

Flowers do not miss the blooming season.

152. 谎言不会具有自洽的逻辑。

Lies do not have self-consistent logic.

153. 我们从自然演绎的时机中获取现实的力量。

We derive the power of reality from the timing of nature deduction.

154. 每一种神奇，都是开启认知的维度。

Each magic is to open up a cognition dimension.

155. 极简是浪漫的境界。

Minimalism is the realm of romance.

156. 春风吹散种子，雨露滋润禾苗。

The spring breeze blows away the seeds; the rain moisturizes the seedlings.

157. 竞争的目标不是毁灭对手而是提高自身。

The goal of competition is not to destroy the opponent, but to improve itself.

158. 孤独是超越所能达到的境界。

Loneliness is the realm that can be achieved by transcending.

159. 不辜负现实，就没有辜负时代。

Live up to reality; live up to the times.

160. 灰度就是现实的深度。

Grayscale is the depth of reality.

161. 创造就是回归现实的节奏。

To create is to return to the rhythm of reality.

162. 用现实塑造梦想。

Shape dreams with reality.

163. 趋势释放现实的力量。

Trends unleash the power of reality.

164. 平衡既是创造的转折，也是毁灭的转折。

Balance is both a turning point of creation and a turning point of destruction.

165. 艺术是心灵的密码。

Art is the code of the mind.

166. 每一种形式都是逻辑演绎的平衡态。

Each form is an equilibrium of the logic deduction.

167. 历史见证每一个趋势所留下的轨迹。

History bears witness to the trajectory left by each trend.

168. 由科学整合技术与需求。

Integrate technology and demand by science.

169. 历史的结局不仅取决于逻辑，而且取决于前提。

The outcome of history depends not only on logic, but also on premises.

170. 艺术是心灵的标尺。

Art is the ruler of the mind.

171. 历史不分胜败，只有趋势。

History does not distinguish between victory and defeat, only trends.

172. 每一种边界和拐点，都是力量的释放。

Every frontier and inflection point is a release of power.

173. 唯有跨界才能获取双重力量。

Only cross-border can achieve dual power.

174. 地理和气象决定生存的方式与现实的节奏。

Geography and meteorology determine the way of survival and the rhythm of reality.

175. 所有的远见都是未来的雏形。

All vision is the prototype of the future.

176. 历史只有趋势，没有彩排。

History has only trends, no rehearsals.

177. 时空流转，不负生机。

Time and space flow and live up to vitality.

178. 所有的积累都是为了时机，所有的力量都是为了超越。

All accumulation is for timing, all power is for transcendence.

179. 把我们带入未来的是勇气而非岁月。

It is courage, not years, that brings us into the future.

180. 绽放就是最好的赞美。

Blooming is the best compliment.

181. 现实之美在于生态，生态之美在于生机。

The beauty of reality lies in ecology; the beauty of ecology lies in vitality.

182. 没有一种认知是多余的。

No recognition is superfluous.

183. 存在本身就是意义。

Existence itself is meaning.

184. 冲锋需要勇气，转折需要智慧。

Charging requires courage; turning requires wisdom.

185. 劳动是人性演绎的原点。

Labor is the origin of the humanity deduction.

186. 有沃野才有奔腾，有绝壁才有飞翔。

Only with fertile land can there be galloping, only with extreme walls can there be flight.

187. 成长是现实的精华。

Growth is the essence of reality.

188. 阳光的价值不是启示，而是成长。

The value of sunshine is not revelation, but growth.

189. 技术集成就是把需求的逻辑转化为产品的逻辑。

Technology integration is to transform requirements logic into product logic.

190. 节能是以跨界的循环突破标准和规范。

Energy conservation is to break through standards and norms with cross-border cycle.

191. 质疑就是回归现实的力量。

Questioning is the power to return to reality.

192. 任何偏见与谎言都无法自洽。

No prejudice or lie can be consistent.

193. 由基础理论整合技术，才能突破规范。

Only by integrating technology from basic theory can we break through the norms.

194. 技术创新就是以逻辑仿真实现概念组合。

Technological innovation is the realization of conceptual combinations through logic simulation.

195. 一切变革的目标，都是提高现实性。

The goal of all change is to improve realism.

196. 共享是社会的模式。

Sharing is the model of society.

197. 宽容是根本性的转折。

Tolerance is a fundamental turning point.

198. 成长是最美的渴望。

Growth is the most beautiful desire.

199. 接受阳光是成长的要义。

Accepting the sun is the essence of growth.

200. 失去普遍性，就失去现实的根基。

Without universality, we lose the foundation of reality.

201. 科学的价值是为技术路径提供拐点、界面、极限。
The value of science is to provide inflection points, interfaces and limits for technological paths.

202. 所有的光辉由内而外。
All the brilliance comes from the inside out.

203. 每一种可持续性，都在开启未来的价值。
Every sustainability unlocks future value.

204. 殖民主义闪烁多元文化的余晖。
Colonialism flashes with a multicultural afterglow.

205. 可持续的意义是被阳光照耀，被万物寄托。
The meaning of sustainability is to be illuminated by the sun and entrusted by all things.

206. 普遍性带来可持续的价值。
Universality brings sustainable value.

207. 生态被季节塑造。
Ecology is shaped by the seasons.

208. 季节被阳光塑造。
The seasons are shaped by the sun.

209. 地理是政治博弈的根源。
Geography is the root of political games.

210. 勇气来自希望而非力量。
Courage comes from hope, not strength.

211. 所有的寒冷、寂静、黑暗无须代价。

All cold, silence, darkness comes at no cost.

212. 所有价值的起点是现实。

The starting point for all values is reality.

213. 成功源于变革而非观察。

Success comes from change rather than observation.

214. 以灰度把握纵深，以纵深控制节奏。

Grasp depth with grayscale and and control rhythm with depth.

215. 每一场技术革命都在把科学的演绎转化为生活的节奏。

Every technological revolution is transforming the science deduction into the rhythm of life.

216. 教育的宗旨是为心灵的成长提供现实可能性。

The purpose of education is to provide realistic possibilities for spiritual growth.

217. 可持续性来自价值创造而非价值转移。

Sustainability comes from value creation, not value transfer.

218. 本能是与生俱来的智慧。

Instinct is innate wisdom.

219. 趋势是通向未来的力量。

Trends are the force to the future.

220. 接收的是光辉，透射的是光泽。

What is received is brilliance, what is transmitted is luster.

221. 多么浩瀚就多么远古。

How vast is how ancient.

222. 期待机遇需要敏锐的抓手而非视角。

Anticipating opportunities requires a keen grasp rather than a perspective.

223. 变革是主动地适应。

Change is active adaptation.

224. 适应是主动地成长。

Adaptation is active growth.

225. 科学的边界在质疑中修正。

The boundaries of science are revised in questioning.

226. 每一次创新都以现实中的问题为起点。

Every innovation takes the problem in reality as the starting point.

227. 科学是探索的进程。

Science is explorative progress.

228. 质疑不是目的，改进才是。

Questioning is not the goal, improvement is.

229. 有灵魂才会有事业。

Only when there is a soul can there be a good career.

230. 没有好的专业，只有好的本事。

There are no good professions, only good skills.

231. 所能驾驭的都是好马。

All that can be harnessed are good horses.

232. 宽容一切，就会走向伟大。

Tolerate everything and you will lead to greatness.

233. 所有喷发的激情，都在诗意中凝固。

All the passion that erupts is frozen in poetry.

234. 没有力量能超越宽容。

No force can transcend tolerance.

235. 自信是由内而外的力量。

Self-confidence is a force from the inside out.

236. 没有一堵高墙能锁住希望。

No wall locks hope.

237. 期待不能翻越空间，但能翻越时间。

Expectations cannot climb over space, but can climb over time.

238. 本能是自然赋予的力量。

Instinct is a force given by nature.

239. 只有被科学所掌握的现实，才能转化为力量。

Only reality grasped by science can be transformed into power.

240. 精确是力量的聚焦。

Precision is the focus of power.

241. 每一个不曾思考的日子，都是对生命的辜负。

Every day without thinking is a failure of life.

242. 艺术和科学都是伟大的探索。

Both art and science are great explorations.

243. 项目实施以科学为先导、技术为后盾、产品为抓手、服务为支撑。

Project implementation is guided by science, backed by technology, grasped by products, supported by service.

244. 历史被责任传承。

History is passed down with responsibility.

245. 掌握逻辑就是掌握现实的力量。

To master logic is to grasp the power of reality.

246. 智慧是借助趋势的策划。

Wisdom is a plan with the help of trends.

247. 没有希望，就没有未来。

Without hope, there is no future.

248. 没有山峰能遮挡翅膀。

No mountain can block the wings.

249. 播种相似，结果不同。

The seeds are similar; the results are different.

250. 持久的回报是成长，成长的回报是结果。

The lasting reward is growth, and the growth reward is result.

251. 通过实践的知识才会闪光。

Knowledge shines through practice.

252. 万物在循环中平衡。

Everything is balanced in cycles.

253. 每一种进化，都有其现实的代价。

Every evolution has its practical costs.

254. 我们每个人都被实践的洪流所塑造。

Each of us is shaped by the torrent of practice.

255. 生命由生态演绎塑造成型。

Life is shaped by ecological deduction.

256. 突变被环境平息并转变成节奏。

Mutations are calmed by the environment and transformed into a rhythm.

257. 成长是被阳光赋予的节奏。

Growth is the rhythm given by the sun.

258. 劳动是构建人性的原点。

Labor is the origin of the construction of humanity.

259. 没有智慧能超越生态。

No wisdom can transcend ecology.

260. 绽放就是最好的时机。

Bloom is the best time.

261. 生活拥有多元化的色彩。

Life has a variety of colors.

262. 光在照耀，风在吹拂，云在飘逸，山在遮挡。

The light is shining, the wind is blowing, the clouds are drifting, the mountains are sheltering.

263. 公平是规则而非平均。

Fairness is the rule, not the average.

264. 可持续性是通向未来的力量。

Sustainability is a force for the future.

265. 创新的目标是获得可持续性。

The goal of innovation is to achieve sustainability.

266. 每一个概念的本质，都在闪光。

The essence of each concept is shining.

267. 思想是感性与理性的交织。

Thought is an interweaving of sensibility and reason.

268. 思想是工具之母。

Ideas are the mother of tools.

269. 雾在弥散，水在流淌，土在滋养，火在燃烧。

The fog is dispersing; the water is flowing; the earth is nourishing; the fire is burning.

270. 树在成长，鸟在飞翔，心在徜徉。

Trees are growing; birds are flying; hearts are wandering.

271. 可持续性是自然演绎的智慧。

Sustainability is the wisdom of nature deduction.

272. 没有超越历史的伟大。

There is no greatness beyond history.

273. 趋势和节奏是可持续力量。

Trends and rhythms are sustainable forces.

274. 每个历史的转折点都在闪光。

Every turning point in history is shining.

275. 可持续性来自现实的趋势和节奏。

Sustainability comes from the trends and rhythms of reality.

276. 燃烧的苦难才会闪光。

Burning suffering will shine.

277. 所有突破点都在边界。

All breakthrough points are at the border.

278. 我们进入每一个空间都需要时间窗口。

We need a window of time to enter every space.

279. 每一束阳光，都有它的时机。

Every ray of sunlight has its timing.

280. 一切在时间中成长。

Everything grows in time.

281. 成长是时间的维度。

Growth is the dimension of time.

282. 智慧并非宏大而是持久。

Wisdom is not grand, but lasting.

283. 坚毅的生命才会闪烁。

Perseverance life will flicker.

284. 融入心脾才会有力。

Integrate into the heart and spleen to be powerful.

285. 探索是灵魂的标尺。

Exploration is the ruler of the soul.

286. 控制了温度，就控制了世界。

Control the temperature, and control the world.

287. 时间会宽容一切。

Time will forgive everything.

288. 公平是社会的可持续力量。

Equity is a sustainable force for society.

289. 阳光的节奏带动生物演绎的节奏。

The rhythm of sunlight drives the rhythm of biological deduction.

290. 唯有细节才能沁入灵魂。

Only the details can reach the soul.

291. 唯有艺术能把现实的苦难转化为社会的力量。

Only art can transform the reality suffering into a force for society.

292. 黑暗是光明的边界。

Darkness is the boundary of light.

293. 独立的灵魂才有自由的光芒。

Only an independent soul can have the light of freedom.

294. 刻意的灵魂才会升华。

The deliberate soul will sublimate.

295. 风雨是戏剧的前奏。

Wind and rain are the prelude to the drama.

296. 热泵是工业文明的灵魂。

Heat pump is the soul of industrial civilization.

297. 社会从公平中获得持久的力量。

Society gains lasting strength from equity.

298. 艺术隔着理想和现实的距离。

Art across the distance between ideal and reality.

299. 掌握能源的逻辑，就能获取无边的力量。

If you master the logic of energy, you can gain boundless power.

300. 创造价值与分配价值有着不同的未来。

Creating value has a different future than distributing value.

301. 实践是人文逻辑的出发点。

Practice is the starting point of humanistic logic.

302. 文明的本质归结于实践的逻辑。

The essence of civilization comes down to the logic of practice.

303. 每个灵魂，都有她的频率和密码。

Every soul has her frequency and password.

304. 伟大的行程也有她的归途。

The great trip also has her way home.

305. 每个生命，都有她的色彩和光泽。

Every life has her color and luster.

306. 创新的本质是在更深层次上回归自然。

The essence of innovation is to return to nature on a deeper level.

307. 创新的本质是在更深层次上回归现实。

The essence of innovation is to return to reality on a deeper level.

308. 从人性的普遍性中获取普世价值。

Derive universal values from the universality of humanity.

309. 那些普遍轮回的必然性，正是我们所依赖的上帝。

The inevitability of those universal samsara is the God we depend on.

310. 历史由意志和责任编织。

History is woven by will and responsibility.

311. 普遍性的价值，才具有革命的意义。

The value of universality has revolutionary significance.

312. 文明的每一种形式都以温度为标志。

Every form of civilization is marked by temperature.

313. 质疑的目的就是在变局中回归真相。

The purpose of questioning is to return to the truth in the changing situation.

314. 每一种忽略，都是一种聚焦。

Every neglect is a focus.

315. 人类总是以勇气和智慧构建文明。

Human beings have always built civilization with courage and wisdom.

316. 建筑就像一列车厢，承载时光的流转。

The building is like a train car, carrying the flow of time.

317. 真实性是科学的灵魂。

Authenticity is the soul of science.

318. 人类用意志把握时机并实现目标。

Humans use their will to seize the moment and achieve their goals.

319. 时空没有止境，探索没有止境。

There is no end to time and space, and there is no end to exploration.

320. 读懂云彩的来龙去脉，也就读懂能源的奥秘。

Read the ins and outs of clouds, and also read the mystery of energy.

321. 语言无法描述自然的神奇。

Language cannot describe the magic of nature.

322. 文明是一种智慧，也是一种期望。

Civilization is both a wisdom and an expectation.

323. 科学体现在仿真与计量的吻合。

The science lies in the alignment of simulation and measurement.

324. 能源是现实演绎的起点。

Energy is the starting point for the deduction of reality.

325. 人生在阳光和风雨中穿行。

Life travels through the sun and the wind and rain.

326. 探索在寻求真理的同时，也在迎接未来。

Exploration is also embracing the future while seeking truth.

327. 每一种宽容都是和谐的力量。

Every tolerance is a force for harmony.

328. 每一种过滤都是一种选择。

Every filtration is an option.

329. 每一种节奏都是可持续的力量。

Each rhythm is a force for sustainability.

330. 真诚是灵魂的窗口。

Sincerity is the window to the soul.

331. 那些能自我迭代的事物都是不朽的。

Things that can iterate on themselves are immortal.

332. 雨雪是生命不可承受之轻。

Rain and snow are unbearable lightness of life.

333. 凋零并非结束，而是新一轮开始。

Withering is not the end, but the beginning of a new round.

334. 探索是接近未来的方式。

Exploration is the way to get closer to the future.

335. 我们度过一天的方式，几乎就是度过一生的方式。

The way we spend our days is almost the way we spend our lives.

336. 每个瞳孔的背后都是灵魂的深渊。

Behind each pupil is the abyss of the soul.

337. 每一片树叶都有它演绎的灵魂。

Each leaf has its deductive soul.

338. 期待的临界点是焦虑。

The tipping point of expectation is anxiety.

339. 传递能量就是传递价值。

To transmit energy is to transmit value.

340. 每一段历史，都要尊重它的起点。

Every piece of history must respect its beginnings.

341. 资本以人性的弱点为逐利的手段。

Capital uses the weakness of humanity as a means of pursuing profits.

342. 生存方式演绎人性。

The way of survival deduces the humanity.

343. 艺术开启灵魂的密码。

Art opens the code of the soul.

344. 远处都是人生，近处都是生活。

The distance is life; the near is live.

345. 色彩是生命散发的光芒。

Color is the light that life emits.

346. 胜利不是鲁莽冲锋，而是安全回归。

Victory is not a reckless charge, but a safe return.

347. 有艺术加持的地方就会有灵魂。

Where there is the blessing of art, there will be a soul.

348. 热泵正在从消费形态转变成为能源形态。

Heat pumps are shifting from consumption to energy.

349. 问题的缘由高于问题的解答。

The reason for the question is higher than the answer to the question.

350. 捷径不会有伟大的前景。

Shortcuts will not have great prospects.

351. 教育的目标是唤醒潜能而非积累知识。

The goal of education is to awaken potential, not to accumulate knowledge.

352. 技术集成是以科学的途径回归现实。

Technology integration is to return to reality with a scientific way.

353. 回归现实才能跨越和腾飞。

Only by returning to reality can we leapfrog and take off.

354. 历史的价值在于多变的缘由与深刻的根基。

The value of history lies in its changeable causes and deep roots.

355. 每个人都有向善的一面。

Everyone has a good side.

356. 可持续的跨越就是飞翔。

A sustainable leap is flying.

357. 生命被阳光照耀和演绎。

Life is illuminated and interpreted by the sun.

358. 艺术的力量来自人性的演绎。

The power of art comes from the deduction of humanity.

359. 每一次转折都是为了可持续。

Every turn is for sustainability.

360. 每一种色彩和光芒都在标度时机。

Every color and light is at the scale of timing.

361. 和谐是自由的山峰。

Harmony is the mountain of freedom.

362. 光芒只因现实的折射而绚丽斑斓。

The light is brilliant and colorful only because of the refraction of reality.

363. 独立地感知才会真正地发现。

Independent perception will truly discover.

364. 文学是从人性的弱点撕开缺口。

Literature is tearing apart gaps from the weaknesses of humanity.

365. 不会有快捷的成长。

There will be no quick growth.

366. 时间是成长的代价。

Time is the price of growth.

367. 真正的危机无法预测。

Real crises cannot be predicted.

368. 思想是多元化的光芒。

Ideas are the light of diversity.

369. 只有阳光带来普遍的成长。

Only sunlight brings universal growth.

370. 飞翔是奔腾的进化。

Flying is the evolution of galloping.

371. 我们获得的能力不会超越苦难的深度。

The capacity we gain will not surpass the depth of suffering.

372. 每一个灵魂，都是一种现实的算法。

Every soul is an algorithm of reality.

373. 色彩是现实对于阳光的回应。

Color is the response of the reality to sunlight.

374. 凡是可被预测的事物就不再是危机。

Anything that can be predicted is no longer a crisis.

375. 宽容是对现实的接纳。

Tolerance is the acceptance of reality.

376. 没有超越光芒的色彩。

There are no colors beyond the light.

377. 文明最深刻的部分都是由危机转化而来。

The deepest parts of civilization are transformed by crises.

378. 飞翔始于翅膀的力量超越自身的重量。

Flight from the power of the wings surpasses the weight of the body.

379. 回归现实是智慧的开端。

A return to reality is the beginning of wisdom.

380. 持续飞翔，不致坠落。

Keep flying so you do not fall.

381. 依生态的节奏而演绎是生命的灵魂。

Interpreting according to the rhythm of ecology is the soul of life.

382. 自然演绎是最深的智慧。

Natural deduction is the deepest wisdom.

383. 哲学以思想的逻辑回归现实的逻辑。

Philosophy returns the logic of reality with the logic of thought.

384. 现实正是变革力量的支点和事物演绎的起点。

Reality is the fulcrum of the change forces and the beginning of the things deduction.

385. 科学与人文交织，决定社会演绎的进程和方式。

Science and humanities are intertwined and determine the course and manner of social deduction.

386. 美是自然演绎的绽放。

Beauty is the bloom of natural deduction.

387. 失去现实根基的梦想，只是水中倒影和灿烂的毒素。

Dreams that have lost their roots in reality are just reflections in the water and brilliant toxins.

388. 偏见只是语言的逻辑，而非现实的逻辑。

Prejudice is only the logic of language, not reality.

389. 回归现实，才能通向未来。

Only by returning to reality can we lead to the future.

390. 现实最深刻的部分才能通向未来。

The deepest part of reality leads to the future.

391. 节奏是现实演绎的形式。

Rhythm is the form of reality deduction.

392. 我们从色彩中感知温度与时节。

We perceive temperature and season from color.

393. 真理是危难中的灯塔。

Truth is a beacon in distress.

394. 差异的势能与均衡的动能不断转换，由此形成事物演绎的节奏。

The potential energy of difference and the kinetic energy of equilibrium are constantly converted, thus forming the rhythm of the things deduction.

395. 趋势为我们带来最好的时机。

Trends bring us the best timing.

396. 规则均衡财富，垄断积累财富。

Rules balance wealth and monopoly accumulates wealth.

397. 人文描述现象，科学分析动机。

Humanities describe phenomena; science analyses motivation.

398. 制胜的法则，在于可持续量级压倒偶然性概率。

The law of victory lies in the fact that the magnitude of sustainability trumps the probability of chance.

399. 投资的目标是未来的趋势。

The goal of investment is the future trend.

400. 每一种发展都被动机操纵。

Every development is manipulated by motivation.

401. 多元化动机导致经济理论只是假象。

The pluralistic motivation leads to economic theory being an illusion.

402. 文明使得黑夜是一种璀璨，严寒是一种温暖。

Civilization makes the night a brilliance and the cold a warmth.

403. 宽广的心灵自有山水。

A broad mind has its own landscape.

404. 空间是苍茫的舞台，时间是恒久的逻辑。

Space is the vast stage; time is the eternal logic.

405. 只有对美激动不已，才会面对未来激动不已。

Only those who are excited about beauty will be excited about the future.

406. 文明发展的力量来自：质疑突破科学边界，勇气突破心理边界。

The power of civilization development comes from: questioning breaks through the science boundaries, and courage breaks through the psychology boundaries.

407. 每一种伟大的力量都是由内而外的。

Every great power comes from the inside out.

408. 和谐是可持续的灵魂。

Harmony is the soul of sustainability.

409. 现实的复杂性交织于多元动机和多重目标。

The complexity of reality is intertwined with multiple motivations and multiple goals.

410. 伟大的事物归于平静。

Great things return to peace.

411. 现实之美总是以深刻的形式启示未来。

The beauty of reality always enlightens the future with a profound form.

412. 通向宏大的路径，就是通向未来。

The path to grandeur is to the future.

413. 在回暖时播种，在渐冷时收获。

Sow seeds when warming up and harvest when getting colder.

414. 只有可持续性才能把我们送进理想的未来。

Only sustainability can send us into the ideal future.

415. 诗意凝聚生活的勇气。

Poetry condenses the courage of life.

第 12 章 | 涟漪和波澜被风操纵
Ripples and waves are manipulated by the wind

（2022 年中船齐耀特聘专家 Distinguished expert of CSSC Qiyao）

1. 人类只有突破心理边界，才能突破科学边界。
   Only by breaking through psychological boundaries can human beings break through scientific boundaries.

2. 文明由勇气和智慧缔造。
   Civilization is forged by courage and wisdom.

3. 完整的才是真实的。
   What is complete is true.

4. 每一条道路，都是梦想的轨迹。
   Every path is the trajectory of a dream.

5. 掌握现实的逻辑，才能释放现实的力量。
   Only by mastering the logic of reality can we unleash the power of reality.

6. 崎岖是最美的来路。

Ruggedness is the most beautiful way to come.

7. 技术发明，是科学逻辑与现实逻辑的迭代。

Technological invention is an iteration of scientific logic and realistic logic.

8. 每一种事物，都有它的地理分布和历史沿革。

Every thing has its geographical distribution and historical evolution.

9. 生命力是美的准则。

Vitality is the criterion of beauty.

10. 自由的本质并非遥远目标，而是更多选择。

The essence of freedom is not a distant goal, but more choices.

11. 寒冷，使得每一种期待更加深刻。

The cold makes every expectation more profound.

12. 光芒与黑暗同样会遮蔽我们的双眼，点亮真理的始终是灰度。

Light and darkness can obscure our eyes as well, and it is always grayscale that illuminates the truth.

13. 没有实践我们就会局限在感知和偏见之中。

Without practice, we are limited to perception and prejudice.

14. 生存模式构建力量释放的法则。

Survival mode builds the law of unleashing power.

15. 运动是生命释放力量的方式。

Movement is the way life unleashes its power.

16. 色彩标度事物演绎的时机。

Color scales the timing of the things deduction.

17. 能力决定我们行走的界面。

Ability determines the interface through which we walk.

18. 快乐是被感性释放的节奏。

Happiness is the rhythm that is released by sensibility.

19. 书法彰显心迹的波澜。

Calligraphy shows the waves of the heart.

20. 我们从危机中触碰到的痛点，感知现实的边界。

We perceive the boundaries of reality from the pain points we touch in the crisis.

21. 节奏是系统释放可持续力量的必然形式。

Rhythm is an inevitable form of the system unleashing the sustainable power.

22. 戏剧性变革总是在黑暗和寂静中发生。

Dramatic change always happens in darkness and silence.

23. 涟漪和波澜，都被风操纵。

Ripples and waves are manipulated by the wind.

24. 飞翔与奔驰具有不同的节奏。

Flying has a different rhythm than galloping.

25. 教育要从偏门游戏回归主流现实。

Education should return to mainstream reality from the partial game.

26. 理性的细节决定商业结果。

Rational details determine business outcomes.

27. 逻辑的起点和目标，都是现实。

The starting point and goal of logic are reality.

28. 每个季节都充满时间的内涵。

Each season is full of the connotation of time.

29. 艺术是现实的灵魂。

Art is the soul of reality.

30. 节奏是我们释放力量的形式。

Rhythm is the form by which we unleash our power.

31. 心灵的波澜，就是艺术的法则。

The waves of the heart are the laws of art.

32. 每一条河流，都有它的波澜与浪花。

Every river has its own waves and episodes.

33. 每个时代总是被它的艺术家们所标志和绽放。

Every era is always marked and bloomed by its artists.

34. 风景即是独特的地理，更是独特的时光。

Scenery is a unique geography, but also a unique time.

35. 只有山峰知道云彩的高度。

Only the mountain peaks know the height of the clouds.

36. 我们最终会被自己的贪婪所奴役。

We end up being enslaved by our own greed.

37. 任何事物都因不可持续而终结。

Anything ends up being unsustainable.

38. 每个时代，都有可持续的独特方式。

Every era has a unique way to be sustainable.

39. 人类总是由智慧和勇气突破极限。

Human beings have always pushed the limits with wisdom and courage.

40. 成长的意义就是逐步走向开放，以增加社会价值。

The meaning of growth is to gradually open up to increase social value.

41. 每一片山海，都有追随它的灵魂。

Every mountain and sea has a soul that follows it.

42. 凡是从严寒挺过来的都会被春天接纳，珍惜每一个奋斗的生命。

Anyone who survives the severe cold will be accepted by the spring and cherish every struggling life.

43. 生活的要义就是把生存的代价转化为生活的目标。

The essence of life is to transform the cost of survival into the goal of life.

44. 并非春天赋万物予生机，而是万物从严寒复苏的季节称为春天。

It is not that spring gives life to all things, but that the season when all things recover from the severe cold is called spring.

45. 期望是灵魂可持续的根源。

Expectation is the root of sustainability for the soul.

46. 灵魂总是被温水扼杀，在凛冽中持续。

The soul is always snuffed out by warm water, which lasts in the cold.

47. 先抑后扬，引导万物复苏。

First suppress and then raise to lead all things to recover.

48. 先扬后抑，导致万物衰败。

First raise and then suppress to cause all things to decay.

49. 每一种现实的波动，都在回归价值。

Every fluctuation of reality is returning to value.

50. 真正的危机是无人敢警示危机。

The real crisis is when no one dares to warn of it.

51. 机制可转化成可持续的力量。

Mechanisms can be transformed into sustainable forces.

52. 每个时代拥有的生机，总是被那些伟大的力量所代表。

The vitality of each era is always represented by those great forces.

53. 时间很长久，时节最珍贵。

Time is long, and the season is the most precious.

54. 生机从来不是锦上添花，而是雪中送炭。

Vitality is never the icing on the cake, but charcoal in the snow.

55. 智慧就是以时机赢取时间。

Wisdom is to win time with timing.

56. 时机是趋势留下的时间窗口。

Timing is the window of time left by the trend.

57. 系统性成长，更依赖时机。

Systemic growth is more dependent on timing.

58. 中国与犹太人比智慧，与埃及比历史，与希腊比文化，与美国比经济，与印度比人口，与俄罗斯比空间站，与加拿大比国土。

China compares wisdom with Jews, history with Egypt, culture with Greece, economy with the United States, population with India, space stations with Russia, and land with Canada.

59. 那些爱惜羽毛的燕子，飞不到终点。

Those swallows that cherish their feathers can not fly to the destination.

60. 被现实煎熬过的灵魂才会成熟。

It is only the soul that has been tormented by reality matures.

61. 在凛冽中绽放就不止于生命。

Blooming in the cold is more than life.

62. 有轮回的时节，再无起始。

There is no beginning in the season of reincarnation.

63. 实践是认知的不竭来源。

Practice is an inexhaustible source of cognition.

64. 每一场社会实践的胜利，都是一种方法论的胜利。

Every victory of social practice is a victory of methodology.

65. 每一种文化属性，都是在规则之内突破人类极限。

Every cultural attribute pushes humanity limits within the rules.

66. 美丽面前有陷阱，潇洒背后是灾难。

There are traps in front of beauty, and disasters behind the dashing.

67. 历史是现实演绎中最持久的逻辑。

History is the most enduring logic in the deduction of reality.

68. 生态是现实演绎中最多元的逻辑。

Ecology is the most pluralistic logic in the deduction of reality.

69. 我们在多大程度上回归现实，就能在多大程度上再现事物演绎的逻辑。

We can reproduce the logic of the things deduction to the extent to which we can return to reality.

70. 实践的主要矛盾正是社会演绎的逻辑根源。

The main contradiction of practice is precisely the logical root of social deduction.

71. 矛盾的科学意义是分析事物演绎的逻辑根源。

The scientific significance of contradiction is to analyze the logical roots of the things deduction.

72. 能使我们清醒的不是黎明而是苦难。

What awakens us is not dawn but suffering.

73. 胜败取决于现实力量转向目标的时机。

Victory or defeat depends on the timing of the turn from realistic forces to the target.

74. 整合需求比整合技术更需智慧：因为创新的方法论意义，首先体现在准确把握并重新定义用户的原始需求，从而把登天的理想变成登山的现实，也把登天的绝望变成登山的可能。

Integration needs is more intelligent than integration technologies: because the methodological significance of innovation is first reflected in accurately grasping and redefining the original needs of users, so as to turn the ideal of ascending to the sky into the reality of climbing the mountain, and also turn the despair of ascending to the sky into the possibility of climbing the mountain.

75. 简化是创新的可持续原则：工业过程的长期可靠性，基于每个部件和每个步骤的极简化。

Simplification is the sustainable principle of innovation: the long-term reliability of industrial processes, based on the minimalization of each component and each step.

76. 技术用于节流，科学用于开源。

Technology is used for throttling; science is used for open source.

77. 经济性是技术准入市场的门槛，也是平衡成本与效率的要求。

Economics is the threshold for technology to enter the market, and is also the requirement to balance cost and efficiency.

78. 产品研制就是需求组合，科学推导，技术集成，系统整合。

Product development is demand combination, science derivation, technology integration, system integration.

79. 只有蜜蜂才懂绽放的含义。

Only bees understand the meaning of bloom.

80. 工业制程的原则是由规则创造细节，再由细节确保可靠。

The principle of industrial processes is that rules create details, and details ensure reliability.

81. 军事化和工业化的相似之处，是基于规则产生协同的力量。

Militarization and industrialization are similar in that they create synergistic forces based on rules.

82. 科学创新是社会发展的机会，与其说是技术整合，不如说是社会协同。

Scientific innovation is an opportunity for social development, not so much technological integration as social synergy.

83. 每一场革命的历史意义，都是由更加广泛的社会协同去释放现实的深层力量。
The historical significance of each revolution is to release the deep forces of reality by a broader social synergy.

84. 唯有历经实践中的每一个痛点，才能深刻体会上帝造物的法则。
Only by going through every pain point in practice can we deeply appreciate the creation laws of God.

85. 技术创新是以经验和理论整合需求和技术。
Technological innovation is the integration of needs and technologies with experience and theory.

86. 每一种希望，都是心灵的居所。
Every hope is the dwelling place of the heart.

87. 信心不仅是生命之源，也是智慧之源。
Faith is not only the source of life, but also the source of wisdom.

88. 智慧是由信心驱使生命可持续的策略。
Wisdom is a strategy that drives life sustainability by faith.

89. 逻辑是被现实所约束的路径。
Logic is a path constrained by reality.

90. 人生在苦难中发芽并成长。
Life sprouts and grows in the midst of suffering.

91. 现实的每一种局限都是一种警醒。
Every limitation of reality is a wake-up call.

92. 我们所能挺过来的苦难都会转变成智慧。
All the suffering we can survive will be transformed into wisdom.

93. 运动塑造逻辑，逻辑塑造灵魂。

Movement shapes logic; logic shapes the soul.

94. 善良是每个人的归途。

Kindness is way home of everyone.

95. 只有智慧能把苦难转化为契机。

Only wisdom can turn suffering into opportunity.

96. 翅膀不仅被风召唤，而且被风塑造。

Wings are not only summoned by the wind, but also shaped by the wind.

97. 热工系统优化原则：耦合仿真热力、流体、传热，贯穿设计热源、负载、负荷，实现产品均衡、稳定、高效。

Thermal system optimization principle: coupling simulations of thermal, fluid, heat transfer, throughout designs of heat sources, charges, loads, to achieve product balance, stability and efficiency.

98. 创新是以组合方式运算现实概念而构建逻辑通道。

Innovation is to build logical channels by operating real concepts in a combinatorial way.

99. 语言是表述词汇，逻辑是推导概念。

Language is the expression of vocabulary; logic is the derivation of concepts.

100. 掌握逻辑，预见未来。

Master logic and foresee the future.

101. 每一种力量，都有它释放的节奏。

Every power has a rhythm that it releases.

102. 正义基于规则而非目标。

Justice is based on rules, not goals.

103. 人性是伟大策略的原点。

Humanity is the origin of great strategies.

104. 最少的宽容高于最大的苦难。

The least tolerance is higher than the greatest suffering.

105. 人性是万事之因。

Humanity is the cause of everything.

106. 伟大策略是对人性的深刻预判。

The great strategy is a profound prejudgment of humanity.

107. 最深刻的人性是共情。

The deepest humanity is empathy.

108. 不是花要在春天绽放，而是绽放的季节叫春天。

It is not that flowers bloom in spring, but that the season to bloom is called spring.

109. 节能的本质是基于科学而突破规范。

The essence of energy saving is to break through the norms based on science.

110. 宽容使文明具有可持续性。

Tolerance makes civilization sustainable.

111. 所有的绽放都是对生命的尊重。

All blooming is a respect for life.

112. 更全面、更系统、更核心，才会成为传统行业的终结者。

Who is more comprehensive and more systematic and more core will become the terminator of traditional industries.

113. 目标是对方向赋值。

The goal is to assign a value to the direction.

114. 节奏是每一种守恒所释放的结果。

Rhythm is the result of the release of every conservation.

115. 生命总是在它的自由端绽放。

Life always blooms at its free end.

116. 每一种稀缺都是期望，每一种过量都是毒素。

Every scarcity is an expectation, and every excess is a toxin.

117. 每一次转折都是成长。

Every turn is growth.

118. 美是生命力的表达。

Beauty is the expression of vitality.

119. 摧毁希望才是战争的终极目标。

Destroying hope is the ultimate goal of war.

120. 灾难不可怕，可怕的是不确定性。

Disasters are not terrible; what is terrible is uncertainty.

121. 每当科学遇见需求，就会开启一个技术整合的新时代。

Every time science meets demand, it opens a new era of technological integration.

122. 当技术融合于艺术，就会赋产品予灵魂。

When technology is integrated with art, the soul will be given to the product.

123. 敏捷制造：作为提升价值的有效途径，而把特殊工艺需求分解成为标准化流程和标准化产品，从而实现技术集成的最大获利。

Agile manufacturing: as an effective way to enhance value, decompose special process requirements into standardized processes and standardized products, so as to achieve maximum profit from technology integration.

124. 成长并非追逐光芒，而是让自身发光。

Growth is not chasing light, but letting yourself shine.

125. 创新源于思想的维度和实践的深度。

Innovation stems from the dimension of thought and the depth of practice.

126. 适应性变革才能释放可持续力量。

Adaptive change unleashes the power of sustainability.

127. 每一种浪漫，都在释放它的情怀。

Every romance is releasing its feelings.

128. 逻辑的完整性体现在事物兴起、持续、衰落的过程中。

The integrity of logic is reflected in the process of things rising, continuing, and declining.

129. 持续跌落是飞翔的起源。

Continuous falls are the origin of flying.

130. 逻辑是连接现实的通道。

Logic is the channel that connects reality.

131. 互联网创造信息对称、产品直达、渠道公开、资源透明的崭新时代，从而把扁平化机会留给最高效的技术、最深刻的思想、最奉献的人类。

The Internet has created a new era of information symmetry, direct product access, open channels, and transparent resources, thus leaving flattening opportunities to the most efficient technology, the most profound thoughts, and the most dedicated human beings.

132. 刚毅的灵魂总是被柔软的心灵所缓冲。

The resolute soul is always buffered by a soft heart.

133. 自由是被逻辑约束的选择。

Freedom is a choice constrained by logic.

134. 延绵不绝、生生不息，呈现自然选择的智慧。

It goes on and on, demonstrating the wisdom of natural selection.

135. 没有预防的智慧，就要付出拯救的勇气。

Without the wisdom of prevention, the courage to save is required.

136. 面临灾难，人类总是以勇气补偿智慧。

In the face of disaster, human beings always compensate for wisdom with courage.

137. 永远不要被一厢情愿所麻痹，因为驱动事物演绎的逻辑是唯一的，不受人类愿景的任何影响，所以探索真理就成为我们仅有的责任。

Never be paralyzed by wishful thinking, because the logic that drives the things deduction is unique and unaffected by the human vision, so the search for truth becomes our only responsibility.

138. 人类对于自然的任何偏见，都要付出勇气来偿还。

Any prejudice of human beings against nature must be repaid with courage.

139. 倘若灾难依然不能使我们清醒，那就注定是一场真正的灾难。

If disaster still does not wake us up, it is destined to be a real disaster.

140. 每一次深刻的变革，都在把文明带进高潮。

Every profound change is bringing civilization to a climax.

141. 文明是历史传递的驿站。

Civilization is a station for the transmission of history.

142. 灾难会警醒人类进入新的维度、新的路径、新的崛起、新的世界。

Catastrophe will alert humanity to a new dimension, a new path, a new rise, a new world.

143. 文明总是被它经历的苦难塑造成型。

Civilization has always been shaped by the suffering it has experienced.

144. 人类在化解灾难的过程中变得更加强大。

Humanity has become stronger in the process of defusing disasters.

145. 孤独是灵魂独立的标志。

Solitude is a sign of the soul independence.

146. 每一只雏鸟，都以跌落作为生命的洗礼。

Every chick falls as a baptism of life.

147. 生命是人类最真挚的渴望。

Life is the most sincere desire of human beings.

148. 节奏是自然演绎的频率。

Rhythm is the frequency of nature deduction.

149. 节奏呈现逻辑演绎的力量。

Rhythm presents the power of logical deduction.

150. 经典承载着可持续的普遍性。

Classics carry sustainable universality.

151. 热爱生活就要热爱它跌宕的全部。

To love life is to love all its ups and downs.

152. 从灰度感受纵深，从色彩感受时节。

Feel the depth from grayscale and feel the season from color.

153. 最大的愚蠢是自以为聪明，最大的聪明是自以为愚蠢。

The biggest stupidity is thinking its own smart, and the biggest cleverness is thinking its own stupid.

154. 伟大的事物总是赋万物予生机。

Great things always give vitality to all things.

155. 计算正确不代表假设恰当。

A correct calculation does not mean that the assumption is appropriate.

156. 人为灾难源于词语代替概念、科普代替科学、计算代替假设。

Man-made disasters stem from words replacing concepts, popularization of science replacing science, and calculations replacing hypotheses.

157. 所有伟大思想都把普遍人性作为逻辑演绎的原点。

All great ideas take universal humanity as the origin of logical deduction.

158. 自卑是转折的起点。

Low self-esteem is the starting point of the turn.

159. 自由是每个阶层的共情。

Freedom is the empathy of every level.

160. 概念思考和词语思考，注定具有不同的回路和深度。

Thinking with concepts and thinking with words are destined to have different circuits and depths.

161. 伟大事物由于深具普遍性而成为构建生态的必要条件，并且是驱动现实生机的本源。

Great things, because of their deep universality, have become necessary conditions for building an ecology, and are the source for driving the vitality of reality.

162. 伟大事物不仅是构建生态的必要条件，而且是驱动发展的充分条件。

Great things are not only necessary conditions to build an ecology, but also sufficient conditions to drive development.

163. 驱动事物演绎的是真理而非愿景。

It is the truth, not the vision, that drives the things deduction.

164. 那些兼具必要性和充分性的事物注定是伟大的。

Those things that are both necessary and sufficient are destined to be great.

165. 定量的状态和定性的趋势基于现象的本质。

Quantitative states and qualitative trends are based on the nature of phenomena.

166. 最小的行动强于最大的假设。

The smallest action is stronger than the largest assumption.

167. 色彩是生命的表达。

Color is the expression of life.

168. 包容是驱动一切变革的伟大力量。

Inclusion is a great force driving all change.

169. 每一门科学，都开启一个探索和思想的维度。

Every science opens up a dimension of exploration and thought.

170. 和平中的警醒和危机中的展望，代表一个民族的灵魂。

Vigilance in peace and outlook in crisis represent the soul of a nation.

171. 掌握灰度就是探测维度的纵深、标度科学的计量、检测产品的工具、控制信号的反馈、表现艺术的手法、运营公司的进程。

Mastering grayscale is to probe the depth of the dimensions, to scale scientific measurement, to detect products with tools, to control the feedback of signals, to express art by techniques, and to run the the process of a company.

172. 我们总是从柔软之处开启灵魂的窗口。

We always open the window of the soul from the soft place.

173. 灵魂总是呈现在事物发展的拐点。

The soul always appears at the inflection point in the development of things.

174. 唯有艺术能够把自由精神植入文化，并散发理想主义光辉。

Only art can implant the spirit of freedom in culture and radiate the glory of idealism.

175. 自然在用亘古与浩瀚启示真理。

Nature is revealing truth with eternity and vastness.

176. 伟大正是那些为现实发展带来普遍性和持续性的事物。

Greatness is precisely those things that bring universality and sustainability to the development of reality.

177. 没有什么能够比生机更加璀璨。

Nothing can shine brighter than vitality.

178. 锁不住的是春风。

What can not be locked is the spring breeze.

179. 美是自洽的逻辑。

Beauty is self-consistent logic.

180. 每一种生命，都是现实必然性的叠加。

Every life is a superposition of the inevitability of reality.

181. 回归现实不仅是科学的终极目标，也是探索真理的起点。

Returning to reality is not only the ultimate goal of science, but also the starting point for the search for truth.

182. 给它阳光就会灿烂是生命的伟大特征。

Giving it sunshine and shining is the great feature of life.

183. 适应和变革是成长的基因。

Adaptation and change are genes for growth.

184. 每一种璀璨，都是形式的意境和色彩的光芒。

Each brilliance is the artistic conception of form and the glow of color.

185. 洞察力决定未来。

Insight determines the future.

186. 历史以它的波澜壮阔检阅人类的进步。

History examines human progress with its magnificence.

187. 自主蔓延和成长呈现生命的伟大。

Autonomous spread and growth present the greatness of life.

188. 人类总是被巨大利益所诱惑和猎杀。

Humanity is always tempted and hunted by great interests.

189. 炒股靠趋势挣钱，投资靠周期挣钱，科技靠变革挣钱；要想获得机会就要把握文明发展的脉络和节奏，因为生命的机会都是在节奏之中展开和蔓延。

Stock speculation earns money by trends; investment earns money by cycles, and technology earns money by change. If you want to get the opportunity, you must grasp the context and rhythm of civilization development, because the opportunities of life are all unfolding and spreading in the rhythm.

190. 节奏不仅是生存的形式，也是进化的形式。

Rhythm is not only a form of survival, but also a form of evolution.

191. 熵减决定进化，守恒形成节奏。

Entropy reduction determines evolution, conservation forms rhythm.

192. 以美绽放，是生命复制和蔓延的自然选择。

Blooming with beauty is a natural selection for life to replicate and spread.

193. 教育通过建立自我迭代机制，从而使得每个人都会具有主宰实践的可能。

Education establishes self-iteration mechanisms so that everyone has the possibility to dominate practice.

194. 哲学决定人类实践的方式。

Philosophy determines the way humans practice.

195. 每一种逻辑，都在传播一种力量。

Every logic spreads a force.

196. 科学只是相对真理，其仿真计算的精度在于假设的准确。

Science is only a relative truth, and the accuracy of its simulation calculations lies in the accuracy of its assumptions.

197. 社会科学的复杂性在于多种逻辑的交织，而非单一逻辑的因果；因此次要原则服从首要原则，可能危机让位必然危机，局部利益服从全局利益，近期危机让位长远危机。

The complexity of the social sciences lies in the interweaving of multiple logics, rather than the cause and effect of a single logic; therefore secondary principles are subordinated to primary principles; possible crises give way to inevitable crises; partial interests are subordinated to overall interests, and recent crises give way to long-term crises.

198. 每个民族都被地理赋予勇气，被历史赋予智慧。

Every nation is endowed with courage by geography and is endowed with wisdom by history.

199. 回归现实就是回归其演绎的逻辑。

To return to reality is to return to the logic of its deduction.

200. 无端美化不仅是偏见，而且是毒剂。

Unwarranted glorification is not only prejudice but also poison.

201. 美不仅是自然的选择，而且是生活的希望。

Beauty is not only a natural choice, but also a hope for life.

202. 文学呈现人类生活的勇气和力量。

Literature presents the courage and power of human life.

203. 节奏是被逻辑约束的自由。

Rhythm is freedom constrained by logic.

204. 失去多少自由就失去多少平等。

You lose as much equality as you lose as much freedom.

205. 所有的坚强都被意志塑造。

All strength is shaped by will.

206. 探索的伟大意义在于重构实践的路径，以提升文明的价值。

The great significance of exploration lies in reconstructing the path of practice to enhance the value of civilization.

207. 数学是逻辑之母。

Mathematics is the mother of logic.

208. 我们在多大程度上把握现实，就在多大程度上拥抱未来。

The extent to which we grasp reality, the extent to which we embrace the future.

209. 每个时代，都以它的色彩为标志。

Every era is marked by its color.

210. 当我们还原色彩的同时，也就还原了一个时代。

When we restore the color, we also restore an era.

211. 我们不可能为奔腾的河流按下暂停键。

We can not press the pause button for a rushing river.

212. 每一种美，都有它的逻辑根源。

Every beauty has its logical roots.

213. 人类智慧并非体现在科学，而是体现在科学的选择和应用；人类灾难并非源自于科学，而是源自于科学的选择和应用。

Human intelligence is not embodied in science, but in the choice and application of science; human disasters do not stem from science, but from the choice and application of science.

214. 开放性的意义在于条件和目标都是系统应用的前提。

The significance of openness is that both conditions and goals are the premise for the system application.

215. 每一种绝望，都在开启另一种希望。

Every despair opens up another hope.

216. 没有触底的灾难塑造不了智慧。

Disasters that do not touch the bottom cannot shape wisdom.

217. 色彩是现实演绎的标尺。

Color is the yardstick of the evolution of reality.

218. 本质是逻辑演绎的根源。

Essence is the root of logical deduction.

219. 设计的不确定性是条件而非逻辑。

Design uncertainty is the conditions rather than the logic.

220. 一切物理学近似都是系统开放的窗口、科学探索的价值、相对真理的不确定性、宗教信仰的尊严。

All physical approximations are the windows of systematic openness, the value of scientific exploration, the uncertainty of relative truth, and the dignity of religious belief.

221. 无论恒久，世界都在那里。

No matter how permanent it is the world is there.

222. 假如没有偏见，人类就不需要上帝。

Without prejudice, humanity would not need God.

223. 各有各的圈层，各有各的节奏，各有各的目标，各有各的结果。

Each has its own circle, own rhythm, own goals and own results.

224. 逻辑在运动中迭代。

Logic iterates in motion.

225. 历史和地理是现实演绎的前提。

History and geography are prerequisites for the deduction of reality.

226. 历史发展的每一个拐点都被勇气突破。

Every inflection point in the development of history has been broken by courage.

227. 差异是演绎的动力，均衡是演绎的目标。

Difference is the driving force of deduction, and equilibrium is the goal of deduction.

228. 抓住主要矛盾的主要方面，不仅是系统整合的前提，也是逻辑演绎的条件。

Grasping the main aspects of the main contradiction is not only the premise for system integration, but also the condition for logical deduction.

229. 生命需要勇气来绽放。

Life blooms with courage.

230. 生活如同溪流一般倾其所有、尽情流淌。

Life pours out all it and flows freely like a stream.

231. 只有伟大的事物能为现实带来普遍的必然性。

Only great things can bring universal inevitability to reality.

232. 每一种逻辑，都在传递生存的法则。

Every logic transmits the law of survival.

233. 运动激活自然演绎的灵魂。

Movement activates the soul of nature deduction.

234. 历史总是被自然和人文的法则所更迭，并由此形成波折。

History is always changed by the laws of nature and humanity, and the resulting twists and turns.

235. 逻辑是被现实条件所约束的传递函数。

Logic is a transfer function constrained by reality conditions.

236. 最高境界的传热是传质。

The highest realm of heat transfer is mass transfer.

237. 科学的力量应当被人文的力量所释放。

The power of science should be unleashed by the power of humanity.

238. 苦难是没有能力整合的逻辑。

Suffering is logic that does not have the ability to integrate.

239. 生态是全面、系统、持续的伟大力量。

Ecology is a comprehensive, systematic, continuous great force.

240. 建筑为每座城市留下了灵魂。

Architecture leaves the soul for every city.

241. 逻辑是现实演绎最深刻的根源。

Logic is the deepest root of reality deduction.

242. 阳光照耀普世的生命，海洋激励不屈的人生。

The sun shines on universal life; the ocean inspires an indomitable life.

243. 逻辑是人的觉悟，条件是神的觉悟。

Logic is the consciousness of man, condition is the consciousness of God.

244. 每一座伟大的城市，都是历史和地理的交集。

Every great city is the intersection of history and geography.

245. 生命总是被奔腾的速度赋予节奏。

Life is always given rhythm by the galloping speed.

246. 竞争是回归价值的必然路径。

Competition is an inevitable way back to value.

247. 自由是被现实约束的轨迹。

Freedom is a trajectory constrained by reality.

248. 适应性是生存的法则。

Adaptability is the law of survival.

249. 系统优化就是以过程的均衡实现性能的超越。

System optimization is to achieve performance transcendence with process equilibrium.

250. 现实的必然性被逻辑所贯穿。

The inevitability of reality is permeated by logic.

251. 焦虑会使我们错失过程所释放的精彩。

Anxiety can cause us to miss the brilliance unleashed by process.

252. 没有恰当的条件，就没有准确的结果。

Without the right conditions, there can be no accurate results.

253. 偏见会割裂我们与现实的必然联系。

Prejudice can sever our inevitable connection to reality.

254. 从机头思维迈向机组思维，再从机组思维迈向系统思维，注定是一个破壳成长的残酷过程，也是迈向节能生态的门槛。

From machine head thinking to unit thinking, and then from unit thinking to system thinking, it is destined to be a cruel process of shell breaking growth, and it is also the threshold towards energy-saving ecology.

255. 科学的局限性在于前提的狭隘和边界的脆弱。

The limitations of science lie in the narrowness of premises and the fragility of boundaries.

256. 科学应用与科学本身同等重要。

The application of science is as important as the science itself.

257. 回归现实的勇气令人激动，期待未来智慧的召唤。

The courage to return to reality is exciting, and the wisdom to look forward to the future is calling.

258. 文明是人文与科学的系统整合。

Civilization is the systematic integration of humanities and sciences.

259. 飞翔很精湛，进化很智慧，生命很珍贵。

Flying is masterful; evolution is wise, and life is precious.

260. 必然的趋势中饱含激情和诗意。

Inevitable trends are full of passion and poetry.

261. 逻辑是自然的选择，智慧是人类的选择。

Logic is the choice of nature; wisdom is the choice of man.

262. 历史按照气候周期和地理分布而演绎。

History has evolved according to climatic cycles and geographical distribution.

263. 智慧是以可持续性为目标的系统整合。

Wisdom is the systems integration with sustainability as the goal.

264. 真理是文明演绎的精华。

Truth is the essence of civilizational deduction.

265. 人文是驾驭科技应用的灵魂。

Humanities are the soul of driving the application of science and technology.

266. 秩序是以和谐为目标的逻辑。

Order is the logic of harmony as the goal.

267. 生态演绎是自然选择的智慧。

Ecological deduction is the wisdom of natural selection.

268. 最高境界的传质是季风与河流，最高境界的辐射是阳光与星辰。

The highest realm of mass transfer is monsoon and rivers; the highest realm of radiation is sunlight and stars.

269. 一切都因生机而美。

Everything is beautiful because of vitality.

270. 文明被实践赋予可持续性。

Civilization is endowed with sustainability by practice.

271. 节能技术趋势：通风优先于空调，新风优先于回风，回热优先于热泵。

Trends in energy-saving technologies: ventilation is preferred to air conditioning; fresh air is preferred to return air; heat recovery is preferred to heat pumps.

272. 热泵始终是规模回热受限的补充，而非节能系统的主导。

Heat pumps are always complementary to limited scale heat recovery, rather than the dominant for energy-saving systems.

273. 胜利注定带有奔腾的节奏和气息。

Victory is destined to come with a galloping rhythm and atmosphere.

274. 每一场胜利都是一部智慧与勇气的交响。

Every victory is a symphony of wisdom and courage.

275. 梦想总是被智慧和勇气所绽放。

Dreams are always bloomed by wisdom and courage.

276. 进化是自然演绎的迭代。

Evolution is an iteration of natural deduction.

277. 缺乏可持续性就会被时代的波澜所淹没。

Lack of sustainability will be overwhelmed by the tides of the times.

278. 音乐呈现成长的完整和节奏的持续。

The music presents the integrity of growth and the continuation of rhythm.

279. 以技术集成实现系统整合是人类赋予现实的创造力。

Achieving system integration with technology integration is the creativity that human beings give to reality.

280. 没有站位就没有视角。

Without standing, there would be no perspective.

281. 系统高于局部，趋势高于机会。

The system is above the locality; the trend is above the opportunity.

282. 文明最大的奢华是想象力。

The greatest luxury of civilization is imagination.

283. 人类的探索是从实践开始。

Human exploration begins with practice.

284. 表述逻辑的词汇才是概念。

The vocabulary that expresses logic is the concept.

285. 哲学被实践锻造，被现实归一。

Philosophy is forged by practice and unified by reality.

286. 成功只有方法，失败只有原因。

Success has only the method; failure has only the cause.

287. 科学的最高境界是理论与实践的统一。

The highest state of science is the unity of theory and practice.

288. 胜利就是最好的辩论。

Victory is the best debate.

289. 历史由胜利者代言。

History speaks for the victors.

290. 历史在偶然性的装饰下充满必然性。

History is full of inevitability under the decoration of contingency.

291. 正义只是胜利者的观念。

Justice is only the idea of the victor.

292. 哲学是被现实危难所整合的结果。

Philosophy is the result of integration by real dangers.

293. 科学是自然的辩证。

Science is the dialectic of nature.

294. 归纳需求以整合技术是科学家的使命。

To summarize needs to integrate technology is the mission of scientists.

295. 突破与变革是探索的使命。

Breakthrough and change is the mission of exploration.

296. 一切失败都是重构哲学的洗礼。

All failure is a baptism of reconstruction philosophy.

297. 利益不仅是文明的期待，更是文明所要承担的风险。

Interests are not only the expectations of civilization, but also the risks that civilizations have to bear.

298. 真理唯探索者和实践者所有。

Truth is owned only by explorers and practitioners.

299. 实践是理论回归现实的过程。

Practice is the process of returning to reality from theory.

300. 生态是自然界的系统整合。

Ecology is the system integration of nature.

301. 必然性基于普遍性。

Inevitability is based on universality.

302. 生机是成长的时间窗口。

Vitality is the window of time for growth.

303. 每一条道路都是探索者的遗产，每一座桥梁都是探索者的勇气。

Every path is the legacy of the explorer, and every bridge is the courage of the explorer.

304. 为适应而改变是可持续性法则。

Change for adaptation is the law of sustainability.

305. 竞争是逻辑迭代与系统整合的途径。

Competition is the path to logic iteration and system integration.

306. 持续闪亮的事物都是由于自带温度。

Everything that keeps shining is due to its own temperature.

307. 心灵的梦想，都是成长的期待。

The dreams of the heart are the expectations of growth.

308. 忠于自己才是最好的别人。

Being loyal to yourself is the best other.

309. 历史就是伟大事物的成长与交替。

History is the growth and alternation of great things.

310. 科学不断深化并在更大范围整合实践，技术不断重构并在更大范围回归现实。

Science continues to deepen and integrate practice on a larger scale, and technology continues to reconstruct and return to reality on a larger scale.

311. 生命的成长体现时间的价值。

The growth of life reflects the value of time.

312. 生态是能量自洽的循环与流转。

Ecology is the self-consistent cycle and flow of energy.

313. 生态的力量在于自然演绎，文明的力量在于系统整合。

The power of ecology lies in nature deduction, and the power of civilization lies in system integration.

314. 资本终究会被暴利带入歧途。

Capital will eventually be led astray by extravagant profits.

315. 危难背后必有转机。

There must be a turning point behind the crisis.

316. 迎接季风就会成长为海鸥。

When you meet the monsoon, you will grow into a seagull.

317. 历史被每一个时代注入了灵魂。

History is injected into the soul by every era.

318. 整合使得科学和技术被赋予系统的价值。

Integration allows science and technology to be given the value of system.

319. 生物进化的价值不是单元积累而是系统整合。

The value of biological evolution is not unit accumulation but system integration.

320. 生态演绎与系统整合的必然性，在于事物耦合的价值大于事物本身的价值。

The inevitability of ecological deduction and system integration lies in the fact that the value of the coupling of things is greater than the value of the things themselves.

321. 生存方式决定生物形态和生态地位。

The mode of survival determines biological morphology and ecological status.

322. 词语的逻辑不代表概念的逻辑。

The logic of words does not represent the logic of concepts.

323. 孕育希望和勇气是文化产业的责任。

Nurturing hope and courage is the responsibility of the cultural industry.

324. 科技是每个时代的标志。

Science and technology is the hallmark of every era.

325. 生存是自然的逻辑。

Survival is the logic of nature.

326. 欲望使艺术富于张力，需求使科学富于张力。

Desire makes art full of tension; demand makes science full of tension.

327. 每一种快乐，都要预支另一种艰辛。

Every kind of happiness has to prepay another hardship.

328. 节奏源自系统输入与输出的延时和错位。

Rhythm stems from delays and misalignment of system inputs and outputs.

329. 科学是回归现实的逻辑，技术是整合需求与系统。

Science is returning to the reality logic; technology is the integration of needs and systems.

330. 科学是技术集成与系统整合的基石。

Science is the cornerstone of technology integration and system integration.

331. 实践的终极胜利就是征服自己。

The ultimate victory of practice is to conquer yourself.

332. 系统整合的灵魂在于需求所引导的边界条件。

The soul of system integration lies in the boundary conditions guided by requirements.

333. 变革与进化是自然界不朽的灵魂。

Change and evolution are the immortal souls of nature.

334. 自然演绎的逻辑是必然性的根源。

The logic of natural deduction is the root of necessity.

335. 生命是最高效率的系统整合。

Life is the most efficient system integration.

336. 可持续的力量用于进化而非毁灭。

Sustainable forces are used for evolution, not destruction.

337. 逻辑的价值在于连接现实。

The value of logic lies in connecting reality.

338. 清澈的灵魂才会有悲伤。

Only a clear soul will have sorrow.

339. 现实演绎的节奏在被那些伟大的事物所操纵。

The rhythm of reality is being manipulated by great things.

340. 文化是人类可持续的力量。

Culture is a sustainable force for humanity.

341. 逻辑就是现实的必然性。

Logic is the inevitability of reality.

342. 希望始终是我们面向未来的力量。

Hope is always our strength for the future.

343. 生物进化是现实演绎的变革与升级。

Biological evolution is a change and upgrade of reality deduction.

344. 在演绎中进化是现实的终极力量。

Evolve in deduction is the ultimate power of reality.

345. 科学赋予文明可持续的勇气。

Science gives civilization the courage to sustain itself.

346. 逻辑是现实演绎的内核。

Logic is the core of reality deduction.

347. 创新源自系统的构建与逻辑的重组。

Innovation comes from the construction of systems and the reorganization of logic.

348. 翅膀使得跌落不再是奔向死亡。

The wings make the fall no longer a rush to death.

349. 湖水止于涟漪，不再流淌。

The lake stops at ripples and no longer flows.

350. 整合现实与未知是探索者的责任。

It is the responsibility of the explorer to integrate reality and the unknown.

351. 系统进化取决于现实开放的程度。

Phyloevolution depends on how open reality is.

352. 没有现实演绎的时间毫无意义。

Time without realistic deduction is meaningless.

353. 现实的苦难把我们塑造成型。

Real suffering shapes us.

354. 我们所具有的力量定义梦想的边界。

The power we have defines the boundaries of dreams.

355. 思想的深度不会超越实践的深度。

The depth of thought does not exceed the depth of practice.

356. 苦难是最真实的启蒙。

Suffering is the truest enlightenment.

357. 所有的美好都是一种时机。

All the beauty is is a kind of timing.

358. 挑战的价值是把可能性转变成为现实。

The value of a challenge is to turn possibilities into reality.

359. 勇气是文明进步的灵魂。

Courage is the soul of civilization progress.

360. 勇气和智慧是文明的标志。

Courage and wisdom are the hallmarks of civilization.

361. 经验为知识整合提供平台。

Experience provides a platform for knowledge integration.

362. 灰度呈现层次的价值和过程的意义。

Grayscale presents the hierarchy value and the process meaning.

363. 萃取和升华是认知的终结者。

Extraction and sublimation are the terminators of cognition.

364. 海洋和沙漠只能由飞翔去跨越。

Seas and deserts can only be crossed by flying.

365. 科学在为每一项技术划定边界。

Science is drawing boundaries for every technology.

366. 适应性变革是生命最深刻的自由。

Adaptive change is the deepest freedoms of life.

367. 所有的诗意都在被人类的宽容所释放。

All poetry is being released by human tolerance.

368. 深潜的鱼儿才知冷热。

Only deep diving fish know hot and cold.

369. 能量孕育着一切。

Energy breeds everything.

370. 回归现实才会拥有未来。

Return to reality to have the future.

371. 不是阳光的期待，便是阳光的结果。

If it is not the expectation of sunlight, then it is the result of sunlight.

372. 生活的快乐要配得上生活的艰辛。

The joy of life must be worthy of the hardships of life.

373. 每一条河流，都有自己跌宕的一生。

Every river has its own life of ups and downs.

374. 音乐的伟大源自逆流而行的坚韧灵魂，正是这些灵魂把人类的苦难变成一种启示性的节奏。

The greatness of music comes from the tenacity of the soul who swims against the current, and it is they who make human suffering a revelatory rhythm.

375. 逻辑是由能量转换成为力量的通道。

Logic is the channel through which energy is converted into power.

376. 只有人类能把现实的苦难打造成文明的节奏。

Only human beings can turn real suffering into the rhythm of civilization.

377. 胜利者在把现实的苦难转化成历史的节奏。

The victors are translating real suffering into the rhythm of history.

378. 奔驰以感受风的流畅，飞翔以感受风的沉浮。

Gallop to feel the flow of the wind; fly to feel the ups and downs of the wind.

379. 美是自然演绎的必然性。

Beauty is the inevitability of natural deduction.

380. 精简源自提炼，提炼源自本质。

Simplicity comes from refinement, and refinement comes from essence.

381. 时间的价值由路径决定。

The value of time is determined by the path.

382. 运动才会拥有平衡与节奏。

Only movement will have the balance and rhythm.

383. 审美就是不断感知可持续的力量。

Aesthetics is the constant perception of sustainable forces.

384. 可持续性是现实的终极力量。

Sustainability is the ultimate force of reality.

385. 每一片土地，都有自己的云彩。

Every piece of land has its own clouds.

386. 时常感动的心灵注定是鲜活的。

Those hearts that are always touched are destined to be alive.

387. 色彩是逻辑演绎的结果和生命活力的尺度。

Color is the result of logical deduction and the scale of life vitality.

388. 色彩的价值无法被语言超越。

The value of color cannot be surpassed by language.

389. 如何安放心灵是每个人的生存智慧。

How to place the mind is the survival wisdom of everyone.

390. 设计是以规范满足需求，而发明则是以科技满足需求。

Design meets needs with specifications, while invention meets needs with technology.

391. 灵魂是系统整合的精华。

The soul is the essence of system integration.

392. 被阳光照耀，被阴影庇护，被雨露滋润。

Illuminated by the sun, sheltered by shadows, moisturized by rain and dew.

393. 所有的伟大都是力量的标志。

All greatness is a sign of strength.

394. 脆弱的平衡缺乏可持续性。

The fragile balance lacks sustainability.

395. 生命以自然进化的特征传达其生命力。

Life communicates its vitality with the features of natural evolution.

396. 生命以美传达生命力。

Life conveys vitality with beauty.

397. 为生命赋能的是太阳而非星辰。

It is the sun, not the stars, that empowers life.

398. 逻辑是力量的不竭源泉。

Logic is an inexhaustible source of strength.

399. 阳光的节奏就是生态的节奏。

The rhythm of the sun is the rhythm of ecology.

400. 效率是可持续性的标志。

Efficiency is a sign of sustainability.

401. 审美就是以变换的视角去链接未来。

Aesthetics is to link the future from a changing perspective.

402. 均匀性提高效率。

Uniformity increases efficiency.

403. 均匀性是可持续的力量。

Uniformity is a sustainable force.

404. 所有的简洁都是深刻的结果。

All simplicity is a profound result.

405. 吸收快的学生未必成为高产出的教授。

Students who absorb quickly do not necessarily become high-output professors.

406. 均衡是可持续的力量。

Equilibrium is a sustainable force.

407. 科学是现实的逻辑，数学是抽象的逻辑，哲学是辩证的逻辑，审美是感知的逻辑。

Science is the logic of reality; mathematics is the logic of abstraction; philosophy is the logic of dialectics, and aesthetics is the logic of perception.

408. 持续变革就是对未来赋值。

Continuous change is about assigning value to the future.

409. 桥梁起始于跨越的梦想。

Bridges begin with dreams of crossing.

410. 科学的价值不在于经典，而在于可持续的活力。

The value of science lies not in the classics, but in sustainable vitality.

411. 可靠性是效率的一部分、成本的一部分、维保的一部分。

Reliability is part of efficiency, part of cost, part of maintenance.

412. 没有落差，就无需翅膀。

Without a drop, no wings are required.

413. 形式是逻辑演绎的路径。

Form is the path of logical deduction.

414. 艺术的价值在于启迪。

The value of art is in enlightenment.

415. 每个人的个性被实践塑造。

Each person's personality is shaped by practice.

416. 黑暗被光明引导，光明被色彩引导。

Darkness is guided by light, and light is guided by color.

417. 独特的个性才会以灵魂绽放。

A unique personality will bloom with a soul.

418. 未来被梦想所预言。

The future is predicted by dreams.

419. 每个人都在以醒悟的节奏迎接未来。

Everyone is greeting the future at an awakening pace.

420. 所有的经典，都以灵魂的付出作为代价。

All classics come at the cost of the soul.

421. 随能量而循环，由力量而节奏，是自然演绎的选择。

Cycle with energy, rhythm by power, is a natural deduction choice.

422. 能够流转就会自建循环，拥有能量就会自带节奏。

Being able to move will build its own cycle, and having energy will bring its own rhythm.

423. 逻辑的节奏归于现实的循环。

The rhythm of logic is attributed to the cycle of reality.

424. 循环是现实可持续的路径。

Circulation is a sustainable path of reality.

425. 河水在每条山谷就已决定了去向。

The river determines its destination in each valley.

426. 河水并非流经每一片土地。

The river does not flow through every piece of land.

427. 每一份主动性工作，都自带诗和远方。

Every active job comes with its own poetry and distance.

428. 每一朵浪花，都由河床决定。

Every wave is determined by the riverbed.

429. 苦难源于科学与逻辑的外延：科学必然符合逻辑，但逻辑未必符合科学。

Suffering stems from the extension of science and logic: science necessarily conforms to logic, but logic does not necessarily conform to science.

430. 并非每一条河流都通向海洋。

Not every river leads to the ocean.

431. 增长的极限受制于树根而非树梢。

The limits of growth are limited by the roots, not the treetops.

432. 所有的绽放都是成长的时节。

All blooms are times of growth.

433. 能使你成长的才是真正的照耀。

What makes you grow is what really shines.

434. 可持续才是历史的赢家。

Sustainability is the winner of history.

435. 色彩是多元化的标志。

Color is a sign of diversity.

436. 伟大的意志拥有无尽的前沿。

Great will has endless frontiers.

437. 每一种形式，都在揭示它的逻辑。

Each form reveals its logic.

438. 每只鸟的激情藏在它的欲望中。

The passion of each bird is hidden in its desires.

439. 质疑本身就是证伪，是一切逻辑深化的原点。

Questioning itself is falsification, the origin of all logical deepening.

440. 播种体现为形式，收获体现为色彩。

Sowing is reflected in form; harvest is reflected in color.

441. 能量通过逻辑转换为力量。

Energy is transformed into power through logic.

442. 可持续的普遍性是伟大的标志。

Sustainable universality is a sign of greatness.

443. 把握灰度，就是把握现实的进程。

To grasp the grayscale is to grasp the process of reality.

444. 熵是最具科学和哲学双重意义的概念，对其全面理解和应用有待于科学家和哲学家的共同努力。

Entropy is the concept with the most scientific and philosophical meaning, and its comprehensive understanding and application requires the joint efforts of scientists and philosophers.

445. 历史的进程体现人类回归自然的智慧和勇气。

The course of history reflects the wisdom and courage of mankind to return to nature.

446. 每一种节奏，都在传播一种力量。

Every rhythm transmits a power.

447. 充分的必要性就是我们的上帝。

Sufficient necessity is our God.

448. 充分的必要性是伟大的标志。

Sufficient necessity is the symbol of greatness.

449. 完美不是极限而是可持续。

Perfection is not the limit but sustainability.

450. 运动赋予我们适应自然的灵魂。

Movement gives us a soul adapted to nature.

451. 逻辑是被条件所约束的运动路径。

Logic is the path of motion constrained by conditions.

452. 诗和远方承载多样性的魅力。

Poetry and distant places carry the charm of diversity.

453. 独特的必要性就是我们的上帝。

Unique necessity is our God.

454. 蜜蜂知晓绽放的含义。

Bees know what bloom means.

455. 勇气是灵魂的推手。

Courage is the push of the soul.

456. 真理源自普遍的样本与科学的统计。

Truth comes from universal samples and scientific statistics.

457. 现实演绎就是最优算法。

Realistic deduction is the optimal algorithm.

458. 任何努力的模仿，都赶不上自我成长。

Any imitation of effort cannot catch up with self-growth.

459. 历史由逻辑的必然性所深刻连接。

History is profoundly connected by the inevitability of logic.

460. 拥有实践，就拥有一切试错和成长的机会。

With practice, all the opportunities for trial and error and growth are in hand.

461. 跨越深刻苦难的同时，也就跨越了未来。

As we cross deep suffering, we also cross the future.

462. 精彩人生，是你的思想不可逆转地改变世界。

A wonderful life is when your thoughts irreversibly change the world.

463. 神明的力量，由命运激发。

The power of the gods is inspired by fate.

464. 美的旋律，具有成长的意义。

The melody of beauty has the meaning of growth.

465. 每一种坚强，都是独特的。

Each kind of strength is unique.

466. 成长，是自然界最可持续的力量。

Growth is the most sustainable force of nature.

467. 对光明的计量，是从黑度开始。

The measurement of light begins with blackness.

468. 节能的本质，是让能量就地循环。

The essence of energy conservation is to circulate energy in situ.

第 13 章 | 成长是人类最伟大的生意
Growth is the greatest business of human

（2023 年中船齐耀特聘专家 Distinguished expert of CSSC Qiyao）

1. 节奏把我们从过去带进未来。

   Rhythm takes us from the past into the future.

2. 每一种旋律，都是真理的节奏。

   Every melody is the rhythm of truth.

3. 理解苦难，才会理解人性。

   To understand suffering is to understand humanity.

4. 安全是底层智慧，妥协是顶层智慧。

   Security is the underlying wisdom, and compromise is the top wisdom.

5. 欺骗的本质，就是以真实场景隐藏虚假条件。

   The essence of deception is to hide false conditions with real scenes.

6. 自由的路径，被现实的可行性链接。

   The path of freedom is linked by the feasibility of reality.

7. 空洞的事物，只剩外壳。

Empty things are only shells.

8. 普遍性由逻辑组合，特殊性由逻辑迭代。

Universality is composed by logic, and particularity is iterated by logic.

9. 设计的本质在于恰当的假设，而非正确的计算。

The essence of design is to make the right assumptions, not the right calculations.

10. 假设是现实迭代的逻辑接口。

Assumptions are logical interfaces for realistic iterations.

11. 普遍的生机源自持久的照耀。

Universal vitality comes from lasting illumination.

12. 阳光以普遍的照耀塑造生态。

Sunlight shapes ecology with its universal illumination.

13. 绽放是生命选择的时机。

Bloom is the timing choiced by life.

14. 绽放是成长的标志。

Bloom is a sign of growth.

15. 一切有关成长的价值，都是要成为最好的自己。

All the value of growth is to be the best of yourself.

16. 美感的根源正是成长的逻辑。

The root of beauty is the logic of growth.

17. 总有一代人，开创并见证历史。

There is always a generation that makes and witnesses history.

18. 所有的节奏都在争取时机。

All the rhythms are fighting for timing.

19. 收获是成长的价值。

Harvest is the value of growth.

20. 成长是收获的代价。

Growth is the price of harvest.

21. 所有的悲伤，都是因为自己不够强大。

All sadness is because you are not strong enough.

22. 随风起舞，就要感知风的节奏。

To dance with the wind is to perceive the rhythm of the wind.

23. 色彩见证时光的变奏。

Colors witness the variation of time.

24. 道德不会超越生存逻辑。

Morality does not go beyond the logic of survival.

25. 聪明以逻辑为本，智慧以时机为本。

Intelligence is based on logic; wisdom is based on timing.

26. 现实演绎的本质是逻辑迭代。

The essence of reality deduction is logical iteration.

27. 逻辑迭代，为现实发展提供无限可能。

The iteration of logic provides unlimited possibilities for realistic development.

28. 经历严寒，才会感知温暖。

Experiencing the cold will make you feel warmth.

29. 由逻辑传递普遍性，由条件迭代特殊性。

Universality is transmitted by logic and specificity is iterated by conditions.

30. 每一种美，都是由条件所迭代出的神奇。

Every beauty is a miracle that is iterated by conditions.

31. 我们在选择利益，规则在选择我们。

We are choosing the interests, and the rules are choosing us.

32. 每一种利益，都包含其规则与时机。

Every interest contains its rules and timing.

33. 北方压制南方，源于人类对生存的渴望。

The North oppresses the South, stemming from the human desire for survival.

34. 无论涟漪还是波涛，自由都是回归水平面的里程。

Whether it is ripples or waves, freedom is a mileage back to the horizontal plane.

35. 时光在轮回中蔓延，历史在希望中递进。

Time spreads in reincarnation, and history advances in hope.

36. 发展取决于逻辑迭代而非逻辑本身。

Development depends on logical iteration, not logic itself.

37. 成长是人类最伟大的生意。

Growth is the greatest business of human.

38. 规则由底层逻辑决定，发展由顶层逻辑决定。

Rules are determined by the underlying logic, and development is determined by the top-level logic.

39. 每一座桥梁，都有它值得跨越的理由。

Every bridge has its reasons worth crossing.

40. 所有的科学都是逻辑，所有的技术都是条件。

All science is logic; all technology is condition.

41. 国家版图就是文化影响力的边界。

The national map is the border of cultural influence.

42. 神明并非逻辑，而是逻辑迭代的时机。

The gods are not logic, but the timing for logical iteration.

43. 节奏是力量传播的形式。

Rhythm is the form of power transmission.

44. 节能的本质就是让能量滞留系统。

The essence of energy saving is to let the energy trap the system.

45. 逻辑是自然的选择，时机是神明的选择。

Logic is the choice of nature; timing is the choice of the gods.

46. 每一条河流，都是可持续性的典范。

Every river is a model of sustainability.

47. 不同企望，有着不同的苦难。

Different aspirations have different sufferings.

48. 复杂的逻辑简单化，简单的逻辑复杂化。

Simplify complex logic, and complicate simple logic.

49. 回归自然，是最高品位的文化。

Returning to nature is the highest grade culture.

50. 思想自由是经济发展的根源。

Freedom of thought is the root of economic development.

51. 一切有价值的发展都是逆向循环：文明发展的代价是反自然，资本赢利的代价是反人性。

All valuable development is a reverse cycle: the price of civilization development is anti-nature, and the price of capital profit is anti-humanity.

52. 所有的欢乐与悲伤，固有其节奏。

All joy and sorrow have their own rhythm.

53. 只有自信，无法摧毁。

Only self-confidence cannot be destroyed.

54. 艺术不止于技术。

Art is more than technology.

55. 波动回归于守恒。

Volatility returns to conservation.

56. 文化，是每座城市不可或缺的灵魂。

Culture is the indispensable soul of every city.

57. 每一种可持续的波动，都隐藏着增长的价值。

Every sustainable fluctuation hides the value of growth.

58. 研发是资本通过逆向循环而提升营收和估值所必然支付的代价，是最可持续的资本开支。

R&D is the inevitable price of capital to increase revenue and valuation through reverse circulation, is the most sustainable capital expenditure.

59. 一切叫嚣与谎言，都来自利益攸关者。

All clamor and lies come from stakeholders.

60. 地理是现实演绎的根源。

Geography is the root of the deduction of reality.

61. 逻辑决定效率，条件决定输赢。

Logic determines efficiency, conditions determine win or lose.

62. 生存高于成长，成长高于赢利。

Survival is higher than growth, and growth is higher than profit.

63. 成长的价值是可持续，而非赢利。

The value of growth is sustainable, not profitable.

64. 一切伟大变革，都以其独特形式作为标志。

All great changes are marked by their unique forms.

65. 美，是一切成长中最富启示性的部分。

Beauty is the most revealing part of all growth.

66. 守恒，是成长的极限。

Conservation is the limit to growth.

67. 每一种进化，都由周期性波动推进。

Every evolution is driven by cyclical fluctuations.

68. 纵向波动的振幅，决定横向进化的速率。

The amplitude of longitudinal fluctuations determines the rate of lateral evolution.

69. 纵向波动的振幅，决定横向成长的速率。

The amplitude of longitudinal fluctuations determines the rate of lateral growth.

70. 回归现实，就是最好的格局。

Returning to reality is the best pattern.

71. 创造价值的始终是落差，而非高度。

Value is always created by gaps, not heights.

72. 一切进化，由波动驱使。

All evolution is driven by fluctuations.

73. 只有诗意能把每一场波折，转化为持续的动力。

Only poetry can transform every twist and turn into continuous motivation.

74. 诱导不仅是热力学第二定律的本质，也是生物与文明进化的本质。

Induction is not only the essence of the second law of thermodynamics, but also the essence of the evolution of organisms and civilizations.

75. 回归现实才会具有进化的意义。

Only when you return to reality will it have evolutionary significance.

76. 光明，是黑暗中的渴望。

Light is the desire in darkness.

77. 技术的本质，是由条件所迭代的科学。

The essence of technology is science being iterative by conditions.

78. 可持续的普遍性，是走向伟大的开端。

Sustainable universality is the beginning of greatness.

79. 每一种历史的均值，都是对现实的支撑。

Every historical mean is a support for reality.

80. 普遍性是由趋势传播的节奏。

Universality is the rhythm of the spread by the trend.

81. 技术集成是由条件所迭代的科学。

Technology integration is the science of being iterative by conditions.

82. 现实定位是理性的前提。

Realistic positioning is the premise of rationality.

83. 缺乏对自然的理解与响应，是苦难的缘由。

Lack of understanding and response to nature is the cause of suffering.

84. 传播普遍性是伟大的标志。

Spread universality is a sign of greatness.

85. 由苦难提炼的诗意，是人类所能拥有的最大勇气。

The poetry distilled by suffering is the greatest courage that human beings can have.

86. 现实的可能性，体现为历史的均值。

The possibility of reality is reflected in the historical mean.

87. 现实由历史的均值所支撑。

Reality is supported by historical averages.

88. 经济体现为欲望与恐惧所形成的波动。

The economy is reflected in fluctuations caused by desires and fears.

89. 无论向左还是向右，都是为了更好地向前。

Whether left or right, it is all about better forward.

90. 艺术，始终是生活实践的结果。

Art is always the result of life practice.

91. 地理，是深具文化属性的科学。

Geography is a science with deep cultural attributes.

92. 每一束光芒，都有它穿越的里程。

Every ray of light has its miles traveled.

93. 词语和逻辑，是利己主义者所能达到的极限。

Words and logic are the limits of what an egoist can achieve.

94. 唯有照耀，能够带来普遍的生机。

Only the light can bring universal vitality.

95. 唯有照耀，能抵达遥远和穿透内心。

Only light can reach the distant and penetrate the heart.

96. 嘲笑未来，是不可饶恕的无知。

To laugh at the future is unforgivable ignorance.

2023 年 1 月 29 日

图书在版编目（CIP）数据

科学箴言录 / 俞乔力著 . --5 版 . -- 北京：作家出版社，2023. 5

ISBN 978-7-5212-2245-6

Ⅰ . ①科… Ⅱ . ①俞… Ⅲ . ①科学知识—青少年读物 Ⅳ . ① Z228.2

中国国家版本馆 CIP 数据核字（2023）第 052969 号

科学箴言录

作　　者：俞乔力
责任编辑：佳　丽
美术编辑：薛　怡
选题策划：新天地文化
出版发行：作家出版社有限公司
社　　址：北京农展馆南里 10 号　　**邮　　编**：100125
电话传真：86-10-65067186（发行中心及邮购部）
86-10-65004079（总编室）
E-mail:zuojia @ zuojia.net.cn
http://www.zuojiachubanshe.com
印　　刷：三河市北燕印装有限公司
成品尺寸：170 × 240
字　　数：360 千
印　　张：28
版　　次：2023 年 5 月第 1 版
印　　次：2023 年 5 月第 1 次印刷
ISBN 978-7-5212-2245-6
定　　价：78.00 元